THE
LEARNING
AND
PERFORMANCE
OF
PHYSICAL
SKILLS

THE PRENTICE-HALL FOUNDATIONS OF PHYSICAL EDUCATION AND SPORT SERIES

JOHN E. NIXON

Series Editor
Stanford University

John D. Lawther

Pennsylvania State University

THE
LEARNING
AND
PERFORMANCE
OF
PHYSICAL
SKILLS

Second Edition

PRENTICE-HALL, INC., ENGLEWOOD CLIFFS, N.J.

Library of Congress Cataloging in Publication Data

LAWTHER, JOHN DOBSON (date).
   The learning and performance of physical skills.

   (The Prentice-Hall foundations of physical education
and sport series)
   Originally published under title: The learning of
physical skills.
   Includes bibliographical references and index.
   1. Motor learning.   I. Title.
BF295.L33 1977   152.3'34   76-20598
ISBN 0-13-527325-0

© 1977 by Prentice-Hall, Inc., Englewood Cliffs, New Jersey

Printed in the United States of America

10 9 8 7 6 5 4 3 2 1

PRENTICE-HALL INTERNATIONAL, INC., *London*
PRENTICE-HALL OF AUSTRALIA PTY. LIMITED, *Sydney*
PRENTICE-HALL OF CANADA, LTD., *Toronto*
PRENTICE-HALL OF INDIA PRIVATE LIMITED, *New Delhi*
PRENTICE-HALL OF JAPAN, INC., *Tokyo*
PRENTICE-HALL OF SOUTHEAST ASIA PTE. LTD., *Singapore*

Contents

Series Preface

It is a professional privilege and pleasure to introduce The Prentice-Hall Foundations of Physical Education and Sport Series of textbooks. This revised series has been expanded to include more comprehensive books written by well known authorities in various foundational areas of physical education and sport.

As knowledge and experience expands in the various foundational areas of physical education and sport, young scholars are electing to specialize in detailed study and research, not only in the traditional fields, but also in the newer foundational areas. This series is well represented with books written by selected authors who bring scholarly expertise and proven literary skills to their assignments in both the traditional and emerging areas.

Because of the recent rapid expansion of specializations within the general field of physical education, and also because the term "sport" is gaining broad recognition and use as an area of intensified study, research, and practice, the scope of the revised series has been extended. There are differences in definitions of these terms among physical educators, sport leaders, and scholars around the world. Some authorities now conceive of the term "sports" as being separate, or different, from the term "physical education." Others still retain the traditional definition that sport constitutes one of several domains of human activity typically included within the overall definition of physical education, along with such terms as "dance," "aquatics," "gymnastics" and "designed exercise."

Each volume has been expanded, enabling authors to provide suitable conceptual depth concerning the specialized subject matter. One of the major contributions of the books in the revised series is their completeness and careful coverage of the latest theories, facts, and concepts which make up the body of knowledge of the area under discussion.

Each book is now a complete text in its own right. No longer should the books in this series be regarded as supplementary to other textbooks.

The central purpose of the revised Foundations of Physical Education and Sport Series has not changed. These textbooks present warranted generalizations from related fields of knowledge which contribute to a sophisticated understanding of physical education and sport.

These generalizations form a basis for educational decision making and policy formulation by teachers, coaches, and administrators in educational institutions as well as in other public and private agencies which organize and conduct physical education and sport programs.

Physical eduaction currently is defined as the art and science of voluntary, purposeful human movement. Its central concern is the individual engaging in selected motor performances and the significance of these experiences. Thus, physical education and sport are broad interdisciplinary subjects. Scholars and practitioners of these areas need to be familiar with the most contemporary hypotheses being generated in the closely related disciplines which explain phenomena associated with human movement. Disciplines which provide the most relevant foundational knowledge in physical education and sport include anatomy, anthropology, aesthetics, biology, history, kinesiology and biomechanics, neurology, physiology, psychology, and sociology.

With rare exceptions, scholars of other academic disciplines have not devoted their major attention to investigations which concern important phenomena in physical education and sport. The historian has virtually neglected the history of sport in general history books. Few sociologists have elected to conduct careful research in selected aspects of sport or physical education as a major scholarly commitment.

Nonetheless, a vast accumulation of knowledge in the foundational fields is rapidly appearing in many countries around the world in the form of research reports, scholarly articles, books, pamphlets, and other literary formats. Most of this knowledge has not been accumulated systematically nor reported and interpreted accurately on a broad scale to members of the physical education and sport disciplines. This difficult task of selecting and reporting relevant generalizations from any one academic discipline, and commenting on their meanings requires a physical education scholar who also has a background of graduate study and research in the related disciplinary field.

The authors of books in this revised series are recognized, distinguished physical education and sport researchers and scholars and are acknowledged specialists in the foundational fields covered in their respective books. Each volume reports and synthesizes recent knowledge into understandable and usable form for students, teachers, coaches, and administrators. The reader is instructed in the vital process of developing his or her own *principles* of physical education and sport as knowledge and understanding accumulate from these foundational fields. Comprehensive bibliographies list basic references and source materials for further study and research.

Most, if not all, of the authors have had extensive intercultural experiences in other countries and thus are highly qualified to bring to the series the perspective of varied societal norms and cultural values as well as to expose the student to a greater range of relevant academic and professional literature than typically has been the case in past American textbooks in this field.

This series is appropriate for courses in the Foundations or Principles of Physical Education at both the undergraduate and graduate levels. Individual volumes are written to serve as definitive texts for relevant subject matter courses or seminars. These books are also valuable for collateral reading and provide excellent resource materials for students working on special assignments, individual study projects and related research compilations and reviews.

Overall, this series provides an important source of scholarly literature which contains the latest scientific, behavioral and humanistic insights about the subject matter of physical education and sport. It also provides the foundational knowledge necessary to guide the selection of teaching and coaching practices which will be of most educational benefit to participants in programs of physical education and sport.

JOHN E. NIXON

Preface

A basic purpose of physical education is the acquisition of physical skills. Health and physical fitness are important aspects of physical education but are meaningless unless they help bring about improvement in human function, and human function implies expression. Expression is of necessity physical; and skill in that expression involves the social, recreational, and sport skills, as well as artistic expression in the dance. It also involves the achievement of precision in body-control skills for vocational as well as leisure pursuits.

A motor skill is a temporally ordered sequence of relatively discrete component actions hierarchically structured to bring about a successful outcome. Skill learning is the readjusting of subsequent motor responses on the basis of one's idea of desired result when compared to current feedback. In motor-skill teaching, the general strategy provided by the teacher makes no attempt to explain the activities of the individual muscle groups. Often a verbal plan is used to initiate early attempts by the learner, but the verbal crutches are later discarded as the skill is made automatic; that is, seldom are there verbal correlates of highly skilled action. Finally, motor learning can only be studied indirectly through progressive measures of performance.

The adjustment of motor behavior to life's purposes, needs, and demands requires development of a myriad of skills. The overt expression of skills results in performances that are for the most part automatic, adapted responses to learned cues. When the incoming cues are familiar, they can immediately activate the response of the subject without the intervention of conscious awareness of sensory controls. Much overt skill response flows out preprogrammed from motor-memory storage. Many skill responses that involve a considerable time span are proprioceptively and unconsciously monitored. For the most part, overt skill responses are performed too rapidly for conscious awareness, although conscious awareness may occur as an introspection of what has occurred or a comparison of this feedback with a mental idea of the desired result. Many of the changes and readaptations that occur as skill learning progresses are accomplished below the awareness level of consciousness. However awkward and slow the conscious monitoring of skill movements is, it often has great value in short-cutting *beginner's* skill learning to help avoid the waste of pure trial and error. Later the conscious monitoring of many *well-learned* skills tends to produce a performance too slow for effecting one's purpose and, more often than not, interferes with the smooth flow of appropriate subskill continuities.

This text is an attempt to summarize available evidence and research on skill learning and performance. I am deeply grateful to those authors and publishing firms who have so generously permitted uses of quotations from or references to their publications. I am also deeply obligated to former students for the thought and discussion that have helped develop this book.

J.D.L.

One

Human Learning and Progressive Adaptation

Six thousand years of recorded experience of man has been abstracted, summarized, epitomized and passed on as an inheritance, much of which man can acquire without the blunders and frustrations of primary experience.

It took the human race thousands of years to develop the ability to read and write; now, given educational opportunity, nearly every child can read and write. Some children actually learn to read by the age of four. The modern high school graduate has a store of knowledge which surpasses that of the most learned of the ancients. With regard to physical development, we are today bigger and stronger, and we possess more physical skill than any preceding generation in history. The average college man of today is three to four inches taller and fifteen to twenty pounds heavier than his predecessor of just sixty years ago.

The modern giants of sport far surpass in size the outstanding athletes of the past. Some professional basketball players, for example, are more than seven feet tall. Defensive tackles and ends in professional football are usually well over six feet in height and range in weight from 250 to well over 300 pounds. Moreover, sport records are constantly being established and quickly bettered. The four-minute mile, considered an impossible achievement in the early part of the twentieth century, is today being surpassed in almost every important track meet. The pole vault record has now passed eighteen feet and the shot put, seventy feet. Even in archery, in spite of William Tell and Robin Hood, the modern archer is far more skillful than his predecessors.

Increase in human growth is due to our application of the heritage of knowledge about health and nutrition, as well as to economic conditions that permit its application to each succeeding generation. The improvement in so many types of physical performance is due to our ability to communicate and to pass on our experiences to succeeding generations. The child can profit from the cumulative, epitomized, abstracted experience of centuries. Fortunately we, in contrast with animals, can learn much of this handed-down knowledge without suffering all the handicaps and failures of the original experiences. Our "learning by doing" can be arranged by teachers so that it is accomplished faster, more safely, less painfully, and more efficiently.

It is readily observable that the actions of human beings, their ways of thinking and behaving, change with training and experience. They modify their responses to various situations, often to remarkable degrees, after motivated practice and meaningful experience. Moreover, many of these changes become relatively persistent, either in terms of the nature of response or, more likely in the learning of physical skills, in terms of progressive adaptation. Responses become more and more precise, more and more effective in bringing about desired results, and more and more automatic in adapting to varying conditions.[1]

It is necessary to define learning as change due to training and experience in order to make it distinct from change due to growth or its opposite, deterioration caused by senescence. Moreover, persistence or relative permanence should be considered a criterion of learning in order to discount temporary changes in performance due to fatigue, change in motivation, or physiological fluctuation.

THE PHYSIOLOGICAL BASES OF LEARNING

We know that changes in response occur after meaningful experience or motivated practice, but the physiological basis of this learning can still be described only hypothetically. Perhaps the most commonly accepted hypothesis is that the human brain and nervous system are analogous to an electronic computer into which are fed data from the various sense organs and sensory nerve endings, and out of which flow currents that activate responses computed in terms of past experience, present wishes, and the many and varied incoming data. The extremely complex nervous system, with its innumerable input and outflow mechanisms, defies complete analysis, although we do know something of its system of *proprioceptive* facilitation with continuous *sensory feedback;* the cord and midbrain *servomechanisms;* and the sensory, motor, and large association areas of the brain itself. All are connected through *internuncial neurons* to outlets of peripherally disposed motor units. Herrick once estimated that "the human cerebral cortex alone contains some 9270 million nerve-cells . . . which stretch away for great distances . . . connecting each cell with many different nerve-centers" and that "the total number of possible nervous pathways is, therefore, inconceivably great." [2]

This system, with its extremely complex integrative areas, may develop with experience into a marvelous "electronic computer" that continuously takes in data from the various sensory nerves, reassembles these data in terms of previous experience already programmed into the computer, and turns out response solutions. Inflowing sensations are received, analyzed, and synthesized; the computed adjustment is then sent on, for action, through the efferent nerves and the associated musculature. Actual overt responses are continually readjusted, at times even after they are initiated, as additional incoming cues arrive, and they are acted upon in terms of the great amount of past experience already programmed into this computer. The individual's accumulating experiences, as life goes on, make possible finer and finer "computations" and response adjustments in terms of this richer experiential background. [3]

Unconscious Motor Memory Storage and Release; Proprioceptive Monitoring

Many movement patterns are learned until automatic, and thereby stored in unconscious motor memory. They are then released as automatic responses when the appropriate situation occurs. One makes many of the movement patterns of eating, dressing, driving a car, or catching a dropped object, for example, without conscious monitoring. These motor-memory patterns are often discharged so rapidly as to exclude any monitoring by either exteroceptive or proprioceptive feedback. This motor-memory storage of automatic patterns, plus proprioceptive guidance of longer time spans of automatic activity, equip one for rapid, adjusted motor response to many aspects of life while the mind is free for other considerations. [4] Legge says, "Proprioceptive information has the great advantage of freeing vision for monitoring more distant events." [5]

Henry comments about the rich store of unconscious motor memory available for acts of neuromuscular skill that might be "thought of as a memory storage-drum phenomena, to use the analogy of the electronic-computer." He implies that "such memory must be different from ideational or perceptual memory since conscious imagery is indefinite and largely excluded." These neural patterns, structured, unconscious motor-memory programs, can be released voluntarily at reception and recognition of an appropriate stimulus situation; however, the guidance of the specific, learned motor program through the proper centers, subcenters, and nerve channels does not involve conscious direction. [6]

Discrete Interval Between Responses. When stimuli for these automatic motor responses or response changes occur in rapid succession, there exists a discrete interval of time before changes can be made to a subsequent stimulus. This *latency period* before a subsequent response can occur is hypothesized by Henry to be dependent on the complexity of the original response being processed in the memory storage.[7] This delay period has been variously reported to range from 100 milliseconds (0.1 sec) to 400 milliseconds (0.4 sec) or more. Kroll hypothesizes that delay of subsequent response (to these closely spaced stimuli) is relatively independent of the quality of the individual's simple reaction time.[8] Siegel explored Henry's hypothesis in an experimental study and reported a confirmation of it, but no evidence that endorsed Kroll's hypothesis. Siegel reported that, in subsequent responses, in attempts to amend a response to a stimulus already received, individuals maintained the same relative position in speed of subsequent response as they had in individual simple reaction-time ranking.[9]

Conscious Awareness in Retrospect

Various writers have called motor-memory storage a motor-memory *trace* or *engram* that furnishes and releases the chosen program; that is, provides the organized and integrated pattern for the skill release. Stimulus selection and sensing from the stimulus display, recognition, and decision making, of course, precede the effector action. In skills the processes from environmental stimuli up to effector action are usually so fast as to exclude consciousness except as an awareness in retrospect. Conscious awareness can occur after the act as an introspection by the subject of his own behavior; for example, a person may experience a near-accident while driving a car. He slams on the brakes and stops suddenly. Only after the act is over does he think about it and feel a bit of emotional upheaval. In fact, consciousness may review past experience in preparation for future acts, or examine the results of acts completed. It can be awareness of something already sensed, or of past experience. It does not seem to be an accompaniment of ongoing skilled action, but an awareness of differences between intention and result.

THE MONITORING OF MOTOR ACTS

There seem to be three degrees of guidance of motor acts: (1) *exteroceptive,* most commonly visual, in which external sensing guides movement adjustment; (2) *proprioceptive feedback,* cerebellar and unconscious, in which the movement occurring sends back stimuli for the next stage; and (3) *motor-memory discharge,* in which the total action is set beforehand and so discharged from the motor-memory storage centers. In this last type, an act may be run off so rapidly that there is too little time for proprioceptive feedback; hence the act is preprogrammed and is a motor-memory storage discharge. Ballistic movements are one example; they have been classified as "open-loop" action because they occur too rapidly for sensory feedback of the ongoing action to modify that action.

Open and Closed Loop

One meaning often implied in the use of the term "open loop" is that a set input stimulus flows directly into a *consistent* response; that is, a specific input stimulus always produces the same response. The word "loop" comes from the idea of nerve-current flowback arriving in time to affect the ongoing action. In the open loop, no such influence is supposed to occur. Gibbs says open loop, when defined as consistent response to a set input stimulus, is an impossibility because of the variations in the multitude of physical and physiological factors affecting any muscular activity from moment to moment (see also pages 11–12).[10]

Integrated units of skill, which include serial chaining and proprioceptive monitoring, are closed-loop responses. At the more advanced stages of skills, subroutines are linked together into hierarchies of action, and each subroutine stimulates release of the subsequent (perhaps partially overlapping) routine. The monitoring of the action, when it is *not* too fast for feedback, is mostly proprioceptive (cerebellar) and below conscious awareness level (closed loop). Schmidt hypothesizes that all responses in skills involve both closed and open loop responses, "with the fast responses being controlled in the open-loop manner during the movements, and with the closed-loop corrections being executed between responses." [11]

The motor-memory released action is usually considered open-loop action; that is, without concurrent feedback—the results of learning and programmed patterns.[12] The memory drum will have a rich store of motor-memory patterns by the time a high skill level is attained. The perceptual trace of the act then furnishes the data for comparison of intent with result. Comparison comes as a result of feedback and is the guide to readjustment of subsequent responses. Woodworth illustrates this perceptual-trace use by remarking that ordinary singers or violin players tend to grope around a little after reaching the neighborhood of a note, guiding themselves by a sense of pitch.[13]

Servomechanisms
and Feedback:
Readjustments During Response

The infant reaching for a button on the floor or a piece of lint on the carpet can be seen to be readjusting his movements during the action as his hand approaches the object, with corrections continuing until his fingers and thumb arrive and take hold of it. This early adjustment of prehension is a simple example of the servomechanism of the human body, with its continual feedback of cues and the subsequent automatic readjustment. This feedback to readjust the hand movement so as to make precise contact with the object is exteroceptive (visual sensing, in this case). As the child develops in body control skills, more and more movement patterns come under proprioceptive guidance (automatic and cerebellar).

Proprioceptive guidance depends heavily on responses to sensory impulses received from nerve endings in the muscles, tendons, and joints. These afferent sensory stimuli originate in the tissues of the body, and are often activated by movement. In the beginning of motor learning, exteroceptive sensing (from vision, hearing, touch) is consciously relied upon for motor guidance, and the individual performs with attention to details of execution. Once the act is mastered (becomes skilled behavior), it is performed automatically, with chief guidance from proprioceptive sensing. Conscious attention to details of movement at this stage will have a disrupting effect on smooth performance.

Proprioceptive sensing includes impulses from both primary and secondary nerve afferents in the muscles. Some are facilitatory (annulospiral and flower-spray endings) and some are damping (Golgi end organs and Renshaw internuncial cells) in their effect on the muscle action. In automatic motor acts, the proprioceptive feedback from peripheral areas helps in motor adjustment, and the motor act is adjusted to the specific posture of the moment as recorded and fed back proprioceptively.

Proprioception becomes one of the most highly developed senses, although its activity is mostly beneath cortical awareness. There is some confusion about this type of sensory guidance or monitoring because of much popular talk about "getting the feel of the act." Actually, the monitoring of a skilled movement through proprioception is cerebellar, subcortical, and largely unconscious. The error is not in the statement about "feel" but in the assumption that this "feel" registers at the awareness level of consciousness and acts as a conscious monitoring agent during the act. What awareness of "feel" occurs must be an introspection of what has already occurred, and such "feel" analysis is very vague, indeed. The only proprioceptive sensing that seems slow enough to permit conscious awareness is the sensory inflow from the joints. The Pacini corpuscles respond as a result of movement, and the Ruffini corpuscles respond with a frequency characteristic of each position assumed. However, the response rate is so slow as to reach awareness level in the cortex as an introspection of the part movement or assumed position already taken.

Children's hunting and pursuit games and later the more sophisticated readjustments in team games of relatively continuous action all involve readjustment of responses to additional cues arriving during the action. The almost automatic readjustment of the highly skilled gymnast after he or she has made an error in a free-exercise routine disguises the error so that it seems to be part of the succeeding routine—a routine that flows from and through the error deviation and makes the whole a continuity and a harmony of movement. Only feedback and loop control that is largely automatic could effect such rapid readjustments of acts already underway. Of course, wide previous experience in such adjustments must be "programmed" or the readjustments cannot be made.

MOTOR LEARNING HIERARCHIES

We have already defined learning as relatively permanent change in behavior resulting from experience, as contrasted with changes due to growth, aging, fatigue, or temporary physiological fluctuations. Now we need to define that particular category of learning called *motor learning*. Motor learning is usually defined as learning in which bodily movements play a major part; it is a term used to describe an adjustment of responses to some environmental situation, a considerable part of which consists of patterned muscular contractions, both static and dynamic. The bodily movements involved are patterns of responses to recognized stimuli; that is, they are perceptual-motor responses.[14] The stimuli may be visual, auditory, kinesthetic, or any combination of sense stimuli.

Learning Is Adaptation and Progression

The relatively permanent change in behavior resulting from experience and training, called learning, is both a process of adaptation to the environment and a progression from simple to more complex and sophisticated adjustments. Just as sounds develop into words and words grow with use into wider and more explicit meanings, so the simple balance and movement skills combine into the more complex skills of posture and the innumerable body-control acts. Skills advance in hierarchies of development. As McGeoch says, "After small amounts of learning early in the life of the individual, every instance of learning is a function of the already existent learned organization of the subject; that is, all learning is influenced by transfer." [15]

Perhaps an example from physical development will clarify Mc-Geoch's point. Children learn to balance themselves on two feet and transfer much of this balance skill into the development of walking ability; then they utilize the additional balance and body control gained from the walking development to accelerate their acquirement of ability to run. Running progresses until it includes ability to make quick changes in direction. Now they can utilize much of this learning to play hunting and chasing games. These various balances and mobility controls are next built into more complex hierarchies of skills in group play. Note the many static and dynamic postural and movement controls on which they build sociomotor skills in dual sports, team contests, or the various dances.

The Nature of Learning Changes with Age

Hebb says that "the first learning of primates is extremely slow, and very different from that at maturity." He continues:

There are two kinds of learning. One is that of the newborn infant, or (as it still may occur in exceptional conditions in adults) the visual learning of the adult reared in darkness or with congenital cataract; the other that of the normal adult. [16]

Hebb then calls attention to Senden's account of the extremely slow perceptual learning of a patient who was born blind and was then given sight after motor and speech habits had developed. [17] Later he describes the very slow perceptual learning of Miner's highly intelligent patient who had congenital cataracts but had sight restored at adulthood by an operation. Hebb states: ". . . two years after operation [the patient] had learned to recognize only four or five faces and in daily conferences with two persons for a month did not learn to recognize them by vision." [18] The parallel between these two adult cases and the early primary learning of the human infant is apparent.

One must remember that the human infant works steadily at motor learning from birth on. The preponderance of this type of incremental learning during the first year or two of life must not be overlooked in the analysis of human motor learning. The simple integration of movements into useful patterns may continually progress. Each succeeding skill is made up of and built on the base of such simple skills as the individual already possesses, providing they can be used appropriately. Although the new skill, the new step in the hierarchy, is made up of simpler, already learned skills, the new unit is more than an aggregate of the old skills. It is a fusion somewhat like that of a chemical compound in which the various elements are not recognizable in their new form. Each stage of learning is built on the already learned organization, so that the very nature of the learning process changes. As Hebb says:

> It is proposed that the characteristics of learning undergo an important change as the animal grows, particularly in higher mammals; that all learning tends to utilize and build on an earlier learning, and, finally, that the learning of the mature animal owes its efficiency to the slow and inefficient learning that has gone before.[19]

Let us look more carefully at this development in infancy, at its slow rate and its nature. Newborn infants develop the ability to raise their heads, coordinate eye movements, raise head and upper trunk together, and reach out and grasp things. Posture develops posteriorly until they can sit erect. Soon they begin to crawl and then to walk. The development of these controls is both posterior and outward (gross to small musculature) in direction. For the first fifteen months, these developments seem to progress in the same sequence in all infants.

The rate of development of the so-called phylogenetic movements (grasping, reaching, creeping, or crawling) shows little or no acceleration in specially trained children. Training is, however, essential for the learning of ontogenetic types of activities (using eating utensils, buttoning clothes, toilet routines, cutting out pictures, and, at higher levels, swimming and skating). The ontogenetic types of behavior seem to be highly dependent on training and experience for their development. In general, as the skill increases in complexity, the value of special training and experience becomes evident. Although phylogenetic developments seem to progress at about the same rate in an infant regardless of special practice or of adults' attempts to teach and accelerate, the rate of achievement varies from infant to infant. These variations, except in extreme degree, have little significance for the prediction of developmental limits in future traits or abilities. There is no agreement as to the extent to which learning is involved in the infant's acquiring the ability to make individual movements. Some think that a large part of this early development is due to maturation. The child does begin to move in the womb long before birth, as all mothers know.

Early Movement Development. Before birth, surface stimuli in the human embryo elicit movements of distant muscles. From birth on, the infant is making almost innumerable movements in response to myriad stimuli, and is slowly establishing in the "cell assemblies" (in the motor-memory drum) simple movements and movement patterns in response to specific stimuli. During the infant development period, the child tries out, to some degree, almost all his musculature, although much of this activity is gross-muscle action with little individuated, precise control. This early random activity and gross-muscle action of the infant's extremely active period of life is responsible for much improvement in motor control. Gradually the child acquires patterns such as reaching and grasping a sensed object, and dynamic and static postural balances involved in sitting erect, crawling, creeping, standing, walking, and other types of locomotion. Very early in infancy the child begins to sort out and put together movements into simple action patterns.

The more or less random movement is the infant's response to internal and external environmental stimuli and results in changes in the nature of these movements. To the extent that the direction of this change and its limits are predetermined by genetic constitution, it should perhaps be considered maturation, although in the sense that this change depends on environmental stimuli for its development, it might be looked upon as a kind of physiological learning. As Huisinga stated long ago (1938),[20] physical play and exploratory urges are innate and occur not only in the human but also in lower species of animal life.

No real distinction can be made between maturation and learning in the infant's development because hereditary factors are only developed in response to environment, and acquired factors can only be secured through a modification of already-existing structure. In all maturation there is learning, and in all childhood learning there is hereditary maturation.[21] The degree to which movement development is due to maturation or to learning (and the distinction is a matter of degree, not kind) is unimportant if we keep in mind that any kind of growth depends on a fostering environment.

The distinction between maturation and learning during infancy is academic. What we need to know is that new adjustments may be learned and/or may be individuated from what was previously a gross-action response. Most of the basic skills demanded by society (eating skills, toilet skills, conduct with others) are subject to adjustment through environmental experience. Eating with a cup or spoon are acquired more rapidly if the child is permitted much practice without forcing and without much censure for failure to achieve adult standards. The mother who gets too upset over the mess the child makes may retard learning. As a child begins to be mobile and branch out in play, it needs equipment, space, opportunity, and occasional help or encouragement.

The child's motor development or motor learning is chiefly trial and revision in terms of results, with very little conscious awareness of just what motor readjustments are taking place. Of course, even at advanced ages, much motor movement and skill learning goes on without conscious awareness of the specific changes being made. The gradual integration of simple movement patterns into more complex units is a relatively slow process but is greatly hastened by the extremely active nature of the healthy child.

Automation, Then Integration.   The simple movements and movement patterns have to become relatively automatic before the child can combine them into more complex units. He or she tends to readjust and combine the various simpler components until some success is achieved without being aware at the conscious level of the various readjustments. At the early age, a more complex unit—riding a tricycle, for example— is not possible until the child has developed to relative automaticity the static and dynamic balances and controls involved in standing, walking, climbing, and certain arm and leg controls. Note that the simpler movements must be relatively automatic before they can be combined into the higher motor units. The integration of the larger units to produce automatic performance is also a linking without conscious awareness of how the component movements are tied together; that is, a result of trial and continual revision in terms of results.

Problem Solving.   When children get a gross-framework idea of the higher hierarchical unit (from seeing a more-skilled child ride the tricycle, perhaps), they seem to learn more rapidly; however, their imitative attempts involve errors between the simpler automatic components until they get a cue or stumble on which simpler automatic pattern to release next. Because selection of successive components to make up the higher unit often involves some sensory or ideational cue before release of the next component, it is not pure trial and error. The stimulus that releases the next component is not a result of conscious analysis, but merely a cue tied to a simpler automatic muscular pattern. The cue to which they respond may be incorrect and produce an error which, as results become apparent, is usually then discarded for another, different automatic pattern. This simple trial and revision in terms of results is a kind of primitive problem solving.

Individual Differences.   In attempts at imitation, children have only a gross-framework idea. Moreover, each individual performs the act in a slightly different way. Levers are different in length from those of other individuals. Muscles vary from those of others in strength, speed, and precision of control. The muscle attachments to the bones differ among individuals in distance from the joints. The inflow of the various stimuli that activate the neural system are specific and individual to him or her alone. Moreover, every time an individual performs an act with approximately the same result, the sensory data fed into the neural computer, the complex brain wave activity, and the physiological state of response organs will vary.[22] Nevertheless, he or she will put together and adjust an overt expression of a motor-movement hierarchy in attempts to serve a particular purpose. An approximately similar hierarchical motor unit may be expressed on repeated occasions to serve a purpose (to ride the tricycle); but the specific muscles and their specific movements will be adjusted to physiological state, posture, surface transversed, the particular tricycle, and so on.

Individuation. Individuation means additional and more precise movement controls within the gross-movement pattern. Early performances tend to be gross total-body acts involving many extraneous movements and much unnecessary tension of associated musculature. The extraneous movements must be eliminated and the tension of the associated musculature greatly reduced. Observation of a novice attempting almost any skill will reveal this excess movement and excess large-muscle activity, particularly if the skill is one requiring considerable precision. Drawing and handwriting by kindergarten and primary school children are good examples. At first, children tense much of their large musculature and get much of their bodies into the act.

Novices learning sport skills that require precise wrist, hand, and finger control will reveal difficulties in separating the timing, the force, and the direction of the act from the handicapping effects of gross bodily muscular activity. Individuation to divorce the excess of movement, unnecessary for the immediate purpose, is part of motor learning. Integration of these partially individuated movements into patterns of response to the playback of perceptual cues develops to some degree during their individuation, so that greater individuation often means progressive adaptation.

LEARNING A NEW MOVEMENT VS. MOTOR PATTERN LEARNING

In method of attack, the problems of isolating and controlling specific movements and of learning skills (motor pattern learning) are quite dissimilar. For most efficient practice in skill learning, at least at the earlier stages, attention is not on the specific movements but on the purpose, object, or goal and only on a gross-framework idea of an action pattern to attain the goal. When the person tries to hit a target by throwing, he or she learns fastest by focusing on the target, with only a gross-outline idea of the total throwing act present in the periphery of his or her attention. However, when that person tries consciously to individuate a movement for the purpose of learning to separate out and voluntarily control that movement, he or she focuses attention on the specific body part in which he or she is trying to isolate the contraction. The process is first to exercise the muscle through some gross act that includes some of the specific muscle movement. This action may strengthen the specific muscle toward which the training is being directed, a procedure often necessary in reeducation work with the disabled. Once the muscle can be made to act with the attention focused on it, the individual practices to divorce it from the gross act and gradually train it to act as a prime mover.

The yogi of India trains himself in voluntary control of body-part movements that most of us never learn or have any need to learn. Some dancers have developed the ability to move certain parts of their bodies which in the average person are not under individuated control. During World War II, some soldiers quartered on Pacific islands for long periods of time learned to individuate muscles under tattoos of hula girls on their forearms so that the figures seemed to come alive. The easiest example of a new movement individuation for the average person to try to learn is that of wiggling the ears. Most people have never individuated the movements involved in this rather ludicrous act.

Some of the speech sounds of foreign languages seem to involve muscle movements which the average student has never subjected to individuated voluntary control. Hindustani has some speech distinctions which the untrained ear cannot even detect. The trilled r of French involves movement individuation unfamiliar to many American children; so do the rr in Spanish and the umlaut o (ö) in German. Verbal explanation is of little help to the novice in these areas. Highly skilled and complex motor performances, whether piano playing, ballet dancing, or new and novel routines in gymnastics, may include an individual movement of some body part over which we have not developed independent (individuated) control. The recent development by tumblers and divers of double and triple twists in the air probably includes some such learning.

Procedures for Individuating Body-Part Movements

Certain procedures are helpful in learning to separate out a new movement and control it voluntarily; that is, in learning to move independently a body part that has always moved in conjunction with others (ring finger, for example). If the body part is not subject to voluntary control, we move the associated parts and try to move the new part with them (move jaw and scalp muscles to move ear). We try to focus attention and strong emotionally toned stimuli toward the part we wish to move until we can get some kind of spill-over of energy into the musculature of that part; thereby we produce the movement and also see, feel, and identify it (the seeing may be with the help of a mirror). Our next problem is to relax so that the tension will leave the associated but extraneous musculature. From here on, one should practice in an attempt to improve. In her "Electromyographic Demonstration of Facilitation," Partridge clarifies this process of strengthening and individuating a muscle movement.[23] Because of reflex linkage, activity may be produced by impulses arising proprioceptively in other components of the synergy. This is the basic principle involved in the individuation of movement.[24]

This description of the adult trying to learn to isolate a new movement and to subject it to voluntary control must not be taken as an explanation of the child's learning of movement individuation. The child has no background in associated musculature, little experience in consciously focusing attention on and recognizing movement sensations from a specific body part, and little awareness of how to go about such learning. Yet the child does develop movement individuation as a part of many skills.

Single Motor-Unit Control

Experiments during the last decade in the learning of control of single motor units *within a muscle* illustrate but do not explain some characteristics of motor learning. The term "motor unit" as used in this sense means a group of striated muscle fibers *within a specific muscle* which is attached to only one motor neuron. Fibrous connective tissue within the muscle acts as insulation for a motor unit. The experimental procedure is to insert a fine-wire intramuscular electrode (25 to 75 microns in diameter) into the muscle. The insertion instrument is a sterilized hypodermic needle. The changing voltage of the motor unit, the myoelectric potential, is then picked up and amplified by an electronic circuit that can be connected to an oscilloscope and to a loudspeaker and audioamplifier. Knowledge of success in activating the motor unit appears to the subject as the spikes on a cathode-ray oscilloscope or the sound from the loudspeaker.

A gentle "twitch" of a single motor unit does not produce a movement visible to the naked eye. Subjects learn by trying to produce the desired effect on the oscilloscope or loudspeaker. They work until they get the desired results, as indicated by the "artificial" feedback. Subjects say they don't know how they are doing it and cannot explain the success except to state that they thought about a motor unit as they had seen and heard it personally (Basmajian, pp. 277, 267). Subjects have learned to control separate motor units *within the same muscle*, independently of each other. They learn to isolate individual units, speed up or slow down rate of firing, turn them off or on in set patterns or in response to commands.[25]

It is perhaps a fair hypothesis to state that much motor learning, especially by youngsters in free play and unsupervised practice, is somewhat similar in learning processes to the single motor-unit learning just discussed. There seems to be trial and continual revision in terms of knowledge of results without much understanding of the motor-pattern adjustments. It is not even established that rational analysis, with attempts to plan and anticipate the changes to be made, will speed up the rate of motor learning of many aspects of skills (see Polanyi's discussion of indefinable knowledge, Chapter 2). Locke expressed somewhat this idea when he said:

> In the final analysis, skill, from the learner's standpoint, is concerned with results *in the environment* and not process in the performer.[26]

SUMMARY

Human beings today are bigger, stronger, and more skillful in many physical activities than their counterparts in any preceding generation. This progress is due to our ability to pass on experience vicariously to succeeding generations. Health knowledge, especially in nutrition and in the conditioning of the human body, skill forms and procedures, technical knowledge and knowledge of basic mechanics, all have contributed to making modern people highly developed physical instruments.

Our behavior is changed, adapted, and adjusted, often in progressive hierarchies of advancement, through training and experience. The closest analogy we can draw to the physiological nature of the human organism is the servomechanism and the electronic computer. We do know that we have proprioceptive facilitation with continuous sensory feedback and cord and midbrain servomechanisms. We have large sensory, motor, and association areas in which, apparently, experience is programmed for this human computer. These complex integrative areas seem to develop with experience into higher and higher levels of programming. The data that arrive from the various sense organs are then reassembled in terms of previous experience already programmed into the computer, and response solutions are turned out. The experience accmulated by the individual as life goes on (assuming feedback of results and intent to improve) makes possible finer and finer "computations" and response adjustments.

We seem to have a motor-memory storage area in which skilled acts can be stored, then discharged automatically on receiving the appropriate stimuli. If stimuli follow each other in rapid succession, a fraction of a second occurs (0.1 to 0.4 sec) between responses. The automatic responses of skilled acts do not involve concurrent accompaniment of conscious awareness.

There are three types of monitoring of motor-skill acts: exteroceptive guidance, proprioceptive guidance, and preprogrammed motor-memory discharge. When the act occurs too rapidly to permit monitoring of the act by afferent feedback, the action is called open-loop action. Closed-loop action implies monitoring from feedback.

After infancy one builds skill complexities on the postural and body-control bases, the simple skills one already possesses. This progression, this building on an already learned organization, means that the very nature of the learning process changes. The parts one puts together in maturity already have unique associations and meanings, and the learning is now a strengthening of associations between what are, at this stage, not wholly unrelated activities.

Phylogenetic development (for example, postural controls, eye coordination, reaching and grasping, crawling) does not seem to be greatly accelerated by short periods of special training, but ontogenetic development (for example, using eating utensils, performing toilet routines, buttoning clothes, swimming) seems to be highly dependent on training and experience.

The almost ceaseless bodily activity of the infant, plus whatever innate determinants of the direction of development may exist, seem to ensure that the normal youngster will develop most of the muscle contractions (and hence movements) it needs for later integration into physical skills. The integration of these movements into a pattern for some purpose is what we mean by motor-skill learning. Two very early examples of simple integration are the child's picking up an object that catches his attention, or his grasping a bottle and holding it to his mouth. It is impossible to separate maturation influence from learning influences in these early stages.

Individuation is the process of learning to divorce body-part performance and control from activities of the whole body. The body part must work over a dynamic or static postural base. Its performance may be (1) over a still base, (2) adjusted to utilize the momentum of a moving base, or (3) adjusted to offset interfering effects of unsuitable body momentum in diverse directions.

Learning to make a new movement not previously under voluntary control involves securing its movement as a part of a gross act; gradual practice with attention on the part to be moved and with attempts to relax the other muscles of the gross act; and practice until the movement occurs as an individuated act with its own "prime-mover" muscle. This extreme type of movement learning is less common in motor learning after infancy but may be needed in certain rehabilitation cases, in the precise refinements of certain adjustments requiring a high level of skill, or in learning certain foreign language sounds not present in one's own language. Recent experiments in learning to control and individuate single motor units *within a specific muscle* may be somewhat like learning to sort out and bring under voluntary control a movement originally not subject to voluntary control. The procedures for presenting knowledge of the results to the learner seem to indicate considerable similarity.

DISCUSSION QUESTIONS

1. Is the modern individual an inferior specimen compared with the American pioneer?

2. Are the greater longevity, larger size, and better health of our present generation due directly or indirectly to learning?

3. Can the servomechanisms of the body readjust many actions even after they are underway?

4. Distinguish between exteroceptive and proprioceptive feedback.

5. What factors affect the length of the latency period between responses to stimuli occurring in rapid succession? Does one's simple reaction time influence the latency period before a subsequent response?

6. Does the hierarchical development of skills imply transfer?

7. Does the infant learn motor skills as rapidly as the adult?

8. Does training seem to accelerate phylogenetic development? ontogenetic development?

9. Does the child *learn* to make the innumerable movements he performs during infancy?

10. Should one focus attention on the muscular action when learning a motor pattern? when learning to isolate a movement out of a gross act?

11. Does the nature of the learning process change from infancy to maturity?

12. How does the postural base (dynamic or static) affect the motor pattern used to secure the same result (a goal, a basket, a hit, a bull's-eye)?

13. Is conscious awareness a concurrent accompaniment of skill action?

14. Explain Woodworth's point that perceptual trace helps produce the right note in singing or violin playing.

15. Give examples of the building of hierarchical motor units.

16. Does one employ exactly the same muscle patterns on subsequent responses to quite similar cues?

17. Is the learning process for precise motor acts quite different from the learning to control single motor units within a specific muscle? Explain your answer.

18. What part does vicarious experience have in the "learning by doing" of the human body?

NOTES

1. Rushall and Siedentop describe learning as the shaping and controlling of behavior through reinforcement contingency (à la Skinner); and base learning on the relationship of behavior to its consequence. See Brent S. Rushall and Darrel Siedentop, *The Development and Control of Behavior in Sport* (Philadelphia: Lea & Febiger, 1970).

2. C. Judson Herrick, *Introduction to Neurology*, 3rd ed. (Philadelphia: W. B. Saunders, 1922), p. 28.

3. The cybernetic hypothesis of the nature of human behavior controls was first proposed by Norbert Wiener. For his latest discussion, consult his *Cybernetics*, 2nd ed. (New York: Wiley, 1961). See also K. U. Smith and M. F. Smith, *Cybernetic Principles of Learning and Educational Design* (New York: Holt, Rinehart, & Winston, 1966).

4. See statement of William James, quoted on page 54.

5. David Legge, ed., *Skills* (Penguin Books, 1970), p. 11.

6. Franklin Henry, "Increased Response Latency for Complicated Movements and a 'Memory Drum' Theory of Neuromotor Reaction," *Research Quarterly*, 31, 3 (October 1960), 449.

7. *Ibid.*

8. Walter Kroll, "Quality of Simple Reaction Time and the Psychological Refractory Period," *Research Quarterly*, 39, 1 (March 1968), 113.

9. Donald S. Siegel, "The Nature and Significance of the Response

Latency Associated with the Amendment of Movements of Varying Complexity." Unpublished doctoral dissertation, University of North Carolina at Greensboro, 1975.

10. C. B. Gibbs, "Servo Control Systems in Organisms and the Transfer of Skill," in *Skills*, ed. David Legge (Baltimore: Penguin Books, 1970), p. 212.

11. Richard A. Schmidt, "Psychology of Motor Behavior and Sport," in *Proceedings of the National Association for Sociology of Sport and Physical Activity*, 1973, p. 53.

12. "Programmed" is used to mean muscle commands structured before the movement sequence begins, and uninfluenced by peripheral feedback. See the discussion by Steven W. Keele, "Movement Control in Skilled Motor Performance," *Psychological Bulletin*, 70, 6 (1968), 487–503.

13. R. S. Woodworth, "The Accuracy of Voluntary Movement," *Psychological Review Monograph*, 3, 2, Supplement (1899), 56ff. See also Legge, *op. cit.*, p. 147.

14. The implication here is that the stimuli are received and responded to in terms of past learning. However, the use of the word "perception" may be slightly misleading in this case if the assumption is made that the recognition of stimulus occurs at the level of conscious awareness, for a great many of the detailed adjustments of motor responses occur below this level. This point will be developed more fully later in the text.

15. John McGeoch, *The Psychology of Human Learning* (New York: Longmans, Green, 1942), p. 445.

16. D. O. Hebb, *The Organization of Behavior* (New York: Science Editions, 1961), p. 111.

17. M. V. Senden, *Raum- und Gestaltauffassung bei operierten Blindgeborenen vor und nach der Operation* (Leipzig: J. A. Barth, 1932); James B. Miner, "A Case of Vision Acquired in Adult Life," *Psychological Review Monograph*, 6, 5, Supplement (March 1905), 108–18.

18. Hebb, *op. cit.*, p. 114.

19. *Ibid.*, p. 109.

20. Johan Huisinga, *Homo Ludens: A Study of the Play Element in Culture* (Boston: Beacon, 1950), pp. 2–4.

21. See Leonard Carmichael, "Heredity and Environment: Are They Antithetical?" *Journal of Abnormal and Social Psychology*, 20, 3 (October 1925), 257.

22. John Lawther, "Movement Individuation, Motor Pattern Learning, and Creativity," in *Contemporary Psychology of Sport*, ed. Gerald S. Kenyon (Chicago: The Athletic Institute, 1970), p. 630.

23. Miriam J. Partridge, "Electromyographic Demonstration of Facilitation," *Physical Therapy Review*, 34, 5 (May 1954), 227–33.

24. See Ernest Gellhorn, *Physiological Foundations of Neurology and Psychiatry* (Minneapolis: University of Minnesota Press, 1953).

25. See descriptions in J. B. Basmajian, "Microcosmic Learning Single Nerve-Cell Training," *Psychology of Motor Learning* (Chicago: Proceedings of Committee on Institutional Cooperation on Psychology of Motor Learning, The Athletic Institute, 1970), pp. 261–81. See also V. F. Harrison and O. A. Mortenson, "Identification and Voluntary Control of Single Motor-Unit Activity in the Tibialis Anterior Muscle," *Anatomical Record,* 144 (1962), 109–16; and "The Independent Control of Two Individual Motor Units in the Same Muscle." Unpublished study by Garland O'Quinn, Pennsylvania State University, February 1970.

26. Lawrence F. Locke, "Movement Education—A Description and Critique," in *New Perspectives of Man in Action,* ed. R. C. Brown and Bryant J. Cratty (Englewood Cliffs, N.J.: Prentice-Hall, 1969), p. 222.

Two

Aspects of and Factors Affecting Motor Learning and Skill Development, Infancy to Old Age

Learning is cumulative, hierarchical, and self-generative.

In psychology, we often draw conclusions about human behavior from the results of animal experiments. One famous example is the chicken pecking experiment in which chickens were prevented from pecking at grain and other food during their early development.[1] Later on they were compared with chickens who had been allowed experience in pecking. The chickens deprived of the early experience pecked just about as well later on as those who had had the earlier practice. The conclusion was that maturation, rather than learning, produced the precision in pecking. Unfortunately, conclusions similar to those drawn from the chicken experiment and other animal development studies are often drawn about human learning. If the human infant had a chicken brain, with its great lack of association areas and its rather limited sensory areas, such an analogy might make sense.

Normal youngsters have far more complicated brains. They need experience to learn most of their adaptations to life. They take on their early primary adaptations much more slowly than do animals, but the possible adaptations available to them are so far beyond the capability of any animal that comparison leads to about as many erroneous conclusions as correct ones. In other words, human behavior is highly dependent on learning, and the human needs a great quantity of experience in order to acquire primary learnings.

Increase in preschool opportunity to learn motor skills produces greater breadth of interests, more confidence for new ventures, superiority in certain sociomotor skills, better atttiudes; and such superiority tends to persist in later years.[2]

21

Some twenty-five years ago a colleague and I published this statement about the value for youngsters of preschool opportunities to learn motor skills. In this chapter we will consider present thinking about motor-skill training at early ages.

FACTORS AFFECTING RATE AND AMOUNT
OF CHILDHOOD MOTOR LEARNING

Parents will sometimes attempt to foster certain ontogenetic developments that are in immediate demand, such as eating skills and toilet routines. However, several factors tend to cause postponement of more extensive attempts at educating the very young. First, later attempts produce success more quickly because the almost constantly active child has now had more time to acquire postural bases, some eye-hand coordinations, and even a bit more strength as a result of incidental learning. Skills develop in hierarchies, and the higher complexities are more difficult to develop if the component parts (the simpler skills) have not yet been acquired. The lower levels of the hierarchy, the so-called primary learnings of infancy and preschool days, not only take much time to develop but seem to need a much greater quantity of attempts, of trial experiences, before they are acquired.

If the adult attempts to teach a child a skill so complex that adequate postural bases (both static and dynamic) have not yet been acquired, the more complex pattern will develop very slowly, if it is learned at all. Effective methods of teaching change with the level of learning of the learner himself. The methods for the lowest levels require great patience and understanding of both (1) the extra time factor and (2) the quantity-of-experience factor. The youngster will need hundreds of trials over months and months of time.

Jones made an extensive observational study of twenty-four children from the twenty-first through the thirty-third month, then again during the thirty-sixth month and the forty-eighth month. In an analysis of their motor development, she says:

> An integration of the activities began as soon as each activity had reached a stage where all the child's attention was not required in its performance. It seemed that each activity had to become automatic before the child was free to combine activities to any great extent. . . . To a large extent, each activity was repeated over and over, without much coordination between the skills involved.[3]

Jones lists as helpful factors in the child's development a home environment with a playmate one to three years older than the subject, a variety of available play materials, and outdoor play space with opportunity for freedom in locomotor activities. She lists as handicapping factors a full-time maid, relatives other than the parents living in the home, over-protection by adults, and inhibition in locomotor activities at home.

Brief periods of specialized training of infants by adults have not tended to prove advantageous, for later performance reveals no significant difference between briefly trained infants and those without the training. But although relatively limited amounts of practice do not seem to produce permanent superiority, there is some evidence that extensive training does accelerate development. The slowness of early basic learning and the great quantity of experience necessary to produce observable change perhaps account for the findings of such studies. The great amount of incidental learning resulting from the almost constant motor activity of the preschool child greatly overshadows the influence of brief training periods.

Many a fond mother trains her child through iteration and reitera-tion, day after day and month after month, during these preschool years. Her love for the child, her great concern for her child's welfare, and her great pride in even the simplest achievements endow her with the patience that is so necessary during this basic learning stage. When she errs, it is usually either by overprotectiveness, too much help, and therefore further-ing of dependence; or exasperation with the child's slow rate of learning, harshness, and therefore inhibition. The fine line between adequate parental care and guidance and enough freedom for exploration and self-dependence by the child is difficult to determine. The neglected child may progress rapidly in some types of motor development as a result of the necessity for self-help, but at the same time may lose out in social and emotional development.

Infant Training of Johnny and Jimmy

Almost four decades ago Myrtle McGraw published the results of her much-quoted study of the twins, Johnny and Jimmy,[4] and four years later a follow-up study appeared.[5] McGraw was attempting to determine the effect of early training on motor-skill development. From the age of twenty-one days to twenty-two months, Johnny was subjected to a highly stimulating environment. He was given daily opportunity and encourage-ment to engage in both phylogenetic and ontogenetic types of activities—stimuli to various kinds of mobility such as ascending and descending inclined planes, getting on and off pedestals, playing with multiple sticks, manipulating graded stools and boxes, jumping, cycling, swimming, and skating.

Jimmy, in the meantime, was given no specific training and spent most of his time in his crib. At the age of twenty-two months, Jimmy was introduced to the activities Johnny had already experienced. He was given highly stimulating training in activities in which he was less skilled than Johnny. After two and a half months of training, Jimmy had approached Johnny's level of skill, although he never quite attained it. In the follow-up study four years later, their differences were not great, but Johnny still exhibited greater self-confidence and superior ease and skill.

The age at which Johnny acquired various skills is worth noting. By the age of eight months he was swimming 7 feet. At fourteen months he was swimming 15 feet with his face submerged and was jumping from a height of 5 feet. He had been started on roller skates at the age of 350 days and at the age of 694 days had acquired reactions that "consisted primarily of the broad rhythmical sway which is characteristic of a proficient skater." [6]

Two or three of McGraw's statements call attention to certain important aspects of the effects of preschool training. With regard to Johnny's skating ability *before he was two years old,* McGraw says:

> . . . the skating ability is so outstandingly beyond that of any other child of corresponding chronological age that it would be impossible to deny the influence of daily exercise or repetition of performance upon the development of a specific skill of this type. [7]

With regard to the effect of training on the so-called phylogenetic activities, McGraw says:

> While use of the activity will not advance appreciably the day a child begins to walk alone and will not alter the general method of progression, exercise may influence the grace with which he steps, his speed and his mien of progression. [8]

One other point that relates to specificity of training and transfer is worth quoting here because of its implications. McGraw says:

> Although Johnny had enjoyed earlier and more extensive practice in certain activities, he apparently was not greatly benefited thereby in the acquisition of performances of a different order; i.e., when the gross movement patterns were quite dissimilar to those in the early training, Johnny's advantage disappeared. [9]

The results of this study have been challenged in various ways, including questioning whether or not the twins were fraternal rather than identical, and hence could be expected to be as unlike as brothers and sisters (mere siblings). Nevertheless, it does call attention to the very early age at which the infant can learn relatively complex motor skills, and thereby raises serious questions about many of the traditional concepts of readiness.

SOME CURRENTLY
POPULAR CONCEPTS
OF CHILD DEVELOPMENT

Various hypotheses about ways to facilitate the development of the infant and young child have been advanced, particularly with reference to the retarded child or the slow learner. The Domans and Delacato from the Institute for Achievement of Human Potentials in Philadelphia hypothesize that reading readiness depends on "complete neurological organization," properly fostered by the correct sequence of infant developmental motor activity. Delacato proposes that reading difficulty can be treated by proper developmental physical exercise, programmed in terms of the gaps he hypothesizes have occurred in the normal sequence of infant developmental motor development; and that reading difficulty can be prevented from occurring in the primary years if such treatment has been adequately administered in the preschool years. He classifies the causes of "inadequate neurological organization" under three headings: (1) heredity, (2) trauma, and (3) lack of environmental opportunity for complete neurological organization. Delacato believes that 70 percent of those suffering from inadequate neurological organization belong in the third category and that his treatments will greatly help most of them.

Dr. Temple Fay, in his discussion of treatment of spastic types of paralysis, described the prescribed exercise treatments, which were later expanded and used extensively at the Institute for Achievement of Human Potentials. He emphasized the recapitulation theory (repetition in the individual's development of stages gone through in the evolution of the human being) and said:

> . . . the patterns of the past lie far below the cortex and, when this higher level is afflicted, may emerge through proper reflex stimulation to give the crude elements of movement and of power that prevailed before the cerebral hemispheres developed.[10]

Fay described the crawling-pattern exercises utilized in the subject's development as progressing from homolateral, prone, belly-down crawling to the "crossed diagonal pattern" of creeping. He advocated a program of neuromuscular therapy based on our evolutionary past—an application of the values of "reflex movement" or proprioceptive playback to stir up and utilize primordial patterns on which, he hypothesized, our later development is based.[11]

Delacato says he diagnoses the child by examining sequential stages of its infant development. In the reeducation procedure, Delacato has the child start at the developmental level, which he diagnoses as having

25

been the period at which inadequacies arose; he then programs the treatment to have the child put through rather intense training in the precise pattern—ranging from prone, belly-down, homolateral crawling to cross-pattern creeping on hands and knees, for example—until the child has mastered each stage to the doctor's satisfaction. He also stresses training for dominance of one side of the body only—hand, foot, and eye. Some of his theories are these:

1. The necessity for hemispheric dominance
2. The recapitulation theory (ontogeny recapitulates phylogeny)
3. A specific organization of the brain with localization of brain function
4. The great dependence of later intellectual growth on early motor development

Many objections have been raised to Delacato's theoretical basis. One of the better analyses is that presented in the *28th Yearbook* of the Claremont Graduate School Curriculum Laboratory, Claremont, California, 1964, pp. 119–31, edited by Malcolm P. Douglass. In the preceding *Yearbook* (1963), Carl Delacato presented his viewpoints under the title "The Ontogeny of Reading Problems" (pp. 119–25).[12] In the *28th Yearbook,* under the title "Delacato in Review," Dr. F. Theodore Perkins, professor of psychology at the Graduate Center, presents an analysis entitled "Problems Arising from Assertions of Assumptions of Delacato." Then Dr. Leon Oettinger, director of the Department of Electroencephalography at St. Luke Hospital, Pasadena, discusses the theory from the standpoint of pediatrics. Finally, Dr. William J. Hudspeth, Laboratory of Psychobiology, Claremont Graduate School, writes on "The Neurobehavioral Implausibility of the Delacato Theory." Let us examine some of the points made in these studies.

The hemispheric dominance theory was proposed by Orton and Travis in 1929–30 at Iowa; it was later abandoned when training for this dominance did not result in expected improvement. Longitudinal studies of children have indicated that the recapitulation theory is not an accurate description of child development. Franz and Lashley long ago refuted the "localization of brain function" theory; [13] and most of the recent studies of the physiology of motor learning have indicated no such hierarchical organization as Delacato describes. There is not much evidence that early motor development is predictive of later intellectual development. Finally, there are many ambidextrous people who show no evidence of any mental retardation—in fact, many are intellectually brilliant.

Two studies on creeping, laterality, and reading were completed by Melvin P. Robbins. The first, his doctoral study at the University of Chicago, was reviewed in *Rehabilitation Literature,* 27, 7 (July 1966),

210–11; the second was reviewed in the October issue of the same magazine. In the October issue the problem is attacked thus:

> Both [studies] tested certain relations between neurological organization and reading in the light of Delacato's theory; the primary question is whether evidence gathered in a systematic and controlled manner supports the postulated relationship between reading and creeping, as well as that between reading and laterality.

Neither study gave any support to Delacato's theory, and Robbins seriously questions the scientific basis of such a theory.[14] In a later study, Robbins and Glass say that, after a careful review of the theory, one is led to this conclusion:

> . . . the tenets are either unsupported or overwhelmingly contradicted when tested by theoretical, experimental, or logical evidence from the relevant scientific literature.[15]

The Archives of Physical Medicine and Rehabilitation, April 1968, presents a short critical review by seven major medical and health organizations of the Doman-Delacato claims and techniques in which they seriously question them. They state that Doman and Delacato withdrew from one comprehensive, government-supported study designed to test their theory. In the *Journal of the A.M.A.* (October 1967, pp. 385–88), a child psychologist, Dr. Roger D. Freeman, concludes that the sweeping claims for cure and the extreme demands on parents to become practically full-time therapists are unjustified by present evidence. In the *Time Magazine* section on Medicine (May 31, 1968, pp. 50–51), the reports of Doman-Delacato critics are reviewed. *Time* says:

> This month, ten major medical and health organizations have stated categorically that patterning was "without merit" and chided its inventors for claiming cures without documentation. (p. 50)

The interest the Doman-Delacato doctrines have in making better education available to the retarded child is perhaps a worthwhile contribution. At least, there are now many other different types of programs devoted to this aspect of education. The greatly increased amount of stimulation, care, and affection which is lavished on these children, particularly the increase in quantity of sensory input and physical stimulation under the Doman-Delacato program, should produce some improvement. However, the regimens prescribed in this program are so demanding and inflexible as to lead to neglect of other family members' needs and to increase the anxiety of already burdened and confused parents.[16]

Newell C. Kephart has done considerable work in the area of retarded children and has presented the theoretical background for his procedures.[17] He stresses particularly what he calls the gross motor bases which the child must learn first. He theorizes that the young child goes through a very definite sequence of perceptual-motor learning, and that all subsequent more complex learning is built on these early learning experiences. Starting with early learning to sit up and to hold the head up, the child progresses to *differentiation* (called individuation in this text) such as wrist and finger movements of grasping and picking up objects. Kephart cites previous sources which state that posture is the basic movement pattern out of which all other movement patterns must develop. He thinks that the center gravitational line in one's posture is the zero point for direction, space orientation, and movement.

His concept of laterality and its development is quite different from that of the Delacato dominance hypothesis. Kephart wants the child to experience adequate types of learning situations so that the body (not necessarily at the level of conscious awareness) learns to respond with its appropriate parts—arms, legs, or hips, right or left or with limbs from both sides—as the exigencies of the situation demand. In other words, the individual must develop a *body sense* of laterality, of right and left, just as he or she must develop a body sense of up and down and of backward and forward.

Perceptual organization develops to some degree along with the individual's motor patterns and continues to develop a little later. In other words, the infant develops a quantity of body knowledge that is matched later with perceptual experience. The eyes learn to move together and follow the hand until eye-hand directional kinesthesis is developed. Directionality develops from (1) movements of the limbs out from the center of the body toward objects, (2) movement of the body toward objects, (3) the turning of the eyes to follow hand movements, and (4) the matching of the ocular kinesthesis of this eye movement toward an object with hand contact of the object. Later, pursuit games bring on higher levels of this directional development. The progressive matching of motor activity and visual (or auditory) perception develops into space orientation.

Kephart says that the body image is the point of origin of all spatial relationships of objects outside the body. The motor activities of the child teach him "awareness of his body in space and what it can do." Kephart therefore advocates a series of activities through which the motor bases of the backward child may be developed. According to his hypothesis, the proper development of these motor bases will accelerate all later learning, including academic learning. Kephart's listed activities include (1) much chalkboard training to develop eye-hand laterality and directionality; (2) much sensory-motor exercise—balance boards, trampoline, Angels-in-the-Snow, stunts, games, rhythms;

(3) form perception training—puzzles, stick figures, pegboards. It would take too much space here to describe Kephart's proposed developmental program adequately, but we should note that regardless of one's acceptance or rejection of his theories of education, his activity program seems to hold some value for the *physical* development of the child who is greatly retarded in motor abilities.

Kephart developed a perceptual-motor survey that purported to determine areas of weakness in the perceptual-motor development of children. The survey consists of thirty items divided into eleven subtests, with each subtest purporting to measure some particular aspect of the individual's motor development. In 1962 Roach completed a doctoral study at Purdue University in which he attempted to establish the reliability and validity of the survey.[18] Roach compared scores made on Kephart's scale by two hundred normal children from the first through the fourth grades with a group of referrals in the school system who were normal in intelligence but who had been referred to The Achievement Center for Children at Purdue University as nonachievers. Roach reported that 85 percent of the nonachievers scored below 65 on the survey scale, whereas 83 percent of the control group from the regular classes scored about 65.

In 1964 Little completed a study of the same scale in which he compared the survey scale scores of 103 children with IQs ranging from 50 to 79, all of whom had been approved for the special education program of the Indianapolis public schools, with a control group of like ages from the regular classes. He found no statistically significant differences in mean total survey scale scores between the educable mentally retarded children and normal children of approximately the same chronological ages and stated that the proposed cutoff point of 65 on the survey scale did not differentiate the two groups.

Little did find significant differences on five subtests—jumping, identification of body parts, imitation of movements, Kraus-Weber scores, and Angels in the Snow. Little's findings of significant differences in the scores of the respective groups on some items are to be expected, as many other studies have reported positive though low correlations between aggregates of physical measurements and mental ability, particularly at the lower end of the intelligence scale.[19]

We must keep in mind, however, that concomitant variation is not necessarily a cause-effect relationship. We would need different evidence before assuming that motor development produces academic aptitude. The problem is a difficult one. Perceiving just what to do in the physical situation (grasping the idea) may be as much a mental as a physical activity, even in as simple an act as a child's imitation of a parent's motor act. On the other hand, many mental tests have physical performance aspects, particularly for the lower age levels—the cutting with the tiny shears in the Stanford Revision of the Binet-Simon test, for example. Moreover, some of the experts using the so-called motor aptitude tests (Lincoln Revision of the Oseretsky, for example) have reported that such tests involve certain intellectual weightings. When the question of this weighting is added to the criticism of the degree to which these tests are valid instruments for motor aptitude prediction, the problem of individual diagnosis and prescription becomes even more difficult. Of course, it is possible that all we are doing in our attempts at analysis is proposing a false dichotomy of mind and body when in fact the two aspects are inseparable in terms of the young child's learning experience. With respect to the intellectual development of the preschool child, Bruner stated that the first stage

> . . . consists principally in establishing relationships between experience and action; his concern is with manipulating the world through action. This stage corresponds roughly to the period from the first development of language to the point at which the child begins to manipulate symbols.[20]

The reader should compare this discussion of Kephart's theories with the earlier discussion of learning changes from infancy to maturity in Chapter 1. With regard to the development of early learning patterns, Hebb says, "It is reasonable to suppose in general that, the less familiar the situation or the task to be performed, the more important slow-increment learning becomes." [21] As we have seen, Jones calls attention to the fact that each act must become automatic before the child can combine activities.

Readiness

Jones's analysis throws some light on the idea of "readiness"—that lower levels of sensory-motor and perceptual skills must be automatized before the child is ready for the next stage. About the only evidence we have as to readiness is the *average age* at which previous children have shown interest and attacked with success a particular learning area. Some longitudinal studies have attempted to list the developments essential before the next stage can be attacked successfully, and a few tests or scales to check readiness have been attempted, but there is such a wide individual variability that prediction from averages has little value. In many fields (reading, motor skills) we are finding that the child may be "ready" long before the previously assumed age of readiness. Hereditary factors may cause difference in age of readiness. Richness of environmental experience seems to be a very important factor. The child's interest, upon exposure, is a very important determinant. Attempts to force learning on the very young child before necessary bases are developed may actually cause an emotional block to later learning. However, we tend to err more in postponement than in starting too soon, particularly in motor skills. The degree of the child's own interest and attention span is one of the best cues.

This trend toward lowering the age level at which readiness is assumed is becoming apparent in the academic field; for example, the study of languages, science, and mathematics is being moved to much younger ages. With regard to the introduction of the basic notions of science and mathematics even as early as the primary grades, Bruner says: "There is no reason to believe that any subject cannot be taught to any child at virtually any age in some form." [22]

The whole concept of readiness needs to be clarified, for misunderstanding has often delayed and perhaps retarded motor development in children. In analyzing early learning in terms of readiness, we must keep in mind the quantitative aspect of the process of motor learning and we must pay special attention to the large amount of incidental learning and its great importance in motor development. Perhaps the children are "ready" for the particular types of motor development, but the unit of learning with which they are started is too complex for their present level of hierarchical skill development. One is not ready to attempt fielding in the simplest baseball game until one has learned to throw and catch. However, one may be "ready," and have been ready for a considerable time, to learn to throw and catch.

Berelson and Steiner make a generalization about readiness for training that emphasizes not only the relative decrease in efficiency of too early training but also the loss of some degree of effectiveness of training postponed after readiness arrives. They say:

In the learning of complex skills or other abilities requiring training, practice is more effective at the point of maturation—not before, but also not long after, the period of biological readiness. [23]

In the attempts to understand the young child's learning and to foster it or improve its rate, four points stand out from the various observational and experimental studies. They are: (1) what seems to be a very slow rate of progress in primary or sensory-motor learning; (2) the need to automatize each activity before it can be integrated with another activity for a higher stage of learning; (3) the great number of experiences (the quantity of experience) necessary for primary learnings; and (4) the importance of motor experience—manipulating and exploring—as a *means* to learn intellectually as well as physically.

The first point, the slowness of the infant's sensory-motor learning, is perhaps one of the causes of much of the traditional teaching about readiness. It is perhaps illogical to conclude that just because a child learns more slowly at a certain age, he is therefore not ready to learn. The adult learns many things faster than the child chiefly because he or she has already mastered many of the basic elements and merely needs to integrate them into a more complex hierarchy of learning (see pp. 7–9). Moreover, effective teaching and learning methods are quite different at different levels.

The Quantity of Experience

The lives of children reared in a favorable environment are full of extensive and varied sense experiences, wide and fluctuating interests, and almost incessant activity. They repeat the same activity many, many times in reoccurring explorations. They build things and take them apart repeatedly. The sand pile and a little shovel or scoop and bucket furnish many hours of activity. So do pets and their own partly imaginative gardens. They play rough with Dad, tease, chase, or wrestle with brothers or sisters, climb and hang by their legs, move the furniture all around, pound with hammer and nails, try out hoops and balloons, various balls, velocipedes and bicycles, boats and rafts. With adult encouragement, they learn to swim, to roller skate or to ice skate.

Barker and Wright did a study of children's activity by following them around from early morning until late at night and recording their behavior. They found over two thousand different settings in which children reacted. By sampling techniques, they estimated the total number of behavior objects to which the normal eight-year-old can react as approximately 1,200,000. They found some 2,200 distinct activities involving about 660 different behavior objects during a waking day.[24]

Many observational studies of children report that they repeat, rework, iterate, and reiterate. Parents often notice the same iteration in the speech practice of preschool children. When very young, they will repeat or try to repeat the same expression, phrase, or sentence over and over until the nonunderstanding adult becomes impatient and orders them to stop. As many as seventy reiteration trials of a word, phrase, or sentence have been conducted in one sequence of such practice by a child.

Apparently a considerable quantity of experience is essential to many kinds of learning, and single experiences in these types of learning have little effect. Deprivation studies in which subjects are greatly restricted in stimulation have been found to produce rapid deterioration of function.[25] The organism seems to need a certain level of stimulation just to maintain normality and a great deal more to produce permanent change. John Anderson has hypothesized that the child's learning is due chiefly to "a high input and a high outgo," a flow of stimulation and response in which

> . . . single experiences or elements occupy relatively insignificant parts. What determines behavior are the relative proportions of different types of stimulation and the amount of reinforcement that occurs.[26]

The time factor, insofar as it involves quantity of experience, is often overlooked. The normal preschool child seems to be vigorously active in physical play eight or more hours every day. The elementary school child, if unrestricted by parents or other adult controls, will engage in physical play before school in the mornings, at noon, after school in the evenings, most of Saturday and Sunday, with greatly increased amounts of activity during holidays and vacations. Then compare this quantity of experience of the active youngster with the amount of activity time in the school physical education program. The "best" programs devote fifty to sixty minutes a day, five days a week, to physical education. Getting to and from class, showering, and dressing take up a part of this time each day. Students are fortunate if they get forty minutes of class activity each day. This amounts to three hours and twenty minutes, yet they will play at something, active or sedentary in nature, for longer than this outside of school on most school days. Saturday and Sunday will double the amount. In other words, the school time can only become really effective if it encourages, fosters, and even directs much of the time outside of school.

Controlled outside-of-school play, tag, hopscotch, all types of pursuit games, ropes to jump, apparatus to climb and to swing on, mats for tumbling or wrestling, swimming and skating, dancing and team games, plus opportunities to use facilities under guidance, will foster children's development. They need encouragement and guidance from intelligent, interested, and able parents, from recreation and playground supervisors, and from teachers through unorganized and organized extracurricular programs. Community planners must arrange for space and equipment, especially with regard to the more complex skills—skating, swimming, badminton, tennis, team games. Gymnastics with apparatus seem to have more appeal at the younger ages than in the late teens, as does track, although supervision and guidance without pressure or forcing is needed. The appropriate activities will vary with the climate and with the sport skills employed by the adults of the community. Children like to imitate adults, and most youngsters will learn much informally by trial and error, and by playing with, observing, and imitating others, peers or adults.

To expand and follow up a study done in 1954, in 1957 Lehman did a study of the swimming ability of entering college freshmen. In the

1954 study (2,505 subjects), 77 percent passed the swimming test on entrance to college; in 1957 (2,640 male subjects), 88 percent passed. Of the sample from 1957, 12 percent could not swim; 4 percent had learned through private instruction; 28 percent had learned in school or in clubs, camps, Red Cross classes, YMCA programs, and so on. However, 56 percent had learned informally—that is, without any organized or planned instruction. How much informal learning had contributed to the abilities of the other 32 percent who could swim (and had had some instruction) is unknown.[27]

Variety of Experience, Freedom, Self-Dependence

The effect of rich environmental experience in bringing about an earlier arrival of readiness, and hence greater progress by the child, calls attention to the need for breadth and variety, a broad base, in nursery school and kindergarten programs. Several studies have indicated that children who have had nursery and kindergarten training tend to maintain superiority in elementary school work over other groups of children who seem to be their equals in intelligence and social background, but who have not had this school exprience before entering first grade. Studies of children with preschool music training indicate a persistent group superiority in certain aspects of music over those without the preschool training.[28]

Studies comparing higher and lower socioeconomic groups with respect to motor development often report superiority of the lower economic groups in this aspect of development. Even Gesell, who tended to emphasize the importance of maturation in preschool development, reported finding this difference between economic levels. The finding has been reported frequently enough to cause us to question the methods of child motor training in "economically comfortable" families (although there are many exceptions—the statement is based on group averages). Questions have also been raised about the motor development aspects of current nursery schools and kindergartens.

A study by Gesell and Lord compared nursery school children, paired in other factors but with one of the pair from a home of low and the other from a home of high economic status. The age range of the subjects was thirty-one through fifty-two months. In most types of development the higher socioeconomic group was superior, but in the motor developments of self-care—ability to wash hands and face, comb the hair, brush the teeth, button clothes, tie shoes—the lower-class children excelled. The investigators suggested that the skills were learned out of necessity by the low group because their mothers were working away from home during the day.[29] Williams and Scott, in a study of black infants of contrasting socioeconomic backgrounds, reported significantly more acceleration in motor activities by the lower group. They attributed the superiority of the low socioeconomic group to a permissive atmosphere and to the absence of cribs, playpens, high chairs, and similar restrictive equipment.[30]

Similar findings were reported to me from a recent study of a large American city. The findings were quite disappointing to the school authorities, because they had hoped to find higher scores on the various motor-development tests in the schools with better buildings, higher paid teachers, and what they considered to be superior equipment. The points that were overlooked were the differences in restriction, in outdoor play, and in the frequency of necessity for self-care, as well as the absence in the homes of the poor of facilities and equipment for indoor and more sedentary play or entertainment. The poor encountered the frequent necessity for self-care, and were free to play untold hours outdoors in streets and alleys.

School and preschool experiences should be stimulating and should attempt to develop self-reliance and independence of action; moreover, they should challenge the child. Gutteridge reported after an extensive study (1,973 children, 31 trained observers, a sample taken from 14 states) that nursery school, kindergarten, and primary school equipment is not adequately challenging and does not provide varying opportunities or adequate stimulation for developing children's motor abilities.[31]

A few special programs have been designed in an attempt to give the child a developmental background plus freedom and self-dependence. "Movement education" and programs stressing "creativity" are examples. Movement education is supposed to help the children learn "the basic principles of how their bodies move, where they move in space and what their capabilities are." Tillotson says:

> Movement education aims to help children master the understandings and basic movement patterns which underlie all skills so that they can effectively participate in sports, dance well and move efficiently for everyday life situations.[32]

Creativity is supposed to be developed to a higher degree in programs in which freedom and independence of action are stressed, and in which teacher direction as to pattern, style, and form of action is reduced to a minimum.[33]

MOTOR-SKILL LEARNING

Studies of the motor-skill learning of primitive peoples make very clear to us the effects of quantity and variety of childhood experience.

Stumpf and Cozens, in describing the motor skills of the Maori, the Polynesian natives of New Zealand, say:

> Maori children seem to take to water as though it was their natural element, and under favorable circumstances learned to swim as soon as they learned to walk.[34]

In describing the training of the primitive Manus of New Guinea, Margaret Mead says:

> Expecting children to swim at three, to climb about like young monkeys even before that age, may look to us like forcing them; really it is simply a quiet insistence upon their exerting every particle or energy and strength which they possess.
>
> Swiming is not taught: the small waders imitate their slightly older brothers and sisters, and after floundering about in waist-deep water begin to strike out for themselves. Surefootedness on land and swimming come almost together, so that the charm which is recited over a newly delivered woman says, "May you not have another child until this one can walk and swim." [35]

Mead goes on to explain that mere infants are taught how to maneuver boats of all kinds:

> Early in the morning the village is alive with canoes in which the elders sit sedately on the center platforms while small children of three punt the canoes which are three or four times as long as the children are tall.[36]

There is great insistence on mastery of all physical skills by the child as early in infancy as possible:

> The test of this kind of training is in the results. The Manus children are perfectly at home in the water. They neither fear it nor regard it as presenting special difficulties and dangers. The demands upon them have made them keen-eyed, quick-witted, and physically competent like their parents. There is not a child of five who can't swim well. A Manus child who couldn't swim would be as aberrant, as definitely subnormal as an American child of five who couldn't walk.[37]
>
> His whole play world is so arranged that he is permitted to make small mistakes from which he may learn better judgment and greater circumspection, but he is never allowed to make mistakes which are serious enough to permanently frighten him or inhibit his activity. He is a tightrope walker, learning feats which we would count outrageously difficult for little children, but his tightrope is stretched above a net of expert parental solicitude.[38]
>
> In other aspects of adapting the children to the external world the same technique is followed. Every gain, every ambitious attempt is applauded; too ambitious projects are gently pushed out of the picture; small errors are simply ignored but important ones are punished. . . .[39]

This attitude, severe and unsympathetic as it appears on the surface, makes

children develop perfect motor coordination . . . but in the everyday activities of swimming, paddling, punting, climbing, there is a general high
level of excellence. And clumsiness, physical uncertainty and lack of poise,
is unknown among adults.[40]

Mead explains that physical development and skill is so universal
among the Manus that they have no word in their language for clumsiness. They had seen *all* adults finally achieve these great physical skills
and proficiencies. The child's lesser proficiency is simply described as
"not understanding yet." As a child, he learns all the skill necessary for
physical adjustment to life. Mead says:

By a system of training which is sure, unhesitant, unremitting in its insistence
and vigilance, the baby is given the necessary physical base upon which he
builds through years of imitation of older children and adults. The most
onerous part of his physical education is over by the time he is three. For
the rest it is play for which he is provided with every necessary equipment,
a safe and pleasant playground, a jolly group of companions of all ages and
both sexes. He grows up to be an adult wholly admirable from a physical
standpoint, skilled, alert, fearless, resourceful in the face of emergency,
reliable under strain.[41]

Organization and Attention Level

The organization and integration of various movements into a pattern to serve some purpose or achieve some goal is the process of motor-
skill acquirement. Once these discrete component movements are tied
together into a complex unit or whole of temporally ordered sequence,
and this larger and more complex activity becomes relatively automatic
in willed response to appropriate cues, we call it a skill. Exteroceptive
monitoring of the act (particularly and most frequently by vision) is reduced to a minimum; and proprioceptive monitoring (cerebellar and
unconscious) takes over. Learned direction of attention and learned cue
recognition precede the overt aspect of the motor act. So does the decision
of what to do and the motor-memory functioning. Fitts says:

A skilled response is one in which the receptor-effector feedback processes
are highly organized, both spatially and temporarily (sic).[42]

And Higgins says:

The cybernetic brain . . . has the functional characteristics or processes
which provide for information gathering (sensory mechanisms), information
storage (memory), decision-making, information updating, and adaptive
response.[43]

At advanced stages of skill development, the larger and more complex
hierarchical unit is internalized, often with component parts (subroutines)

preprogrammed in the motor-memory drum, and with temporal continuities monitored proprioceptively and unconsciously.

Much skill performance is turned over to the body's automatic control while the attention is on sensing and predicting the next appropriate act. This anticipation permits less attention on the motor act and faster response. The student listens to the lecturer while continuing to write notes of what has already been said. The pianist reads the notes that are to follow those his fingers are executing. The typist keeps his eyes on the script ahead of the words he is actually typing. The typist or reader concentrates on the words, phrases, and sentences, usually grasping word groups instead of individual letters. At times an error, such as a misspelling, may cause him to focus on a detail of the display, although even misspellings are often overlooked in the meaningful integration of the larger unit. This relatively automatic, sequential typing or writing letters of words in the sentences is apparently partly closed-loop proprioceptively guided action. The letters (and occasionally the words) are usually motor-memory discharge—units preprogrammed and released without even proprioceptive monitoring. It would seem that preprogramming, proprioceptive monitoring, and at times a bit of exteroceptive guidance during pauses contribute to extensive note taking or typing.

Once a skill is highly developed, unconscious motor memory and proprioceptive monitoring produce the muscle-movement patterns. Batting or catching a baseball or stroking a tennis ball call forth a succession of already-existing relatively flexible but relatively automatic motor-memory patterns. By "flexible" we mean that these motor patterns are adjusted at the moment to the spatial and temporal cues of the situation.

As skill develops, simple motor components are tied together into larger units, into larger and larger hierarchies of motor response, and reduced to unconscious, automatic motor-memory or proprioceptive control. Sometimes the well-learned skills become so programmed that they run off too rapidly for proprioceptive feedback to influence them. As Lashley says: "An effector mechanism can be pre-set or primed to discharge at a given intensity for a given duration, in independence of any sensory controls." [44] Lashley calls attention to the separate finger movements in piano playing that can occur as rapidly as sixteen per second (0.065 sec each). The reliance here is on nonperceptive motor-memory discharge.

In Jones's study of the development of motor skills in children in the second and third years of life, she notes that each of the simpler activities of the child must become relatively automatic before they can be combined into a larger and more complex unit. In other words, these simple activities must first come under motor-memory and proprioceptive control before they can unite to form larger, more sophisticated skill continuities. The simpler skills, once established in motor memory and linked proprioceptively into functional continuities, can be carried out with exteroceptive cues to release the action. Even when the more complex units are not "ballistic" (when the temporal span is somewhat extended), the performance can be carried out automatically (unconsciously and proprioceptively guided) with the attention on ahead. However, it should be remembered that exteroceptive cues and especially vision are necessary during the early learning of these simpler skills, or what are later sub-routines. As the learning progresses, proprioceptive feedback is relied upon; the simpler acts can be conducted without much visual attention; and then more easily linked into the more complex units or higher hierarchies. When the skill is learned until it is proprioceptively guided, it is reduced to cerebellar monitoring and therefore does not involve conscious attention to the details of the act.

Perceptual Discrimination and Automatic Action

Youngsters about to learn to throw a baseball or kick a football already have all the necessary movements and much of the postural-base control in their repertoire. They now learn a total, more complex, highly integrated continuity of action, a new pattern or a series of new patterns, to fit a new purpose. Adolescents or adults learning to drive a car need to learn to perceive the cues to action, and then to select and integrate the appropriate movements. They have made, thousands of times, all the separate movements they must now learn to integrate into new patterns of action. Their problems are (1) perception, (2) movement selection, and (3) integration of these movements into the unit of action. They must learn not *how* but *when* to press on the accelerator or the brake pedal. They must learn the appropriate degree of force to apply as indicated by the perceived situation. Force and range of movement in turning the steering wheel are learned from the feedback of results and continual revision in an attempt to improve. Each range of movement, each force to apply, and the timing of the respective movements are adjustments learned from playback of results when reacting to perceived situations. Foot and hand movements are integrated into an automatized continuity of responses to successive cue perception. As the skills of driving develop, they involve extensive perceptual learning and subsequent automatic action, such as the discriminative perceptions and reactions to stop signals, speed zones, variations in road width, unevenness of road surface, chance pedestrians, and congested traffic. Successful driving is impossible without continual cue reception and continual feedback of results of initiated adjustments. Much of the movement adjustment and correction becomes automatic response to arriving cues. The driver learns to integrate much of his earlier simpler learning into the complexity of these new skills.

Hierarchical Linking. The integration of simple movements into movement patterns and into progressively more complex units, or larger loops of subroutines (to use the servomechanism language), is basic to high skill development. Bryan and Harter's experiment [45] in the learning of the Morse telegraphic code stressed this letter, syllable, word, phrase progression in the structuring of larger and larger automatic units of receiving or sending. The process of linking these smaller units or subroutines into larger and more complex units is a matter of continued motivated practice.

After much learning of a skill, the memory trace or drum storage of skilled patterns may be so preprogrammed that the temporal span from cue appearance to act execution is decreased and the patterns are established through shorter neural paths. Each movement component in the higher hierarchy serves as a conditioned stimulus for the subsequent component. As skills develop to high levels, they achieve proper activity sequence, correct timing, and smooth transition between the simpler movement components or subroutines. As Gibbs says:

> Learning permits prediction of the results of responses, and the delegation of monitoring from visual attention to proprioceptive mechanisms which function at subconscious level. Highly probable responses are initiated with a minimum of visual attention and a short visual response latency.[46]

Indefinable Knowledge. Just how simple units are linked together to form a higher unit in the skill hierarchy is often unexplainable. Polanyi says: "Indefinable knowledge is still an essential part of technology." [47] He recommends practical courses and apprenticeship to transmit skills. In his example of knowing how to ride a bicycle in terms of "indefinable knowledge," he says that the verbal explanation (". . . adjust the curvature of your bicycle path in proportion to the ratio of your unbalance over the square of the speed") has little meaning to the rider and he goes on to state that there are a number of other factors to be taken into account also, or the rider will fall. Much of our knowledge in skills (if knowledge is defined as relative mastery of performance) is not expressible in words. Polanyi says: "On an inarticulate level, men grope their way toward a skillful performance, unconsciously readjusting the coordination of their muscles in the direction of success." [48]

Another example Polanyi uses to illustrate skills not expressible in words is perhaps better. He speaks about the pathetic attempts of trained scientists "to produce a single violin of the kind the half-literate Stradi-

varius turned out as a matter of routine more than 200 years ago." [49]
Today we find that many a great athlete is unable to describe how he
himself performs unless he has previously studied in detail movies or
tapes of his own performance.

Ad Hoc Responses.   A skill does not seem to be just a great number
of precise and specific acts to be sorted out in the central nervous system
and selected to fit precise and specific situations. Welford says:

> It would appear better to think of the central mechanisms as capable of
> producing a response which is formed *ad hoc* by a kind of "calculation"
> based on many influences derived from the present aims and past experience
> of the subject and the sensory data of various kinds available at the time.[50]

In speaking of the strokes in tennis, he says: "No two strokes are exactly
alike . . . each stroke is in some way computed specially for the occa-
sion." [51] Welford lists the player's posture, movement, intentions, results
of previous strokes, and the external data as factors affecting the internal
calculation.

Gibbs says the input-output relation depends on the initial length
of and load on the muscle, and also varies with fatigue. A given input
signal cannot produce a consistent response, and a simple open-chain
control (S → R) is therefore precluded.[25] It is not possible to initiate
a movement of a definite extent without data on the initial state of the
controlled member—that is, positional data on initial states are needed
for control.

Spatial orientation, environmental conditions, and physiological
conditions all affect the special adjustment for each act. Acts, although
similar in appearance and serving to attain the same goal, are never identical in muscle movements employed. "Every change in body positioning
alters the configuration of the next succeeding efferent response." [53] The
muscles affecting these fine control patterns just discussed are always attached to a postural (and often moving) base to which they must adjust.
The axes of the body, gravity, body orientation, and space relations are
all factors in the adjustments for the final precision of the act. Posture
itself is varied by both proprioceptor and exteroceptor stimuli. Lashley
says:

> . . . there exist elaborate systems of interrelated neurons capable of im-
> posing certain types of integration upon a large number of widely spaced
> effector elements. . . . They form a sort of substratum on which activity
> is built.[54]

In the striking act in games involving a small ball, much emphasis
has been placed on "keeping one's eye on the ball." In the fast, ballistic-

type striking act, the eye direction after the start of the act is a factor chiefly because of its effect on body position and dynamic posture. Shutting the eyes tends to affect balance controls, and turning the head during an act changes the postural pattern over which the act occurs. In driving a golf ball or place-kicking a football, the change of head position seems to change and hence disturb the postural base over which the act is built. If the motor-memory pattern is selected and discharged in agreement with an assumed postural base but the base is changed during the act, a different action pattern will emerge. Changes in the postural base concurrent with the discharge of the motor pattern will of necessity modify the overt motor act. The reader is probably familiar with the effect of turning the eyes and head to focus down the fairway, during the golf drive, before the club makes contact with the ball. As mentioned earlier, if the motor act is performed quite rapidly (a ballistic movement, for example), insufficient time elapses for sensory controls to cause any modification of the motor-memory discharged act.

EARLY TRAINING AND POTENTIAL

Whether or not actual motor-achievement potentiality is increased by more extensive preschool and childhood training is undetermined. Individuals do seem to be able to reach higher final levels, on the average, if they start the developmental practice quite young. Studies of the effects of music training and of nursery and kindergarten training, as well as observations of the development of children of primitive races, all indicate higher levels of achievement by those who start young. During the last fifty years, the average age of those attaining national and international championships in many sports has dropped about eight years. However, studies of these athletes indicate that the number of years of consistent practice before reaching championship achievement has not changed greatly. The athlete still seems to need eight to ten years of consistent practice to achieve the highest peaks. He or she just starts younger. Moreover, with continuing motivated practice, excellence of performance continues over many more years than it did formerly. In other words, high skill levels are achieved at much younger ages and often persist as high efficiency of performance to a much more advanced age than was customarily found even a generation ago.

Perhaps the answer is not that potentiality is increased significantly by childhood training, but that potentiality should be fostered at the first appearance of readiness and may be partially lost if training is postponed until later years. In the generalization by Berelson and Steiner cited before, you will note that they said practice was more effective at a point of readiness—"not before, but also not long after." McGraw was of the opinion that roller skating could be learned most economically at the stage in which the child "was just beginning to gain equilibratory control." [55] Recent studies have indicated significant positive correlations between various measures of swimming and of balance.[56] Many children of nursery and kindergarten age are now found to have great success in learning to swim. Whether it is a balance factor that makes swimming so easy for these young children to learn or whether the ability to learn has something to do with the gross muscular nature and total bodily activity of the skill must await further research.

Training the Adult

Let us look for a moment at the other extreme, the bottom percentiles in motor abilities in the required first year of physical education activities of large American universities. (The pressure of enrollments and the cost of facilities for such programs are tending to eliminate this requirement in some areas.) Several studies have been made of women students, average age about eighteen, who arrive at the university with very inadequate body control in performing the physical activities common to the social and recreational life of their peers. Many experiments have been tried in attempts to improve this low group in some way. "Significant differences" have been reported in improvement of these groups when they are placed in special classes and given instruction that seemed proper to their level of development, as compared to groups of the same level admitted to the regular classes. The improvement of these low groups, even when taught in special classes, is so slight in comparison with the average group that the differences are greater instead of less after each has had a year of training. Most of the low group never seem to attain enough skill to be welcome participants in the various recreational and sociomotor physical activities of their academic peers. They prefer to be scorekeepers or equipment caretakers during the school period, and learn to avoid this whole area of "little success" for the rest of their lives.

The person who arrives at adulthood with very little development of body control, sociomotor, or recreational skills—the so-called "motor illiterate"—rarely has the time, the energy, the patience, or the desire to build the slowly developing bases neglected in childhood. The vigorous physical activity of childhood and the hour after hour, day after day, and week after week of play are gone and cannot be resurrected. Social demands, conventional behavior and inhibitions, academic work, one's job, all combine to interfere with any planned skill-development program. Because few people have the time to build these bases, they avoid situations in which they display extreme inefficiency, or they have little interest in activities in which they "lose face" because of the social stigma of incompetence.

In 1960 Nessler did a study of women entering college who were at the lowest percentile (based on over 1,600 entering women tested) as measured by various motor-skill tests. She put her experimental subjects in special classes in which the first eight weeks were devoted to practice of basic skills and body-control movements, the area in which these students seemed most deficient. The next eight weeks were spent on the fundamentals of badminton. Her control group from the same low percentile was placed in the regular program of required physical education for women.

The activity abilities which Nessler tried to develop in her low groups included ball handling (throwing, catching, bouncing); striking or batting a ball; running, dodging, and changing direction; jumping; and kicking a ball. Nessler concluded at the end of her experiment that, although a skills class adapted in program and method to low-skilled students was more advantageous than the regular class for these students in performance of the specific skills practiced, such a course could not compensate for their vast lack of experience in motor skills.[57]

Docherty made a follow-up study of these same low-skilled students after they had completed their two years of required physical education. She concluded in part as follows:

> Low-motor-skilled students seem to gain in skill and favorable attitude toward physical education from participation in a special activities class adapted to their needs at the specific time of the class; but then seem to gradually retrogress in their skill and attitude as time increases after the culmination of the special class even though they are still continuing to attend physical education classes.[58]

Factors Limiting Adult Motor Learning

Whether this inability to attain average performance is completely due to inadequate background, or discouragement through lack of success, or even an emotional block, a complete loss of interest followed by development of compensating activities; or whether it is partially due to some actual loss of potentiality through long postponement of adequate educational experience is not known. The relative lack of success with this low group, even when extra time for practice is arranged and special rewards are made available (and apparently real interest in improvement is aroused), seems to indicate some deterioration in potentiality through long postponement of training. However, one should remember that only in infancy and childhood does one have the many, many hours of time for vigorous physical play and the excess energy to devote to such activities. Adolescence and adulthood bring many competing activities of a more sedentary nature and many social inhibitions to vigorous physical play, especially for women.

It must not be assumed, however, that average individuals lose much of their ability to learn motor skill after middle age. Normal individuals well beyond middle age can learn motor skills if they want to do so and are not too fearful about trying something new. At first, however, they often lack confidence in their own ability to learn.[59] They tend to be a little slower, a little more cautious, and a bit less keen in their receptor senses.[60] Rapidly paced learning is harder for them than if they are allowed to set their own pace.[61]

Subjects well beyond middle age present a problem as to methods of teaching them gross physical skills, for they seem to experience difficulty in translating the instructor's demonstrations into their own performance. Manual manipulation often seems to be quite helpful.[62] They should be allowed to progress at their own chosen rate, without pressure.[63] They often find equally successful compensatory changes to substitute for certain impairments.[64] They will need clearer, stronger, and perhaps more frequently repeated cues to give them the idea.[65]

If subjects have health and vigor, motivation, and an average background in physical activity, they can learn many industrial, hobby, or recreational skills of a physical nature, even in the sixth and seventh decades of their lives.[66] Many retired people have learned to swim, skate, ski, or even play racket games. They tend to be somewhat slower, but may become quite accurate.[67] Moreover, such learning activity often has real therapeutic value.[68]

SUMMARY

Within the last twenty years, preschool and elementary school emphasis on body control, sociomotor, and recreational skills has been growing. However, the theories as to the type of program most valuable for present-day children and their future development are quite diverse. The various physical development programs of today range from infant training and reconditioning in the Doman-Delacato precise "patterning" doctrine through "readiness training" programs such as "movement education" and the traditional physical education programs (or gymnastic programs in the European terminology) modified and readapted from Jahn and Ling, to the specific skill training of infants in swimming, skating, gymnastics, and other skills.

Some of the problems that must be faced in trying to construct an effective preschool and elementary school motor development program for children follow:

1. Much time and patience are essential for teaching very young children. These early sensory-motor learnings take great quantities of time and great numbers of trial experiences for their very slow development. Children show evidence of more rapid learning after maturation and incidental practice have developed postural bases, eye-hand coordinations, and certain strengths.

2. Methods of teaching older children, especially verbal explanation and description, are not effective at this earlier age.

3. Experimental studies involving brief periods of specialized training of infants by adults tend to reveal no measurable degree of improvement.

4. The fine line between adequate care and guidance by the parents and enough freedom for exploration and self-reliance by the child is difficult to determine. The necessity for self-reliance has been found to hasten certain motor skill acquirements.

5. The smallness of the fraction of total motor-learning time represented by school physical education programs is rarely realized. In almost any day, healthy children participate in more vigorous activity outside class than they do in a whole week of physical education classes. Moreover, they often devote all weekend and most of their holidays to physical activity. What they are permitted, helped, and encouraged to do outside class can be of much more advantage to them in motor-skill achievement than all the practice within the class activity programs.

6. The traditional concept of "readiness," or lack of it, has tended to postpone too long children's participation in useful physical activities they will enjoy, can learn, and will use extensively, once learned.

7. Children need a wide variety of motor experiences, much freedom, and as much self-dependence as possible without too great personal hazard. Oversupervision and overprotection have proved inhibiting in the area of motor-skill acquirement. Studies of primitive peoples have made very clear the effects of quantity and variety of childhood motor experience.

Early motor-skill training seems to be related to higher peaks of skill achievement in later life. Skill, ability to succeed, more opportunity for the more skilled to participate, growth of interest with increase in skill, all may contribute to superiority in skills as an adult for the child who starts younger. Whether or not potentiality for development is increased by preschool training is not yet clear.

Motor-skill foundations (the simple body-control bases), if lacking, are difficult to build in adulthood because they take so much time to acquire and because discouragement results from lack of success. The adult resents appearing clumsy and awkward, and hence loses interest and resorts to compensating activities of a less physical nature. Competing activities of a sedentary nature usually do not permit the adult to devote the time needed for learning the elementary bases of many physical recreational skills. Moreover, society in the United States tends to create social inhibitions to vigorous physical play by adults, especially women.

We often overlook the fact that during infant and preadolescent years children have almost limitless energy. If they are healthy and not denied the opportunity, they practice various body-control and sociomotor skills almost every waking moment. Moreover, never again will they have such a great amount of time for vigorous activity. Never again will they have hour after hour, day after day, and week after week of time to engage in their own play and to pursue their own inclinations toward vigorous activity. As they move into adolescence, their almost irrepressible energy diminishes somewhat; social demands, assigned duties, schoolwork, conventional behavior and inhibitions, all combine to decrease greatly the hours of physical activity that characterized preschool and elementary school years. However, adults can learn motor skills if they want to do so, even well past middle age. Beyond fifty years of age, they tend to be a little slower, to have more difficulty with receptor senses, and do not learn as well under pressure. But with motivation, health, and growth of self-confidence, they can learn to perform many motor skills rather well even into the sixth and seventh decades of life.

DISCUSSION QUESTIONS

1. Do experiments with animals reveal how we learn?
2. Is the human infant slower in motor learning than many animals?
3. Is it advisable to attempt to train the nursery school child in various types of ontogenetic development?
4. Does integration of simple movement activities into larger patterns begin as soon as the child's attention is not required to focus on performance of the simpler activity?
5. Have brief periods of specialized training of infants tended to produce observable improvement over those not so trained?
6. Is quantity of experience the key to childhood adaptation and adjustment in motor behavior?
7. Are freedom and self-dependence basic factors in more rapid motor development of preschool children?
8. Does the child acquire the major part of his or her motor development and physical skills in school?

9. Is postponement of training after "readiness" advisable lest we accelerate the child too much?

10. Did Jimmy, in McGraw's study, achieve the same levels as Johnny even though his training came at a later stage of development?

11. Do the lower economic classes tend to be retarded in motor-skill development?

12. Is there great emphasis on motor-skill acquirement in child training among primitive people?

13. May early training increase potentiality?

14. May a great lack of early training make gross motor-skill acquirement unlikely in adulthood?

15. Can an older person who so desires learn new sport skills? industrial skills?

16. What is the basis for the hypothesis that one can increase, through activity experience, one's specific aptitude for learning a new motor skill?

17. State four reasons why motor development should receive special emphasis in infancy and childhood.

18. Explain why the child seems to need a great quantity of similar experiences, as well as a great variety of experiences.

19. Why do many medical and health organizations oppose the Doman-Delacato "patterning" program?

20. Why is the "general readiness program" opposed by some psychologists? To what extent is motor learning specific? Try to illustrate your answer by examples from motor-skill learning.

21. What are the objections to conscious attention to, and attempts at analysis of, specific movements by the child himself when he is trying to improve in body-control skills?

22. Are the arguments for preschool and primary-grade movement education programs equally applicable to secondary school grade levels? Explain your answer.

23. Distinguish between Delacato's and Kephart's views on laterality.

24. What is the purpose of the Lincoln-Oseretsky scale and what does it measure (mental, physical, or both)?

25. Why do we have difficulty in separating mental and physical measures at the preschool ages, and with mentally retarded children?

26. What are the present trends with respect to the concept of "readiness" stages in children?

27. At what stage of motor learning and performance do the simple motor patterns combine into autonomous and more complex hierarchical units? Describe the changes in levels of consciousness that occur in skill learning.

28. How does the motor-memory discharged response differ from the proprioceptively monitored motor response?

29. What are the basic differences in programs designed for "general readiness training" and "specificity of transfer"?

30. Is creativity more likely to occur at the lower or higher levels of skill acquisition? Defend your answer by examples. Does creativity tend to be specific to an area, or is it a general factor?

NOTES

1. Charles Bird, "The Effect of Maturation upon the Pecking Instinct of Chicks," *Pedagogical Seminary*, 33, 2 (June 1926), 212–34.

2. John D. Lawther and John M. Cooper, "Sub-Committee IV. Methods and Principles of Teaching Physical Education," *56th Annual Proceedings, The College Physical Education Association* (1953), p. 108.

3. Theresa D. Jones, *The Development of Certain Motor Skills and Play Activities in Young Children*, Child Development Monograph No. 26, ed. Arthur T. Jersild (New York: Bureau of Publications, Teachers College, Columbia University, 1939), pp. 66–67, 149–50.

4. Myrtle B. McGraw, *Growth: A Study of Johnny and Jimmy* (New York: Appleton-Century-Crofts, 1935).

5. Myrtle B. McGraw, "Later Development of Children Specially Trained During Infancy: Johnny and Jimmy at School Age," *Child Development*, 10, 1 (March 1939), 1–19.

6. McGraw, *Growth: A Study of Johnny and Jimmy*, p. 163.

7. *Ibid.,* p. 167.

8. *Ibid.,* p. 119.

9. *Ibid,* p. 280.

10. Temple Fay, "Origin of Human Movement," *American Journal of Psychiatry*, 111 (March 1955), 648.

11. *Ibid.,* pp. 649–50.

12. See also C. H. Delacato, *The Diagnosis and Treatment of Speech and Reading Problems* (Springfield, Ill.: Charles C Thomas, 1963).

13. See also Henry E. Garrett, *Great Experiments in Psychology* (New York: Appleton-Century-Crofts, 1930), chap. 14.

14. See also Melvin P. Robbins, "A Study of the Validity of Delacato's Theory of Neurological Organization," *Exceptional Children,* 32, 8 (April 1966), 517–23; and opinions of scientific and professional societies in *Archives of Physical Medicine and Rehabilitation,* April 1968, pp. 183–86.

15. M. P. Robbins and G. V. Glass. "The Doman-Delacato Rationale: A Critical Analysis," in *Educational Therapy,* vol. 2, ed. J. Helmuth (Seattle: Special Child Publications, 1968).

16. R. D. Freeman, "Controversy over 'Patterning' as a Treatment for Brain Damage in Children," *Journal of A.M.A.,* 202 (October 1967), 385–88.

17. Newell C. Kephart, *The Slow Learner in the Classroom* (Columbus: Charles E. Merrill, 1960); and *The Brain Injured Child in the Classroom* (Chicago: National Society for Crippled Children and Adults, 1963).

18. Eugene G. Roach, "The Perceptual-Motor Survey: Normative Study" (Ann Arbor, Mich.: University Microfilms, 1963).

19. Henry Allan Little, "Perceptual-Motor Characteristics of Educable Mentally Retarded Children." Unpublished doctoral dissertation, University of Indiana, 1964.

20. Jerome S. Bruner, *The Process of Education* (Cambridge, Mass.: Harvard University Press, 1961), p. 34.

21. D. O. Hebb, *Organization of Behavior* (New York: Science Editions, 1961), p. 115.

22. Brunner, *op. cit.,* p. 47.

23. Bernard Berelson and Gary A. Steiner, *Human Behavior, An Inventory of Scientific Findings* (New York: Harcourt, Brace & World, 1964), p. 58.

24. Roger G. Barker and Herbert F. Wright, *Midwest and Its Children: The Ecology of an American Town* (Evanston, Ill.: Row, Peterson, 1955), p. 532.

25. W. H. Bexton, W. Heron, and T. H. Scott, "Effects of Decreased Variation in the Sensory Environment," *Canadian Journal of Psychology,* 8, 2 (June 1954), 70–76; Donald O. Hebb, *A Textbook of Psychology* (Philadelphia: Saunders, 1958), p. 276.

26. John E. Anderson, "Growth and Development Today: Implications for Physical Education." Paper presented at National Conference on Social Changes and Implications for Physical Education and Sports Recreation, Estes Park, Colorado, June 1958.

27. Karlton B. Lehman, "Where Entering Male Freshmen Learned to Swim and Their Ability to Swim," Master of Education problem, College of Health and Physical Education, Pennsylvania State University, University Park, 1957.

28. Arthur J. Jersild, *Training and Growth in the Development of Children,* Child Development Monograph No. 10 (New York: Bureau of Publications, Teachers College, Columbia University, 1932); Ruth Updegraff, L. Heiliger, and J. Learned, "Part III: The Effect of Training upon the Singing Ability and Musical Interests of Three-, Four-, and Five-year-old Children," *University of Iowa Studies in Child Welfare,* New Series, 50, 346 (1938), 83–121.

29. Arnold Gesell and E. E. Lord, "A Psychological Comparison of Nursery School Children from Homes of Low and High Economic Status," *The Pedagogical Seminary and Journal of Genetic Psychology,* 34, 3 (September 1927), 339–56.

30. Judith R. Williams and Roland B. Scott, "Growth and Development of Negro Infants: IV. Motor Development and Its Relationship to Child-rearing Practices in Two Groups of Negro Infants," *Child Development,* 24, 2 (June 1953), 103–21.

31. Mary V. Gutteridge, "A Study of Motor Achievements of Young Children," *Archives of Psychology,* No. 244 (May 1939).

32. Joan Tillotson, *Elementary Physical Education Workshop.* Unpublished workshop syllabus used at Brigham Young University, July 1–12, 1968.

33. Movement education and creativity will be analyzed at greater length in Chapter 4.

34. Florence Stumpf and Frederick W. Cozens, "Some Aspects of the Role of Games, Sports and Recreational Activities in the Culture of Modern Primitive Peoples," *Research Quarterly,* 18, 3 (October 1947), 213.

35. Margaret Mead, *Growing Up in New Guinea* (New York: New American Library, 1930), p. 26. Copyright 1930, 1958, by Margaret Mead.

36. *Ibid.,* p. 26.

37. *Ibid.,* p. 27

38. *Ibid..* p. 25.

39. *Ibid.,* p. 27.

40. *Ibid.,* p. 28.

41. *Ibid.,* pp. 36–37.

42. P. M. Fitts, in *Categories of Human Learning,* ed. A. W. Melton (New York: Academic Press), p. 244.

43. Joseph R Higgins, "Movements to Match Environmental Demands," *Research Quarterly,* 43, 3 (October 1972), 328.

44. K. S. Lashley, "The Problem of Serial Order in Behavior," cited from L. A. Jeffres (ed.) *Cerebral Mechanisms in Behavior: The Hixon Symposium,* John Wiley & Sons. Inc., New York, pp. 122–130, and Chapman and Hall, Ltd., London. (Page references to Wiley edition.)

45. W. L. Bryan and N. Harter, "Studies in the Telegraphic Language: The Acquisition of a Hierarchy of Habits," *Psychological Review,* 6 (1899), 345–73.

46. C. B. Gibbs, "Probability Learning in Step-input Tracking," *British Journal of Psychology*, 56 (1965), 233–42. Cambridge University Press. See also Legge, *op. cit.*, p. 185.

47. Michael Polanyi, *Personal Knowledge* (Chicago: University of Chicago Press, 1958), p. 50.

48. *Ibid.*, p. 335.

49. *Ibid.*, p. 53.

50. A. T. Welford, *Ageing and Human Skill*. Oxford University Press for the Nuffield Foundation, 1958. (Reprinted 1973 by Greenwood Press, Westport, Connecticut), pp. 26–27.

51. A. T. Welford, "Obtaining and Processing Information," *Research Quarterly*, 43, 3 (October 1972), 295.

52. C. B. Gibbs, "Servo-control Systems in Organisms and the Transfer of Skill," in Legge, *op. cit.*, p. 212.

53. See discussion in "The Physiology of Motor Learning," by F. A. Hellebrandt, in *Anthology of Contemporary Readings*, ed. H. S. Slusher and Aileene S. Lockhart, Dubuque, Iowa: Brown, (1968), p. 94.

54. K. S. Lashley. "The Problem of Serial Order in Behavior," in Jeffres, *op. cit.*, p. 39.

55. McGraw, *Growth: A Study of Johnny and Jimmy*, p. 241.

56. Elmer A. Gross and Hugh L. Thompson, "Relationship of Dynamic Balance to Speed and to Ability in Swimming," *Research Quarterly*, 28, 4 (December 1957), 342–46; John A. Reeves, "A Study of Various Types of Balance and Their Relationship to Swimming Endurance and Speed." Unpublished master of science thesis, Pennsylvania State University, 1962.

57. Joan Nessler, "An Experimental Study of Methods Adapted to Teaching Low-skilled Freshman Women in Physical Education." Unpublished Doctoral dissertation, Pennsylvania State University, 1962.

58. Ethel Docherty, "The Developmental Progress of Low-skilled College Women in a Required Physical Education Program." Unpublished master's thesis, Pennsylvania State University, 1962.

59. Solomon Barkin, "Redesigning Jobs in Industry for a Maturing Population," *Age Is No Barrier*. Report of the New York State Joint Legislative Committee on Problems of Aging, 1952, pp. 92–96; Pearl Berlin, "The Learning of Swimming by Senior Citizens." Research project co-sponsored by the AUW Recreation Department and Wayne State University, Division of Health and Physical Education, October 20, 1960.

60. Barkin, *op. cit.*; A. T. Welford, *Skill and Age* (London: Oxford University Press, 1951), pp. 121–23; J. A. Williams, "Speed of Movement and Chronological Age." Unpublished master's thesis, Pennsylvania State University, 1958.

61. Welford, *op. cit.*; G. E. W. Wolstenholme and M. P. Cameron, eds., *Aging—General Aspects*, Vol. I, *CIBA Foundation Colloquia on Aging* (Boston: Little, Brown, 1955).

62. Berlin, *op. cit.*
63. Wolstenholme and Cameron, *op. cit.*
64. Frances Hellebrandt, "The Physiology of Motor Learning," *Cerebral Palsy Review*, 19, 4 (July–August 1958), 9–14.
65. Berlin, *op. cit.*, Welford, *op. cit.*
66. Berlin, *op. cit.*; A. J. Carlson, "Education for Later Maturity in the U.S.A.," *Report of the Third Congress of the International Association of Gerontology* (London: Livingston, 1955), p. 611.
67. Hellebrandt, *op. cit.*
68. Berlin, *op. cit.*

Three

The Nature of Learning: Types and Theories

"Learning by doing" means adjustment to feedback.

The changes in human behavior resulting from training, experience, or both, called learning, involve one's entire being. Learning includes both implicit and overt responses, and includes changes in attitudes, emotions, ideas, concepts and generalizations, motor and verbal responses. Unconscious conditionings are likely to accompany much of our purposeful learning. The individual is a unified organism, not a dichotomy—not a bipartite organism divided into mind and body. In our attempt to classify learning into types according to its major aspects, we are emphasizing only what we can observe in active response. However, various concomitant learnings accompany almost any major objective in learning. I learn skills but at the same time I learn to enjoy or dislike them; to compete and to love competition or vice versa; to be concerned about my physical condition lest I be unsuccessful; to react to social pressures and game rules; to cooperate with teammates and opponents; to be emotionally stimulated by certain environmental atmospheres; to like certain associates and perhaps dislike others; to be fearful or courageous in critical situations, and so on.

The degree to which the various parts of the human organism participate in learning may well vary along a continuum, but hypothetically no part is ever likely to reach zero activity when other parts of the organism are engaged. There is adequate evidence that much learning occurs below the level of conscious awareness and involves an involuntary response—as different from purposeful learning as was the conditioning of the iris muscle of the eye to contract at the ringing of a bell in Hulsey Cason's famous experiment.[1] At the other extreme, there is the inductive-deductive approach of the research scholar in the search for truth. The design of an experiment may involve a very considerable amount of creative imagination as well. Yet the research scholar has emotionally toned attitudes which affect his or her work—a strong conviction that one must rely on factual evidence is an example. William James recommended that one reduce the details of daily life to the custody of automatism so that the mind will be free for higher activities.[2] However, human beings function as unitary organisms, not as two halves—an automaton and a "free" mind. The various parts of the human being do not function independently, even though all aspects do not reach conscious awareness.

DRIVE OR PURPOSE

In learning, individuals are faced with situations that stimulate them, raise some tension in them, cause some disequilibrium. Some drive, purpose, or goal is activating them. Completely satiated animals or completely satisfied humans do not strive for further achievement or adaptation. Human progress seems to depend on this dissatisfaction, this discontent, this striving to satisfy needs. Individuals who are completely satisfied and contented make no progress, make no attempt to adjust, adapt, learn. According to Hull,[3] responses that reduce need are thereby reinforced, but if the response does not reduce need, it is inhibited. According to him, reinforcement (reward of response with reduced drive following response) causes an organization in the nervous system that links future stimuli and responses in the sequence in which they occurred when the need was reduced.

KINDS OF LEARNING

For the purpose of this text, we have adopted a functional view of the nature of learning, based on what conditions produce what outcomes. Our conclusions are a synthesis of experimentally or empirically derived generalizations and are eclectic; they are chosen from various experimental findings without concern for underlying theory. Tolman's suggestion that there are a number of different kinds of learning [4] may be a practical hypothesis for us to accept as we study the factors which affect learning, although we should bear in mind that Katona's analysis of the learning of material ranging from pure rote memory to highly organized content indicates a continuity of the learning process rather than discrete types.[5] Perhaps an eclectic view would accept Tolman's view only as emphasis on the major aspect of the learning, with lesser aspects always accompanying the major emphasis.

Perhaps a look at some of the ways that have been used to describe kinds of learning will help us understand its nature and complexity. The division of processes that occur along a continuum, into kinds or categories is an artificial device used to help analysis and understanding.

Latent Learning [6]

In accordance with the stress on incidental learning in Chapter 1, I should like to examine first a type of learning often overlooked—namely, latent learning. Learning seems to occur even when the learner has no intention or any particular drive to learn. The word "latent" does nothing to describe the process or nature of such learning; it merely indicates that performance at the time in which the learning must have been taking place gave no evidence of any change. The fact that responses have been modified is evidenced later in faster learning or better performance. Mere association without any intent to learn may contribute to faster learning at some later date if the later association is accompanied by a drive or purpose. Latent learning seems to occur even when the responses learned were unrewarded.

Perhaps another way to describe latent learning would be to say that the child may be learning to some degree, if he is just being put through the motions of the act by his parents, even though he has no interest and no desire to learn the particular responses. Curiosity and exploratory activity apparently develop in the child an acquaintance with things, certain space orientations, feelings of familiarity, and certain basic perceptual-motor controls—all learnings that have occurred without direct motivation. Hull, who was cited earlier emphasizing the importance of drive in learning, says there is also learning in which no reduction of primary need, by the responses which are learned, takes place. Hull says:

> Careful observation and experimentation reveal, particularly with the higher organisms, large numbers of situations in which learning occurs with no associated primary need reduction.[7]

However, Hull believes that some secondary, associated need may be causing the activity and therefore the learning.

Learning Through Conditioning

Since the time of Pavlov's famous conditioning experiments in which he substituted the ringing of a bell for meat powder as a stimulus to saliva flow in dogs, numerous conditioning experiments have been carried out with both animals and humans. By arranging the situation so that an unconditioned (original) stimulus is contiguous with a neutral

stimulus, one will eventually teach the animal to produce the unconditioned response whenever the neutral stimulus is present. This type of
involuntary-response conditioning has been called *classical* conditioning.

In addition to the many animal conditioning experiments, numerous experiments of this type have been conducted with humans—for
example, conditioning of eyelid blink, galvanic skin response, bladder
control of bed-wetting infants, patellar tendon response, and various vaso-
motor responses. These experiments demonstrate the type of learning in
humans that is called involuntary response conditioning—learning that
occurs without conscious awareness by the subject of the change which
is taking place, except insofar as he observes his own conditioned behavior after the change. Many an old athlete experiences an acceleration
of his heartbeat when he hears a band playing the same tunes played by
bands years before as he was preparing to start a varsity football game.
The response is involuntary and was learned unconsciously. Many of our
feelings, our emotions, our superstitions are changes that have occurred
in us because of this type of learning.

Watson conditioned various infants to fear a rabbit by making its
appearance simultaneous with the occurrence of a loud noise behind the
child's ear. Watson extended his experiments and based his whole psychological theory of the nature of learning, behaviorism, on a conditioned-
reflex hypothesis. This theory was very popular in the third decade of
this century, and persisted until Franz and Lashley established a theory
of the somewhat generalized functioning of the brain (as opposed to
Watson's theory of function by established reflex arcs) through their
brain-part extirpation experiments with primates and lower animals.

Mothers often condition their children to fear various things either
by frightening statements or by revealing their own fears. We acquire
innumerable conditionings through incidental learnings. The sight,
smell, or verbal description of food often causes salivary flow in a hungry
person, revealed perhaps through a number of swallowing acts. How
many conditionings of this type become patterned into our daily behavior is difficult to estimate, but apparently the number is large. Children often become conditioned to react according to certain attitudes in
the classroom, to others on the playground, to still others when adult
company visits their home. Such conditionings are often relatively permanent. Books, pennants, pictures, or other mementos of one's undergraduate days often arouse a feeling of nostalgia, years later.

Much learning is the substitution of a contiguous stimulus for the
original stimulus because of the temporal association of the two stimuli.
Contiguity of the stimuli during some repetitions of the activity causes an
adaptation in which the unconditioned stimulus may be replaced by a
conditioned stimulus. Higher-order conditioning may involve the sub-

stitution of words as conditioned stimuli. I learn to attach a word to the food I want by association. Later I may substitute another conditioned stimulus for this one; for example, milk, *lait, leche, milch*. This temporal learning through association occurs with both involuntary and voluntary responses. Let us now move on to types of learning involving voluntary responses and purposeful attempts at learning.

Trial and Error

Perhaps the next classification along the continuum of learning is what Thorndike has called "trial and error" learning. In this type of learning, individuals are faced with a situation in which they want to do something but do not know how to go about it. They have a drive, a motive, a purpose, a need, or a desire. They try out various responses, guiding themselves as best they can from past experience, but rather blindly if the situation is quite novel. They gradually discard the unsuccessful types of activity and adopt those that seem to bring them closer to the goal. With continued practice, they discard much of the extraneous activity and integrate into a pattern those activities that lead to the goal. Trial and error is quite characteristic of your behavior when you attempt to learn a completely new skill, although imitation of others helps you in your selection of provisional tries.

If you have some background in the relevant area but do not know the specific approach to your new goal, you may very well rehearse many of the activities mentally, discarding some of them as ineffective without expressing them overtly. In other words, there is a more sophisticated type of trial and error in which many of the tries are only mental rehearsals.

Thorndike's theory of bond formation, S $\xrightarrow{\text{(bond)}}$ R, and his emphasis on learning being the strengthening of bonds between stimuli and following responses that were satisfying, has had a great influence on educational practice. The teacher arranges the learning situation so that the students are more likely to make responses satisfying to themselves; of course, the environment is arranged so that these responses are also those desired by the teacher. Students have goals toward which they may have already been stimulated by parent or teacher influence. They try out responses they think will help them toward that goal. For faster learning, they should experience early successes (reinforcements of responses) and more successes than failures. Such success implies teacher guidance as to goals, teacher organization of the learning environment, and encouragement.[8]

Thorndike's association theory is now often classified as a type of conditioning based on the principle of reinforcing the associative bond between the stimulus and the desired response. When it occurs, the desired response is rewarded, thereby strengthening the bond. Failure to reward a response repeated several times is the procedure for eliminating that response.

Research has indicated that both rewarding the correct response and punishing the incorrect response may hasten the strengthening of the desired response. However, the results of studies on the effect of making a wrong response annoying (by means of punishment) in order to eliminate it are somewhat conflicting. Severe punishment seems at times to be deleterious to learning even when applied only to incorrect responses. In some few instances mild punishment may be helpful (mild shock, for example), even if it is applied to the correct response. The causal factor seems to be the attention-getting value of the mild shock to furnish information, playback, as to success. Attention is called to success, and the reward of the success, now attended to, more than compensates for the mild punishment. Information as to success seems to be very important in facilitating learning. Perhaps this is just another way of saying that one will endure a bit of annoyance if one sees that the satisfaction of wants is thereby being attained; that is, the reward more than compensates for the punishment.

Information about degree of success, playback of exact results, and encouragement ("good," "correct," "well done," "fine progress," and so on) all seem to be effective factors in strengthening responses, in favoring the establishment of these responses over those not so reinforced. Throwing or shooting at a target has an instant playback of results; the subject immediately sees the degree of success. A larger target and a shorter distance for the novice permit a higher degree of information playback because he or she needs to hit the target somewhat in order to judge how far off center the hit is.

The continuum of learning from the involuntary response type of classical conditioning through trial and error (Thorndike's connectionism) up to the functioning of the highest level of thought all seem to have association of stimuli with stimuli, and stimuli with responses, by contiguity of occurrence and response reinforcement (reward). Moreover, learning involves attitudes, emotions, and various physiological reactions, whether one is attempting to acquire physical skills or academic learning. We have considered the listed types of learning as change phenomena occurring along a continuum in which the same basic principles apply—drive, contiguity of stimuli, and responses that are satisfying.

Insight Learning; The Gestalt or Field Theory

In the mental trial and error process, we seem at times to "hit upon" a quick solution. One whole school of psychology stresses this process of "suddenly hitting upon" a suitable response. The Gestalt theory of learning emphasizes either conscious or unconscious reorganization of the total stimulus situation into a meaningful unit or pattern (a gestalt). An analogy to the Gestaltist's concept of the reorganization of environmental stimuli received from a situation is provided by the transformation that occurs to produce a stereophonic sound melody as it is organized and transmitted to the human ear from a vinyl disc. The interpreting done by the record player and accompanying apparatus is analogous to the reorganization done within one's being, and the vinyl disc with its indentations is analogous to the external stimulus situation.

As we relate and organize them, external stimuli furnish cues that fuse into meanings. The Gestalt psychologist assumes that the complex of stimuli arriving through the senses is being constantly organized and interpreted into units of meanings (gestalts); and that this organizing, this development of insight, is learning. The Gestaltist, however, in addition to consideration of one's total neural system as a transforming, unifying agent, stresses the *sudden emergence* of meaning in contrast with the gradual adjustment of the association theory. Köhler used as the criterion of insight *"the appearance of a complete solution with reference to the whole layout of the field."* [9]

The Gestaltist says that the whole stimulus situation is organized in terms of figure and background; and that the perception, the meaning, the insight come from the whole pattern, the unified pattern. The organization provides more than just an aggregation of parts; organization itself adds the meaning. Look at the illustrations in Figures 1, 2, and 3. Figure 1 is just an aggregate of dots and curved lines. Figure 2 presents exactly the same lines and dots reorganized into a pattern. Figure 3 is the same as Figure 2 except for the inversion of one curved line, yet the meaning changes.

FIGURE 1.

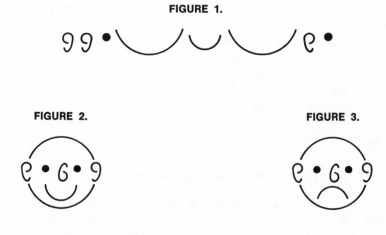

FIGURE 2.   **FIGURE 3.**

The constituent parts of these figures are identical but the arrangement, the relationship of the parts in space, has caused a reorganization of perception—has added meaning. The Gestalt theory emphasizes that the decision on appropriate activity, the solution to problems in a situation which then flows into overt activity by the subject, comes about as the subject "sizes up" the situation and "hits upon" an appropriate response. He has reorganized the incoming stimuli into a meaningful gestalt. Learning is the reorganization of perceptions and adjustment of responses through these insights.

The trial and error advocate would say that in Köhler's well-known experiment, the ape, Sultan, may have tried out some procedures mentally before he went for the box to climb on to reach the fruit.[10] However, so-called insight learning does seem to happen to most people at times. They seem suddenly to "hit upon" a solution mentally, then carry out the conceived idea. It may be that the difference is merely the extent to which the unsuccessful "provisional tries" occur below the level of conscious awareness, if we accept the hypothesis of some reorganization at a subconscious level. We do seem to have ideas that arrive at the level of conscious awareness rather well organized—in fact, so well developed that they often burst forth as an overt expression. Sometimes (perhaps too rarely) we are amazed, or at least delighted, at how cleverly we have expressed an idea after we have spoken "on the spur of the moment"; and sometimes we are disturbed that we should have burst forth with so stupid a statement. In each case, we have expressed the thought without first rehearsing it consciously.

Most analyses of the nature of creative imagination state three basic aspects of the process: (1) acquisition of an extensive background in the content area (of the creation); (2) a period of relaxation (incubation) without awareness-level consideration of the problem, although the drive and interest in the whole problem area may be just beneath conscious focus, and may be undergoing some change; (3) the sudden insight, which may be released in its newly organized form by almost any extraneous cue from the environment.

Many a coach keeps cards in his pocket, or on the lampstand beside his bed at night, to record sudden ideas (insights?) that "pop into" his mind. Some of these "sudden insights" prove to be ingenious ideas after being tried out in practice, but many turn out to be of no value when submitted to the test of team scrimmage. The mature adult tends to use mental trial and error in an attempt to save time, and perhaps the embarrassment or even cost of overt expression of the "errors." Problem solving could very well be considered a form of mental trial and error. When a solution does come to mind, is this insight? As the human mind reduces more and more of its experience to the shorthand of verbal and mathematical symbolism, a much more sophisticated type of implicit activity, of mental overview of the problem and weighing the evidence, can take place. Solutions are more likely to be rapid. Hypothetical solutions or ideas of action will "come to mind" out of a wealth of experiential background stored somewhere in one's memory drums. However, this type of attempt to achieve a purpose or to restore equilibrium to a stimulated nervous system, is just the upper end of the continuum of the learning processes which extend all the way down to activity of the simple classical-conditioning type. In terms of the computer analogy, learning at advanced levels is much different because so much usable adjustment is already programmed into the computer. (Hebb's statement quoted on p. 9 presents somewhat the same view).

APPLICATIONS OF THE GESTALT THEORY

We must not overlook the Gestaltists' emphasis on meaningfulness. Meaning is certainly very helpful in learning, retention, and application of knowledge. In trying to apply the Gestalt theory, the teacher confronts the student with the total situation bearing on the particular adapted reaction desired. The environment is so arranged as to stimulate recall of pertinent previous experience, which brings to the student a realization of the significant aspects and their basic relationships. The student is rehearsed in this situation until the various cues fuse into a meaningful pattern (a gestalt) for him. He gets the idea, he grasps the meaning, his experience fuses into a comprehended relationship. He has learned.

The claims for whole as contrasted with part learning, the idea that the first orientation of the beginner should involve presentation by demonstration of "the general idea" or "gross-framework idea" of the skill, and the hypothesis that one develops a kinesthetic image of the skill pattern through mental rehearsal all seem to be ramifications of the Gestalt approach to learning. Psychologists long ago demonstrated that material which could be made meaningful was much easier to learn than material demanding pure rote memorization. Retention after the same amount of practice is also much greater for meaningful material. But the point must not be overlooked that we have many types of knowledge to acquire, many responses to habituate, that are not meaningful when we must first acquire them.

The Open- and Closed-Loop Theory of Action

When I reach out to pick up a pin, say from the floor, I usually perform the act slowly enough so that I can make finer adjustments during the act. Here I am using exteroceptive (visual) feedback to guide my readjustments. However, it is the nature of skills that some motor acts are performed too rapidly for feedback to monitor the act. Such acts need to be preprogrammed before they start. How much time is needed before the feedback from ongoing action can produce modifications in the action is one of the problems in performance of precisely skilled acts. Once an act is well learned, it may often be preprogrammed in unconscious motor memory and then released too rapidly for any modification of the ongoing action by feedback. If the situation demands action that occurs within three- to four-tenths of a second or less, the act is over before feedback can cause readjustment. When a complex act is well learned (becomes relatively automatic) and has a temporal span and continuity lasting longer than reaction time, it is monitored proprioceptively.

Proprioceptive monitoring is below conscious awareness and allows much faster guidance of a progressing act than does exteroceptive monitoring (adjustment and guidance from visual sensing, for example). Preprogramming and proprioceptive monitoring are generally discussed under the open- and closed-loop theories, open being motor-memory discharge with no feedback monitoring during the act. Closed-loop feedback monitoring includes either exteroceptive monitoring or proprioceptive monitoring during the ongoing action. The word "loop" refers to the current from stimulus to muscle and to the neural afferent feedback from efferent acts, feedback that may modify the action if it arrives during the ongoing action. The "open" in "open loop" implies that this feedback did not arrive in time to affect the act (did not close the loop). As was discussed earlier (see pp. 4–5), open-loop activity means an autonomous response consistent in resulting response-effect for a specific input stimulus and not affected by feedback.

Ballistic movement has been cited as an example of open-loop action. It is released so rapidly that there is no time for feedback to affect it. The rapid motor-memory discharge of a preprogrammed act is generally considered to be an open-loop action; there is no time for or influence of feedback. Poulton says:

> A rapid aiming movement which is completed in about 0.5 s (.5 sec.) cannot contain a voluntary correction, for a voluntary movement has a reaction time (RT).[11]

In other words, ". . . a rapid aiming movement would be unaffected by visual monitoring for there is no time to use this visual information." Note that Poulton's example includes exteroceptive monitoring in this last statement.

In the open loop, a preset program is released *without concurrent external or internal monitoring.* An open-loop example of a response, not modified after being triggered off, might be that of a skilled person aiming and hitting the head of a nail with a hammer. The movement is too fast from onset to completion to permit readjustment of the overt act of swinging. An ordinary person may drive a nail with a rapid, relatively autonomous series of strokes but with enough time between strokes to permit some exteroceptive feedback, hence some aim adjustment between strokes. But aim adjustment between strokes does not mean exteroceptive monitoring from the start to the completion of a single stroke movement. The rapid act is an open-loop act. Once the individual releases a stroke, there is no modification of the preprogrammed act. Knowledge of results tells the performer if the stroke was satisfactory, if the nail bent, or how it sank into the wood, but this feedback occurs after a stroke is completed and before the next one starts.

The viewpoint of Gibbs is that the open-loop movement—one stroke of hitting the nail with the hammer, for example—is described inaccurately if the implication of open loop is that a set stimulus produces a consistent response. His objection is to "consistent response." Body movement and varying posture, internal physical and physiological conditions (variation in muscle stretch, postural angle, fatigue) modify each response and make it specific to the particular condition and situation of the moment (see Gibbs, p. 41 and Welford, p. 41). The objection is not to the concept of an absence of concurrent feedback but to "the set stimulus producing a consistent response." In driving a nail with a hammer, the hammer-head contact with the nail will vary in precision from stroke to stroke. The amateur often has a bruised finger or thumb to indicate an extreme variation. It might be well to compare this viewpoint with Thorndike's S———►R theory.

The Open- and Closed-Skill Continuum

The reader has noted that open loop refers to acts without any feedback during the response. Open skill refers to skill performance consistently monitored by the sensing of external stimuli. Exteroceptive monitoring during an open-skill act is most frequently visual. The open-skill act has spatial and temporal controls monitoring the selection and execution of the movements. Knapp implies that types of skills range in a continuum from open to closed, depending upon the extent to which control of the skilled behavior is determined by external rather than proprioceptive control. She states that the range extends from skills that are predominately perceptual (open) to skills that are predominately habitual (closed). She includes among the closed skills those in which "conformity to a prescribed standard sequence of motor acts is all-important" (such as required exercises in gymnastics or skating). In the open-skills category, she puts those in which "at every instant the motor activity must be regulated by and appropriate to the external situation." The various strokes in a tennis rally might be a good example of what Knapp would call open-skill activity.[12]

In contrast to the regular exteroceptive monitoring of the open-skill act, the closed-skill activity is generally considered to be relatively independent of external environment for any concurrent monitoring and is chiefly autonomous patterning monitored by proprioceptive feedback. One leans over the back of the ring, then explodes through the hops, turns, and extensions of the shot-put skill with only established ring diameter restricting the autonomous act. Even in the continuous nail-driving of the *skilled* carpenter, much of the rather continuous stroking may be proprioceptively guided; that is, his nail-driving tends to be a continuity of stroking without intervening pauses between strokes. His skill has developed along the continuum toward the autonomous, closed-skill performance. The strokes seem to be serially linked, with successive strokes being conditioned responses to the ones preceding.

One interpretation of closed versus open skill states that while the developing skill is largely dependent on external environment for direction and control, it is still an open skill. In other words, even the closed skills go through the open-skill stage in their developmental progress. Those which can later be performed without environmental-stimulus monitoring are then called closed skills. They become patterns of action relatively independent of environmental monitoring (with little reference to the environment); for example, script writing and required exercises in gymnastics or skating have been so classified.

Gentile calls the closed skills those which take place in a stable, unchanging environment in which performance can be carried out successfully with minimum reference to the environment. Gentile contrasts the "stationary regulatory conditions of the environment" in the closed-skill action with the open-skill performance, which is "concomitantly controlled by the temporal/spatial characteristics of the variable regulatory conditions in the environment." [13] Gentile's phrases, "stable, unchanging environment" and "stationary regulatory conditions of the environment," seem to me to be inaccurate in describing closed skills. Many of our so-called skills can flow through in quite varied types of environment without much exteroceptive monitoring. Script writing can be performed relatively automatically in varying situations and with different muscles employed. The attention is on the idea, not on the motor patterns. One writes on the blackboard, at the desk, on a pad at the telephone, or even in the snow. Motor memory and proprioceptive monitoring guide the muscle patterns to form the letters. Each simple part acts as a conditioned stimulus for the next part of the skill—for the forming of the succeeding letters. The rest of Gentile's statement—"with minimum reference to the environment"—seems to be adequate to indicate the internal, proprioceptive monitoring of the closed skill.

Many skills depend on advanced reception of exteroceptive cues even when the stimulus, once received, flows into automatic action with the attention on ahead to catch succeeding cues. Prediction is essential for the fast, smooth action, whether it is in driving a car, fielding a grounder in baseball, or picking holes and dodging through the opponent's defensive line in American football. One talks to a companion, thinks over a speech one is soon to deliver, ponders some of life's problems, or whatnot, while one is driving along familiar highways. It seems to me that, under Knapp's classification, these motor skills would tend to be placed toward the open skills end of the continuum since they are dependent on relatively constant exteroceptive stimulus for guidance. They would be called open skills if one were to define open skills as those in which it is necessary to monitor information from the environment to determine when to discharge the movement pattern; but, as you see, the movement patterns are autonomous, to a great degree either motor-memory releases or proprioceptively guided actions, and in this sense to a great degree closed skills.

Whiting says that many such skills "include components which in themselves are closed skills." The distinction is that they are controlled by proprioceptive information or are preprogrammed in the brain as a whole. Whiting [14] refers to such skills as "closed skills in an open situation." Driving a car would seem to illustrate Whiting's point. The attempt to classify skills as open or closed runs into difficulty if open includes all those that must be initiated by the external environment. Many skills run off autonomously as various successive external cues set off motor-memory programs, interspersed or tied together with some proprioceptive monitoring as the complex activity extends its temporal span. Spaeth comments about the value of trying to classify skills along a closed to open continuum. She says:

> Perhaps a clearer description of the skills continuum can be achieved by first considering the nature of the perceptual activity required, and then noting the degree of habituation attained. [15]

Stereotyping versus Variability in Skill Patterns

In many of the so-called closed skills (putting the shot, required exercises in gymnastics or skating), the individual tries to adopt a stereotyped movement pattern that is as close as he can achieve to his (or the coach's) ideal or model of best performance. At high skill levels, successive skill performances in such skills will resemble each other in the gross action pattern. Moreover, some of the *required exercises* in certain sports require a particular gross-pattern stereotype. The constant variation in the details of every automatic performance was discussed previously. The optional activities in, say, skating or gymnastics allow for much individual variation and creativity in attempts to add fluency, originality, and beauty of expression. There is individual stereotyping, but the movements are quite variable from individual to individual. In such activities, it is the individual's personal idea of performance that he or she wishes to stereotype and then exhibit.

In the so-called open skills, achievement of one's goal in a constantly changing environment (including environmental effects produced by opponents) demands diversity of performance, anticipation, and spatial and temporal predictions, but also the rapid discharge of memory-stored units established from much previous experience. The advanced prediction permits the decision and the triggering off of the selected skill. The senses are focused on ahead to catch cues for subsequent activity, and the skill is an unconscious discharge from the motor-memory drum. When the skill is made up of successive movement patterns generated from unconscious *ad hoc* calculations and proprioceptive monitoring, it is no longer just motor-memory discharge; it now depends on internal feedback and monitoring. One plays a fast series of rallies in a tennis game and constantly adjusts to cues from opponent action and ball path; but automation must take care of most of the stroking because the attention must be ahead of the action. Prediction comes from exteroceptive sensing, but most of the activity must be autonomous functioning of large hierarchical units. One begins to see the great difficulty in trying to use the open- and closed-skill classification.

PERCEPTION

Perception is the organization and interpretation of sensory stimuli in the light of past experience. Perception grows steadily with learning and experience. The mosaics of displays from the different senses combine into a whole—a perceptual unit. The stimuli, arriving from multimodal displays of sensory data, are automatically analyzed, organized, and shaped by the individual's needs, aims, expectations, present physiological state, past learning, and immediately preceding situation.[16] The individual puts stimulus bits or cues together with past experience to make a simplified whole or meaningful unit. A word is seen as a unit, not as several individual letters. In Figure 4, four bits are seen as a face, not as four separate bits.

Past experiences largely determine what cues to expect, how to direct attention so as to catch their earliest appearance, and the meaningful

FIGURE 4.

whole into which they fuse. In motor skills, early reception of anticipated cues often permits their identification to flow into response so rapidly that organizing and interpreting both seem instantaneous and unconscious; that is, the time for conscious awareness occurs only after the act is released, and then only momentarily if at all, for attention is often focused ahead to catch cues for subsequent behavior. Any kind of learning is the adjustment of response to stimuli or stimulus situations. But before we can make the appropriate response, we must perceive (recognize) the stimulus. Even though these recognitions may be subliminal at times, there must be familiarity with the stimulus in order for adapted response to be made.

Motor learning has often been called perceptual-motor learning (see page 7 and particularly note 14). The word "perceptual" is introduced because the stimuli need to be recognized by the subject before he or she can act adequately. The recognition, as well as the adapted action, has to be learned. We call your attention to the slowness of early perceptual learning described in the studies of Senden and of Miner (see Chapter 1). This recognition of the stimulus in its setting and its interpretation makes up a great part of our learning, and seems to increase in importance as we progress up the hierarchical scale of learning complexity and maturity. We learn to recognize people, words, objects, smells, and sounds. We learn to recognize movements of others as being the beginnings of certain acts. Early in childhood we learn to recognize sensations of slight loss of balance and to respond appropriately. Perceptions, once learned and made automatic, are initiated by constants (learned cues) within the total display. In other words, some basic aspect gives the "recognition key" regardless of varying details in the total background. The quick perception is a release interpreted from the associated experiential background already programmed in one's nervous system. The response may be merely a feeling of familiarity, our awareness of meaning, or even a subliminal but completely adapted motor response.

Factors Affecting Perception

The following are usually listed as the physical factors that affect visual perception: size of the object to be perceived, distance to it, its color and brightness, the background against which it has to be seen, the amount of illumination of the object and its surroundings, and, of course, the visual exposure time. Loudness and pitch both affect auditory perception, as do interfering noises. Duration of the stimulus may have some effect. Location on, and movement against the body surface, breadth of area contacted, and intensity affect tactual perception. In each case, amount of experience (familiarity with the type of stimulus) is an important factor.

The surrounding situation, the expectancy of the moment, the emotional state, the direction and level of attention all affect stimuli noted, fused, and interpreted into a perception. In the semantics of much recent research, the complex of developing stimuli to which one's senses are exposed, and which lead to interpretation and decision, are often called "display." The neural fusion of these sensed stimuli into a meaningful unit is perception. One's perception, instantaneous as it often seems to be, is produced by both spatial and temporal factors. It is often a fusion produced from various sense stimuli, memory traces, and environmental conditions, both external and internal.

The different sense modalities (eye, ear, and so on) transmit pertinent cues from displays which then combine to initiate a perceptual whole, a meaningful unit. The basic cues, or so-called constants, fuse into the percept, and the details of the display are unnoticed or relegated to later analyses. The fusion of display constants *from different modalities* into a unit of perception is remarkable not only because of the greater resulting accuracy but also because of its automatic nature. In fact, the combination of stimuli from two or more modalities has been found to produce faster reaction time than the stimuli received from only one sense organ.

As early as 1912, Todd reported that various stimuli combinations of light, sound, and electric shock resulted in faster reaction times than simple reactions to light or sound.[17] Bliss, Townsend, Crane, and Link supported Todd's conclusions. Their studies also reported little or no difference in simple reaction time to visual or tactual (air jet) stimuli, but in choice reactions, decision time for tactual was found to be considerably longer.[18]

Swink [19] made an extensive laboratory investigation of the relative effects on reaction time of stimuli from single and multiple modalities. He reported the following ranking of the various stimuli and stimuli combinations for their effects on reaction time, listed in order from slowest to fastest reaction time: light, sound, shock, light-sound, light-shock, light-sound-shock. Faster reaction times have been found from binaural as opposed to monaural auditory stimuli,[20] and faster reaction times to binocular as opposed to monocular visual stimuli.[21] Part of the cause of the shorter reaction times from multimodal stimuli has been attributed to increased vigilance. It is apparent that a specific perceptual unit is so interrelated in the nervous system to the various receptor senses as to be sensitive to the earliest-arriving stimuli, regardless of the modality. Moreover, the identification may arrive from more than one sense organ and cue in the perception earlier by mutual reinforcement.

Perception in skilled behavior often seems to be immediate even though both spatial and temporal aspects may be responsible for the perceived whole. We perceive, seemingly at once, an opponent's intent as suggested by the beginning of his or her movement pattern, even though the flow of the movement does involve a time factor. The rapidity of well-learned perception implies much previous experience and familiarity. It also implies that the stimuli, which contribute to the pattern perceived, occur approximately concurrently or in fractional-second sequence. One needs only a few constants and past experience to recognize a dog at first glance. Perhaps general size, shape, and quadrupedal factors are some of the constants that meld into the seemingly instantaneous perception. The mere auditory reception of a bark is often all that is needed.

Each new experience with any such percept, any such meaningful whole formed after the stimulus display of the moment, changes or modifies to some degree that perceptual unit. One might say that the perception is refined and retouched by each experiencing. Consider the multitude of experiences that have affected and modified one's perception of "dog." In fact, Welford says that a percept is an organized form affected by each new impression like the modification of a plastic model.[22]

Sensory Reception

There is a form of analysis within the senses themselves. The eye interprets certain waves as light and color. The ear picks up sound waves, lengths, and combinations and interprets them in terms of pitch and intensity. Intensity of light is interpreted by the eye; loudness of sound, by the ear. The visual cortex interprets the display in terms of angles, movements, shape, verticality and horizontality. The peripheral areas of the body pick up tactual contacts, movements, approximate location and areas of contact, pressures, temperatures, and pain. Tastes and smells furnish other stimuli which, with experience, produce learned differentiations and identifications. In contact sports, amount or area of contact, easing and release of pressure (wrestling), are often sensed stimuli that provide cues for action. Audible cues often combine with visual cues to help in perception. Even the adjustment of the posture and balance of the body is greatly helped by visual orientation and reception.

Postural Alertness
and Selective Attention

In many types of skill, the focus of attention on the correct cues and the ignoring of extraneous ones are basic prerequisites for successful performance. When one is wide awake and interested, one is at a higher level of arousal and more sensitive to stimuli. Then general direction of attention toward areas in which pertinent stimuli are expected to occur is a preliminary stage. One orients the body and directs the senses—that is, employs postural alertness and selective attention. Past experience has taught one what body position is best and what cues are most likely to occur. Intent, readiness, preset for the predicted, even imaged act, all tend to speed up response on reception of anticipated stimuli. The track starter gives a preliminary orientation by the commands: "On your marks" and "Get set." The tennis server looks to see if the opponent is attending and seemingly alert and often asks, "Ready?" The middle linebacker in American football takes a flexed knee and semi-crouched position, with a wide stance and weight not too much on his toes (lest the play be a forward pass), then usually focuses on the offensive quarterback's movements. The offensive soccer player with the ball handles it with his feet but keeps his eyes raised enough to sense the movements of the defensive players in front of him.

CUE REDUCTION

A cue is a stimulus from the situation that has attached to it, through learning, an association with adapted response, a feeling of familiarity, or both. Each cue is one "sub-S" (S_1) in the total stimulus situation; to put it another way, each "sub-S" becomes a cue when it is adequate to initiate an adapted reaction pattern (see Figure 5). In the area of perception, we find that prompt recognitions develop and progress in development so that only a very few cues are essential for perception to occur. A person's stride, the sound of his voice, his profile seen at a distance, or

FIGURE 5.

S_1
S_2
S_3
.
.
.
S_N.

71

even the sound of his footsteps as he enters the front hall may be adequate cues to produce recognitions by members of his family. With learning, we decrease the number of cues essential for the prompt recognition we call perception. Think of any environmental situation as one in which various stimuli and various types of stimuli activate sense organs; any smaller number or even only one of the sub-Ss can become the stimulus for prompt recognition (see Figure 6).

FIGURE 6.

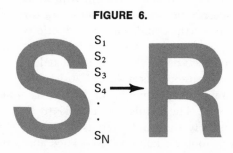

All our lives we learn to substitute a cue, a bit or element out of a total situation, for the original total stimulus situation, and we respond immediately without awaiting or without needing the remainder of the original total situation to produce the appropriate learned response. When the alarm clock clicks, I reach out to turn it off before it has time to ring, even though I am not sufficiently awake to be fully conscious of my act. The noon hour strikes and I get a hunger response although I may be in no need of food after a late breakfast. A red light suddenly appears as I drive along the avenue and my foot pushes on the brake before I have time to think about the reason.

The decrease with learning in the number of cues essential for recognition is due to the filling in of the rest of the stimulus pattern from a mental construct already established from previous experience. The term "mental construct" is merely a verbal symbol to represent the phenomenon characteristic of highly trained perception, which produces the filling in of the whole stimulus situation from a greatly reduced number of cues. The very speed of these trained recognitions indicates their automaticity. Naval fliers in World War II learned to recognize various types of airplanes exposed on the viewing screen for only one two-hundredth of a second.

Cues and "Cue Constants"

A cue is a recognized stimulus within a total stimulus situation which, by itself, has become a substitute for the total stimulus situation in producing appropriate action. Stimulus generalization has often been interpreted as being based on what are called cue constants. Cue constant is a term used to describe an aspect of a situation, person, or object that seems to persist from occurrence to occurrence and thereby serves as a prompt means to produce identification and meaning of the situation, person, or object. Facial expressions to indicate joy, perplexity, or even intense interest seem to possess cue constants. There are cue constants in physical movements or gestures to express disdain, contempt, insult, indifference or lack of knowledge—shoulder shrug with flexed elbows and open palms facing upward, the V sign with the fingers, the nose-thumb motion, and so on. The voice sound of a relative or close friend, the peculiar stride or stance of a well-known person, the neigh of a horse or moo of a cow, the shape of a camel, the outline of a leaf from an oak tree all may become, after experience, cue constants that produce almost immediate identification. A shape outline, a specific movement pattern, or a postural stance may become a cue constant for prompt recognition of a person or object frequently experienced.

Cue constants provoke perception although many details of the display may vary. Postural outline, voice pitch and quality, or characteristic stride in walking may identify an individual before other details are evident. The example of cue constants that cause the perception "dog" (regardless of the species) has already been mentioned. Illusions may result from too few constants or from misinterpretation of such cues as perceptual constants because of expectation or some emotion such as fear or strong desire. Some similarity in shape, color, type of movement, or produced sound may result in either an early perception or an early illusion. How often have you thought you recognized a friend in a crowd or at a distance only to find with closer inspection that you were mistaken!

These examples offer a somewhat different interpretation of stimulus generalization. The earlier statements about "stimuli with considerable similarity" may merely be an indication of cue constants within a somewhat varying display. However, let us be careful about the meaning we read into the term cue constant. Physiological state and external background both tend to affect and bias the degree of "constancy" of the sensed cues. The earlier example of animal-species identification calls attention to considerable variation in the pitch, quality, and range of the so-called identifiable constant. When we get into the problem of species perception, we see the difficulty in using the term in its literal meaning— no two dog barks are the same and no two dogs bark the same, yet the bark is considered a cue constant. We see here the growth and generalization of the meaning of cue constant until it merges into a symbol of meaning (discussed later under concept).

Cue Constants
from Previous Experience

A basic aspect of skill is the direction of attention and the selection of the most important cues in the total display. Past experience has taught which cues are most important in achieving the present goal. The automatic organization of incoming stimuli into a percept or whole suppresses details in the display mosaics. Beginners are often not sure which cues are the pertinent ones. They take more time to scan the stimulus situation, need more cues, have not yet learned to select or recognize the earlier-appearing cues, and need more time to organize them and attempt a decision. For example, beginners must drive a car more slowly until they learn to perceive earlier-appearing cues and more pertinent cues. It takes much practice to learn to recognize early-appearing cues quickly and respond to them automatically.

Skilled Cue Reading

The experienced driver senses the speed of the car, sees the green or red light, the stop sign ahead, other cars, and so on; because of earlier prediction, he or she can make smooth adjustments of the brake, the accelerator, and the steering wheel. The driver's muscular acts are seemingly effortless, automatically performed, and adapted to varying conditions. The skill of an experienced baseball infielder in fielding a hard-hit grounder illustrates early and fast cue reception and recognition. The infielder often has the problem of running to the appropriate position and fielding the ball, then throwing it to the appropriate base. The direction and start of the run must be decided before the ball has traveled far from its collision with the bat. The infielder's final arm and hand movements to catch the ball must be decided from cues appearing during the last part of the ball's flight. Fortunately, the skilled person can add acceleration to a movement already underway without the necessity of one reaction time intervening.[23] Long practice has taught the skilled person what cues are most likely to occur. Anticipatory ability and high probability in prediction can often greatly speed up the expert's response.

After much experience, we do not need to sense details of the display mosaic before recognition. In fact, with practice and experience we learn to substitute, as the stimulus pattern for perception, a very small early-appearing part of the situation for the total situation. A postural change or a preliminary movement may reveal the succeeding act before the act unfolds. Many a teacher catches child misbehavior by slight cues detected from stimuli registering only in the periphery of the eye or by noting a slight but unusual noise. The tennis player catches a slight peripheral-eye glimpse of the opponent's lunge toward the net, so drives a return along the sideline or, if quite deep in the court, lofts a lob for the other baseline. A friend at a distance is recognized by stride and posture before his face can be seen. Only a few cues plus past experience produce quick and early recognition in many cases, thereby enabling appropriate action to be taken in plenty of time. The action flows along smoothly without the irregularity and stops caused by the unskilled person's slower perception of cues.

Expectancy and Perceptual Time. Preliminary preparation or set often affects earlier cue recognition. Expected cues release responses with a minimum of attention. The preparatory set involves not only precise direction and high level of attention but also adjusted posture and applicable muscles on stretch. The decision process has been made in advance and the neural process has therefore been shortened. Lashley says: ". . . an effector mechanism can be pre-set or primed to discharge at a given intensity or for a given duration, in independence of any sensory controls." [24]

In sports, we learn to react to many movements and opponent positions almost as they are initiated—to a change of direction, a jump, a throw, a quick step, a preparatory stance, and so on. The expectation, the alertness, the postural adjustment, and the sensory focus all tend to aid in fast prediction and response from earliest cues. Gibbs states:

> Learning permits prediction of the results of responses, and the delegation of monitoring from visual attention to proprioceptive mechanisms which function at subconscious level.[25]

He adds that the time to amend errors is, therefore, shortened from 0.25 seconds to 0.10 seconds.

Competitive Strategy. As part of game strategy, various devices, such as similarity in delivery form of the fast ball and the "change-of-pace" ball as it is released by the baseball pitcher, are used to make earlier reading of cues more difficult for opponents. Other examples are the very short arcs on the volley in tennis, the late changes and fakes in the spiking of the volleyball, and so on. Shortening as much as possible perceptual time allowed the opponent is a common strategy. The pitcher's throw to first base is often difficult to distinguish from his throw to home plate if one is trying to rely on early cues. The runner at first base has difficulty judging his lead from the base when the pitcher is left-handed; that is, the change in movement pattern is so fast that it greatly diminishes the runner's cue-reading time. In many sports, shorter arcs in striking, misleading preliminary moves, and improbable acts all tend to delay opponent perception or shorten available perceptual time. Expectancy of an occurrence, when accurate, speeds up perception of earlier cues from the start of the occurrence; expectancy when wrong delays perception because of the longer time needed to amend a movement already begun. Considerable postural adjustment may be necessary before the amended movement can be initiated. Sport strategy aims at creating inaccurate perceptions, temporary illusions, wrong decisions as to action, and often involves the attempt to perform the unexpected. Football quarterbacks rely greatly on their ability to delay opponent perception by giving and acting out false cues. Years of practical experience are necessary before prompt and precise perceptions develop; yet adjusted responses to situations in traffic, in industry, and in sport demand rapid, automatic action if the action is to be effective.

Prediction from Early-Appearing Cues

Skill responses must often be determined and initiated in advance of a critical time for their execution. It takes one- to two-tenths of a second, or even longer, to initiate a reaction after the cues appear, then approximately the same amount of additional time to make the movement. For choice reactions and complex movements, the duration of time before the movement can be started overtly is considerably longer. Because of this delay, successful action often requires prediction and advanced initiation of the movement. A baseball thrown by a skilled pitcher may travel from the pitcher to home plate in about half a second, often at a rate of more than 10 feet per tenth of a second. It is clear that the batter must decide on action when the ball is still many feet from home plate.[26]

Drivers of cars keep their eyes scanning well in front of the car's hood, but not on one point. They use what is commonly called "distant" or "diffused" vision: they include a considerable distance and a broad scope in visual scanning, including the road-surface boundary lines. The somewhat distant focus, instead of precise focus on a nearby point, lets them catch any important cues from the large area of the pertinent display. The distant cues allow time to predict desirable action in advance. In other words, the earlier cue reading lets them decide on needed movement and initiate it in plenty of time to solve the motor problem of the moment. Past experience will make them more sensitive to chuck holes, undesirable closeness to road borders, other car approaches, and so on. The cues are turned over to the body (to motor-memory and proprioceptive monitoring) for response; visual attention is kept on ahead for the next cues.

The development of precise airplane bombing in World War II before mechanical computers were available caused much study of what was then called "coincidence-anticipation." Hitting the target involved computation of plane speed and elevation, falling time of the bomb, and, of course, the arc it would follow in dropping from a speeding plane. Ordinary car driving through traffic requires this "coincidence-anticipation" in order to miss instead of hit other cars. Skill in baseball, cricket, or softball requires early cue reading to estimate exact distance, direction, and speed of ball plus reaction and movement time of the batter. Team games with contact maneuvers require anticipation to make or avoid contact, depending on the specific purpose of the player. Even the stopwatch timing of runners or swimmers requires the timer to anticipate so that his own reaction time and movement time do not bias the results. Electric timing has helped greatly in solving this problem.

It is evident that the cues must be read early and the action started if a moving bat is to collide precisely with a rapidly moving ball as it arrives at the preferred contact point. Racket games, volleyball, soccer, and so on necessitate the same advanced prediction and start of movement. Position, velocity, acceleration, and direction must all be predicted in advance of the initiation of movement. There seems to be no substitute for years of motivated practice for developing high skill levels in such acts. Practice must emphasize reading more difficult cues with shorter exposure time for perception; for example, experience against increase in both speed and veering direction of object to be contacted. Prediction of the future position of a rapidly moving object is essential for success in such skills as football forward passing, skeet shooting, shooting game on the run or fly; or in dodging missiles. Whiting [27] states that the interval needed for coincidence-anticipation ranges from 200 milliseconds down to only 50 milliseconds (from two-tenths of a second down to five-hundredths of a second). It seems that skilled performers catch earlier-appearing cues which are already tied with considerable certainty to appropriate responses. They know what to expect and what extraneous factors in the stimulus pattern to ignore.

Peripheral Vision versus Eye Focus

Taxi drivers and schoolteachers seem to rank high in reception and recognition of stimuli received by peripheral vision. Looking to the far distance, with the eyes turned inward as little as possible, seems to allow the subject to see a large area and to observe stimuli sensed in various areas of the periphery. In fact, one can stare ahead, off to a distance, while focusing attention on action seen in the periphery of the eye. In other words, focus of attention is not necessarily foveal focus. A schoolteacher learns to note student behavior when he does not seem to be looking directly at the student. Military sentinels in twilight or semidarkness are often told not to look directly at a suspected movement, but "to sense it out of the corner of the eye." The rods of the retina are supposed to be more sensitive to stimuli than the cones in this semidarkness.

High skill level in juggling three balls seems to be performed with relatively still eyes, much peripheral vision, and much proprioceptive monitoring.[28] Cobb [29] found that hitting targets at a distance (30 feet or more) with a ball was quite dependent on peripheral vision. However, in dart throwing at close targets (9 feet or less), exclusion of peripheral vision had little effect. In many of the motor skills, the background as revealed in the periphery of the eyes aids greatly in cue discrimination. Moreover, we learn to include a broad scope in our visual area in order to cover much of the area of possible cue appearance; for example, the basketball dribbler, when driving toward the free-throw lane on a fast break, must see his teammates simultaneously as they approach the offensive basket from opposite sidelines. Whether one or the other escapes his defensive opponent must be seen on the instant. The pertinent cue in this case is the amount of space between an offensive and defensive player. Focusing on only one offensive player by the dribbler will turn his eyes and conceal the situation of the other. Moreover, an attentive focus shuts out or at least diminishes sensitivity to other stimuli.

Awareness Level in Perception

The old psychological definition of perception as the recognition of a stimulus is much oversimplified, especially as applied to motor skill. We often sense and react to input with very little of the stimulus pattern being recognized at the awareness level of consciousness. Subliminal stimulus patterns and appropriate reactions are not unusual in human behavior. In a visually recognized figure, the background etches out the figure although we may not consciously notice the background. In training pilots to land small planes without instruments, the familiar background of the approach and landing stretch seems to aid in the skill. Guidance cues seem to arise from the background and help the trainees even though they are not aware of noticing them. Athletes usually insist on preliminary practice on an unfamiliar sports area before an important contest, and are not aware of all the cues that familiarity furnishes them.

Very often we organize and interpret stimuli, then react without involving the awareness level of consciousness. As Kristofferson says, "Therefore let it be explicitly stated that some classes of information may be utilized by the organism even though they are transmitted over channels which are not controlled by the attention mechanism." [30] The individual may, after the act, have conscious memory of it and may even attempt to analyze the stimuli that caused the action. Postural and movement adjustments in skills are usually made automatically without any awareness of the stimuli that produced them. Much body control and adjustment involves response to proprioceptive cues, cues that do not register at the awareness level of consciousness. In rapid performance of a motor skill, the awareness aspect is often no more than introspection of what has occurred. In the rapid interchange of conversation, or in quick verbal responses, we often do not know what words were in our response until we have already said them. Then we may correct them if they do not quite express what we wished to say. Sometimes we are startled by the tactlessness or stupidity of our utterances. And sometimes, unfortunately quite rarely, we are amazed at the brilliance or wit of our statements. Welford says: "Consciousness does not seem to be of ongoing action, but rather of the results of past action in relation to future goals." [31]

The adult tying his or her shoelaces, buttoning clothes, or performing many of the innumerable tasks of the daily routine performs much of this kind of activity with proprioceptive monitoring, and hence automatic action. Even when exteroceptive guidance plays some part in initiating the action, much of the action may be subliminal. A woman may go back to see if she turned out the light, turned off the stove, locked the door, or locked the car, only to find that she has already performed the task. This subliminal and largely proprioceptively guided behavior apparently has not registered enough in the awareness level of consciousness to be recalled later.

Stimulus Generalization

In general, stimuli with considerable similarity will tend to evoke the same response. This fact is a part of the problem of stimulus generalization (transfer). A somewhat generalized stimulus may be a great advantage because complete exactness of cue reproduction is not always possible—for example, variation in word pronunciations, especially in a newly learned language. Even variation in dialects of one's own language requires the same type of stimulus generalization to grasp meaning. Script writing varies greatly among individuals, yet we can read many handwritings and recognize their authorship. On the other hand, similarity of stimuli may cause errors in recognition if the cues are too few and the learning has not progressed far enough. Stimulus generalization permits us to transfer responses. We have enough stimulus transfer so that we can dodge or catch various thrown objects as we see them approaching us. In fact, similarity of stimuli, hence stimulus generalization, permits us to adjust to many situations in life which we have never before encountered. We use similarity of stimuli to clarify points to others or to delude them. Acting, punning, pretending all rely on generalization of stimuli to guide the perceptions of our observers. In puns the absurdity of the double meaning comes to us from the stimulus situation. The stimulus similarity may come from similar sounds or from unusual meanings in the particular context; for example, my dog Ben had pups so I now call him Ben Hur.

The fond mother, amused at the antics of her michievous youngster, tries to simulate cues of anger as she scolds or punishes him. Soon the child also learns to give off false cues of pain and repentance when he feels neither. It is often a question of who is fooling whom. The feints and fakes of sports contests are other examples of attempts to fool others through the principle of stimulus generalization. The great base runners in baseball and the great defensive players in team games need very few cues to release appropriate action; but they also have learned great discrimination between cues in order to decrease the number of errors from stimulus similarity.

Another way to look at the principle of generalization of similar stimuli might be to say that the person who generalizes is actually reacting to identical elements in similar situations (Thorndikian theory). When I try to fake a defense in basketball by a head and foot movement to one side, I do make a preliminary part of the movement pattern for the drive past that side of the opponent—the head and shoulder, and perhaps foot, do start a movement in the fake direction. These false cues are taken from the total pattern of the actual act of driving by on that side. I merely cut off the act after slight preliminary moves and drive to the other side. There will of necessity be slight differences in the center of gravity of my body when the drive is inhibited for quick reversal so early. If these slight differences in my center of gravity with relation to my base are apparent to the skilled opponent, he uses them as cues, instead of my fakes, to initiate acts to defeat my purpose. He has had enough experience or training to be highly discriminative in responses to cues from opponents' actions.

DEGREE OF MEANINGFULNESS

Learning is a complex affair and has many aspects. It involves involuntary conditioning, such as modification of pupillary response or fear of snakes. It involves the type of learning described as individuation of movements in the preceding chapter, needed in innumerable types of motor-skill accuracy. It involves many associative bonds; for example, learning names of states, capitals, presidents; conjugations and declensions; names of bones and muscles. It involves comprehension of meaning; for example, one's concept of almost any noun.

Perhaps it is a sound principle of teaching to try to classify the learning problem according to its degree of meaningfulness for the particular learner. Human maze learning, learning to hit the proper keys on the piano or typewriter keyboard, learning one's way across a strange city on foot, even the learning of some of the traditional coordination exercises in physical education all involve learning a kind of serial association without much background of meaningful experience that will transfer and help to strengthen the associative links which must be formed.

Both in school and in life we have to learn many responses that are made a specific way by custom, tradition, or reasons beyond our comprehension. Spelling, multiplication tables, many dates and facts, number of days in each month are examples of this type of learning. A course in anatomy requires much memorization of names. Language study requires memorization of vocabulary, conjugations, and declensions. Remember how long you had to struggle over those foreign-language irregular verbs! Some such learning is essential in most areas of schoolwork. Students learn because they want to succeed in school, to please their parents, to equal or surpass their classmates, and so on. Intrinsic motivation, actual interest in the content itself, is very difficult to achieve in such learning. The best the teacher can do is to convince students that the learning is essential knowledge in the social milieu of which they will be a part, or that it is a prerequisite for some future goal. In the learning of the so-called coordination exercises mentioned above, students learn a serial sequence different for each arm but occurring simultaneously, with perhaps some additional head and trunk movements to add to the complexity, increase the difficulty, and multiply the number of unlike movements to be carried on simultaneously by various body parts. Students practice the exercise not because they see any use for such activity, but in order to secure teacher approval and a passing grade—or perhaps because they docilely accept the teacher's dictum that the activity is a "worthwhile developmental exercise."

The methods used in nonmeaningful associative learning are quite different from those used with meaningful material. They involve much repetition, immediate substitution of correct response for any error, and extrinsic motivation. Recall involves speed, accuracy, and rote memory; but even in rote memory learning, the learner will try to invent some sort of meaningful association, some system of like sounds or of extraneous verbal symbols to hasten learning. There must be some means of tying together the material into the desired sequential order. The memory devices (mnemonic indices) used a generation and more ago may have been an immediate help for recall, but may have wasted much time in later years. For example, if the precise number of days in each month had been memorized in early learning, the adult would have been saved hundreds of repetitions of "Thirty days hath September, April, June and November," up to the final words about February and Leap Year. Having to repeat a multiplication table to recall the product of, say, 7 times 8, or 9 times 12 is another example.

The Concept

An accompanying meaningful vocabulary tends to develop with our skills; we grow in ability to think about the activity in words. We learn to use meaningfully such words as "force," "speed," "accuracy," "balance," "arc of the swing," "reaction time," "movement time"; we also learn to use the names of particular activity patterns such as "kip," "giant swing," "two-and-a-half off the diving board," or "hook shot off the pivot." The nouns one uses in thinking and communicating, whether in physical activity or in academic areas, are call *concepts*.

The very nature of a concept illustrates the extent to which human experience can be abstracted, synthesized, epitomized, and then reduced to the shorthand of verbal symbols without losing the lessons from the great experiential background. Perhaps a short discussion of the nature of the concept will clarify our meaning.

A concept represents a lot of experience fused into a core of meaning. It is a cluster of meaning represented by some symbol. Words such as "dog," "car," "movie," and "ball game" are symbols that represent significant aspects of much past experience in that particular area. We do not need to recall all the specific experiences to use the concept. In fact, we probably cannot recall all the previous experience that added to our meaning of the concept. How many types of dogs passed through your realm of experience to give you your present concept of dog? Your concept of a pivot has probably developed from a background of experience in the hip rotation and shift of weight in golf, the reversal of direction in tennis, the offensive maneuver for direction change in basketball, or the innumerable turns and shifts in center of gravity in the dance.

Generalizations

Moving further along in the continuity of meaning, we come to *generalizations*, relationships of broad applicability between two or more concepts. We have a concept of speed of movement and a concept of force of impact. We generalize that, other things being equal, the force of impact is proportional to the speed of movement; or we may use a heavier bat but swing at the same speed, and therefore increase the force imparted (force equals mass times acceleration). If we swing the bat or racquet faster, we hit the ball harder. If we increase the speed of our body before blocking an opponent, we can hit him more forcefully. In other conditions, if we cannot avoid an undesirable collision completely, we can decrease its seriousness by decreasing our speed as much as possible. This principle applies to bumping into another pedestrian or backing into another car when parking our own. The concepts of speed and force here are joined into a statement of relationship, a generalization.

SUMMARY

The individual is a unified organism and learning involves his or her entire being. In various degrees any learning situation tends to involve attitudes, emotions, ideas, concepts and generalizations, and motor and verbal responses, implicit or overt. A drive or purpose seems to be basic to learning. Learning varies in nature and complexity from classical conditioning to highly rational and meaningful adult learning, and from simple movements to highly complex and integrated movement patterns involving various body-part individuations in a patterned sequence. There is some evidence of latent learning—occurrence of learning without apparent intent, and with no associated primary need reduction. Common classifications of learning are conditioning, associative learning, and insight learning. Perhaps these are just variations in aspects of learning along a continuum.

The old theory of learning as that of a set simulus flowing into a consistent response has been rejected in recent years. Even the theory of open-loop discharge of response from motor memory without time for feedback has been modified somewhat. The various physical and physiological conditions of the moment are supposed to cause some modification of the details of the motor-memory discharge. In addition, there are the closed-loop responses, in which feedback from ongoing action occurs and proprioceptive monitoring guides the response in terms of this feedback.

Categorizing skills as open and closed gives "open" a different meaning. Open skill refers to skill response continually monitored by exteroceptive stimuli; and closed skill refers to skills that are internally, proprioceptively monitored. Skills tend to occur along a continuum from open to closed, depending somewhat on the nature of the skill and its degree of dependence on external, environmental guidance. Moreover, as learning progresses, many skills move toward the closed end of the continuum. Some skills are less dependent on constant changing of external environment, and consequently the response may be stereotyped to a consider degree. The stereotyping may be desirable when a particular prescribed form is preplanned for beauty or required by the rules.

Perception is the organization and interpretation of sensory stimuli in the light of past experience. Various cue constants in the total sensory display are organized into a psychological unit. Both external conditions and internal states affect perceptual interpretation. The stimuli from various sense modalities may combine, facilitate, and speed up perception.

Sensory reception, in itself, is somewhat selective and analytical. Its speed is partly dependent on postural alertness and selective attention. Rapid perception results from learning to recognize the earlier-appearing cues in the display, cues which seem to be relatively constant in that particular percept from occurrence to occurrence. This advanced perception permits prediction of appropriate response and initiation of action in time to meet rapidly changing conditions.

Visual perception is dependent on stimuli received in both the rods of the periphery of the retina and in the cones in the fovea of the retina. Much visual perception is greatly affected in speed and precision by cues received in both these areas of vision. Perception may occur so rapidly and result in such a prompt response that conscious awareness can occur only in retrospect.

Motor-skill learning involves perception of the stimulus situation, movement selection, and integration of selected movements into a unit of action. Much of the movement selection and integration is brought about by adjustment from feedback of results by proprioceptive facilitation. As learning progresses, fewer cues from the stimulus situation are needed to release an adapted response. Moreover, with prediction from early-appearing cues, the initiation of the cue response can occur in time to produce precise and smooth-flowing action.

Stimulus generalization develops so that similar stimuli evoke like responses. Human beings gradually develop symbols to represent great areas of experience. The symbol stands for a concept—a wealth of experience abstracted, synthesized, epitomized into a cluster of meaning and tied to appropriately adapted responses. Generalizations are relationships between concepts.

A background of selected, organized, and interpreted experience (meaning) carries with it many strong associative links. When the material to be learned can be made meaningful in this sense, it is easier to learn, is retained longer, and is much more likely to transfer to new situations. Meaningful material already possesses transferred relationships from previous learning and can be further linked to one's experiences by instructor stimulus of additional past experience relevant to the present situation. When the advanced skill learner sees the purpose or object of the new skill, he or she makes many meaningful adaptations from previous experience. When the material to be learned is lacking in meaning (not clarified by past experience), it must be learned through drill, rote memory, and extrinsic motivation.

DISCUSSION QUESTIONS

1. May one learn without being aware that one is learning?
2. Are mental, physical, and emotional adjustments through experience completely different and isolated types of learning?
3. Are complacency and satisfaction conducive to learning?
4. Do the different categories of learning merely indicate degree of emphasis on certain aspects of the learning—that is, is there a continuity of the learning processes from simplest to highest types of learning?
5. May one be learning in situations in which one has no intention or desire to learn?
6. Does unconscious and involuntary response conditioning occur in the well-educated, normal adult?
7. Are children occasionally conditioned by parents in certain attitudes and reactions without the parents' intent or awareness of so doing?
8. May trial and error learning occur without overt expression of the trials?
9. Is the occasional effectiveness of "punishment" in facilitating learning due to the feedback of information of results of action —that is, clarification of more effective response?
10. Is the "sudden emergence of a complete solution" (gestalt learning as described by Köhler) the typical way that motor-skill learning occurs?
11. Is "insight" merely highly sophisticated mental trial and error?
12. Does the incubation stage in creative imagination imply the

occurrence of a reorganization of the background of information carried on below the level of conscious awareness?

13. Do any of the theories of learning in this chapter encompass the cybernetic hypothesis (electronic computer, servomechanisms, and constant feedback) of human adaptation and adjustment hypothesized in Chapter 1?

14. Are the most suitable teaching procedures for meaningful and nonmeaningful material the same?

15. Is perceptual learning a basic and increasingly important factor in the development of high motor-skill levels?

16. Distinguish between the S————►R learning theory of Thorndike, the open-loop theory as implied in the motor-memory release, and the closed-loop action. Why does Gibbs object to the theory of "consistency of response" to a set stimulus?

17. Distinguish between open-loop theory and open-skill theory. What are the objections to the use of the open- and closed-skill categories for the classification of skills?

18. Distinguish between preprogrammed action discharge from motor memory and proprioceptively monitored action.

19. When and to what extent is stereotyping of one's skill patterns advantageous?

20. What is meant by the term "psychologically simplified whole" in perception?

21. Do perceptions occur only at the awareness level of consciousness? Are there various levels of consciousness?

22. What physical and physiological factors affect perception?

23. Do stimuli arriving from various modalities tend to slow up reaction time? How do you explain your answer?

24. Give examples of analysis within the senses themselves (eye, ear).

25. What adjustments may one make in order to obey a command to "Pay attention"?

26. How does expectancy affect the speed of perception? the accuracy of perception?

27. Explain the importance in skilled performance of prediction from early-appearing cues, and give examples.

28. Discuss the uses in skills of peripheral versus foveal vision.

NOTES

1. Hulsey Cason, "Conditioned Pupillary Reaction," *Journal of Experimental Psychology*, 5, 2 (April 1922), 108–46.

2. William James, *Talks to Teachers on Psychology* (New York: Holt, Rinehart & Winston, 1961).

3. Clark L. Hull, *Principles of Behavior* (New York: Appleton-Century-Crofts, 1943), pp. 383ff.

4. Edward C. Tolman, "There Is More Than One Kind of Learning," *Psychological Review*, 56, 3 (May 1949), 144–55.

5. George Katona, *Organizing and Memorizing* (New York: Columbia University Press, 1940).

6. See Donald Thistlewaite, "A Critical Review of Latent Learning and Related Experiments," *Psychological Bulletin*, 48, 2 (March 1951), 97–129.

7. Hull, *op. cit.*, p. 387.

8. The old stimulus-response chain of skill learning is no longer accepted, and the concept of feedback has taken over. This concept will be discussed later in this chapter in the section on open- and closed-skill learning.

9. Wolfgang Köhler, *The Mentality of Apes* (New York: Harcourt, Brace & World, 1925), p. 190.

10. *Ibid.*

11. E. C. Poulton, "On Prediction of Skilled Movements," *Psychological Bulletin*, 54 (1957), 467–78; also quoted in *Skills*, ed. David Legge (Baltimore: Penguin Books, 1970), pp. 101–02.

12. Barbara Knapp, *Skill in Sport* (London: Routledge and Kegan Paul, 1967), p. 152.

13. A. M. Gentile, "A Working Model of Skill Acquisition with Application to Teaching," *Quest*, 17 (January 1972), 6, 11.

14. H. T. A. Whiting, "Overview of the Skill Learning Process," *Research Quarterly*, 43, 3 (October 1972), 273.

15. Ree K. Spaeth, "Maximizing Goal Attainment," *Research Quarterly*, 43, 3 (October 1972), 338.

16. A. T. Welford, "Obtaining and Processing Information," *Research Quarterly*, 43, 3 (October 1972), 300.

17. See W. H. Teichner, "Recent Studies in Simple Reaction Time," *Psychological Bulletin*, 51 (1954), 128–49.

18. J. C. Bliss, J. T. Townsend, H. D. Crane, and S. W. Link, *Tactual Perception: Experiments and Models* (Menlo Park, Calif.: NASA Report No. NAS 2-2751, Stanford Research Institute, December 1965).

19. J. R. Swink, "Intersensory Comparisons of Reaction Times Using an Electropulse Tactile Stimulus," *Human Factors,* 8 (1966), 143–45.

20. W. M. Smith, "Sensitivity to Apparent Movement in Depth as a Function of Stimulus Dimensionality," *Journal of Experimental Psychology,* 43 (1952), 149–55.

21. These statements of relative reaction times to stimuli from various modalities are reviewed by W. J. Wargo et al. in *Human Operator Response Speed, Frequency, and Flexibility* (Santa Monica, Calif.: Report No. NAS 12–103 by Dunlap Associates for Electronic Research Center, NASA.)

22. A. T. Welford, "On the Nature of Skill," in *Ageing and Human Skill* (Oxford, Eng.: Oxford University Press for the Nufield Foundation, 1958), pp. 17–27. See also Legge, *op. cit.,* p. 28.

23. A. T. Welford, "The Obtaining and Processing of Information," pp. 303–04. See also L. R. T. Williams, "Psychological Refractoriness of Two Serial Motor Responses," *Research Quarterly,* 44, 1 (March 1973), 32; and his article in *Journal of Motor Behavior,* 3, 4 (1971), 289–300.

24. K. S. Lashley, "The Problem of Serial Order Behavior," quoted in Legge, *op. cit.*

25. C. B. Gibbs, "Probability Learning in Step-input Tracking," *British Journal of Psychology,* 56 (August 1965), 233–42. See also Legge, *op. cit.,* p. 185.

26. A. T. Slater-Hammel, "Velocity of Fast Balls and Curve Balls," *Research Quarterly,* 21, 3 (March 1952), 95–97.

27. See the extensive discussion in W. T. A. Whiting, *The Acquiring of Ball Skill: A Psychological Interpretation* (Philadelphia: Lea & Febiger, 1969).

28. James Gallagher, "The Study of Eye Movements and Visual Focus During the Learning of Juggling." Unpublished master's thesis, Pennsylvania State University, 1961.

29. Robert A. Cobb, "The Effects of Selected Visual Conditions on Throwing Accuracy." Unpublished doctoral dissertation, Springfield College, 1969. See also C. T. White, "Eye Movements, Evoked Responses and Visual Perception," *Acta Psychologia* 1967, pp. 337–40.

30. Alfred B. Kristofferson, *Attention in Time Discrimination and Time* (Report prepared under contract No. NAS 2–1790 by Bolt Beranek and Newman, Inc., Cambridge, Mass., for Office of Technical Services, Department of Commerce, Washington, D.C.).

31. Welford, "Obtaining and Processing Information," p. 309.

Four

Methods in Early Stages of Skill Learning

Early skill develops by aping, mimicry, and bodily attempts to express gross-framework ideas.

Before beginning the discussion of methods, certain facts about procedures in motor learning should be mentioned. For example, at times even a child seems to be able, merely from observing an adult engaged in relatively simple activities, to imitate in what resembles, at least in gross pattern, the action of the adult. Many acts are performed somewhat effectively and rather promptly by imitation after direct observation. In this connection we should mention a principle long established by physiologists—namely, that movements, not muscles, are represented in the cortex; in other words, suprathreshold stimulus of the cortex releases more or less integrated movement patterns. Moreover, a muscle itself may be stimulated from various parts of the cortex.

Next we should mention that many highly skilled individuals are unaware of exactly how they perform particular skills. Much of the learning of skilled behavior goes on beneath the level of conscious awareness. Let me quote a few psychologists on this point. In 1927 Bowdlear, in summarizing one of his studies, said:

> Man would be at a decided disadvantage if he could not learn by trial and error since often the thing he has to manage is very difficult to learn through rational analysis. Much motor skill is acquired by doing the best you can; getting into trouble, varying your procedure, and gradually "getting the hang of the thing" without ever clearly seeing what are the conditions of success.[1]

Bartlett stated this more succinctly when speaking about the muscular part of a skilled operation: "The more efficient it is, the less is known about it." [2] U. T. Place, a British psychologist, states the same idea in this way:

> Close attention to his own activity will be of no avail to the unskilled person because he has not learnt to discriminate between the relevant and the irrelevant features. . . . On the other hand an acute consciousness of the details of his own activity in relation to the environment may actually detract from the efficiency of performance in the case of an individual who has learnt to make many of the adjustments involved automatically. Thus we say frequently of someone whose skill is already well developed that his performance suffered because he paid too close attention to what he was doing.[3]

Bartlett comments on the fact that key cues only rise to awareness in the execution of certain skills, that the bulk of what is happening proceeds at levels below consciousness.[4]

The assumption here is that there are various levels of consciousness, from the focus of attention (used here to imply the awareness level) to the unconscious. The latter implies content that cannot normally be brought to the awareness level; that is, to conscious attention. For example, varying levels of consciousness are active when one is driving a car while talking to a companion and, at the same time, considering other matters not covered by the social conversation. One adjusts the brake or the accelerator and rotates the steering wheel according to incoming cues. The actions are largely automatic and only the stronger cues from the highway cause attention to focus completely on driving. Of course, if one drives with too great inattention, one becomes a hazardous driver. The way in which we direct our attention (or perhaps at times the way in which our attention is directed by interest, strength of competing stimuli, and so on) affects the vividness of our consciousness, the difference in clearness of objects and of the various other factors in the environmental situation.

Two instances in my own experience may be helpful in illustrating the pattern nature and the fact that the performer has only a gross-outline awareness of much motor behavior. While a graduate student at Columbia over a generation ago, when it was still safe to walk alone at night through the poorer parts of the city, I used to take a subway down to Chatham Square and walk across town to Greenwich Village. This stroll was a post-midnight means of relaxing after several hours of study. One night, while browsing through Pell and Mott Streets, I noted a poor crippled hunchback lurching along with a very irregular hitch and limp. Four street urchins playing in the street at this late hour, perhaps because it was too hot to go to bed or because they had no responsible parents to guide them, paused in their play and observed the cripple, apparently with some interest. Then as he passed them, they fell in behind in a line, imitating his lurching, hitching stride so well that an observer could not help recognizing the close resemblance. They seemed to be a family group of queer creatures, all with the same grotesque means of locomotion. A hundred feet down the block, the urchins dropped off and returned to their former play and the cripple was now apparently out of mind as well as out of sight.

Some years later I was reclining not far from the first tee at a country club golf course. Four men of very mediocre golfing ability, and with quite varied builds and stature, stepped up to the tee and took their first drives. Each had his peculiar stance and form, affected perhaps by too much time at the table or by too frequent playing of the "nineteenth hole." After they had gone on down the course, one of the caddies who had been waiting for a job back in the shade of a nearby tree stepped up to the tee and proceeded to give his fellow caddies such a close imitation of the drives of the four men that no one who had observed would have failed to identify each one being imitated. True, there was a bit of exaggeration of the varied mannerisms, but only enough to etch out more clearly the one being imitated.

It seems likely in each of these cases that the imitations were improvisations of the moment, previously unpracticed. The gross-pattern imitation illustrates the way a human body may respond in unified movement patterns to what is merely a retained general idea of an observed action.

HOW SHOULD WE START THE BEGINNER?

In motor-skill learning the best results seem to be obtained when the learners' first attempts are endeavors to grasp and respond to the unit idea, the general idea, the gross-framework idea of the pattern that will accomplish the purpose. They seem to learn more readily during motivated practice if they delegate the major part of the movement adjustment, the filling in of the gross framework, to lower levels of consciousness. Attention is directed not to the details of the movements but rather to the general-impression memory of the gross outline of the skill. In other words, conscious awareness should not attend to the movements that make up the act, but should focus on the desired results and allow the lower levels of attention to control the movements. This imitative behavior, this activity in which the novice attempts to approximate the gross act, seems to be possible, at least to some degree, as soon as the individual has acquired the primary sensory-motor adaptations of infant and nursery school development. It is not uncommon to see a four-year-old attempt imitations of what seems to be a gross-framework idea of the behavior of the adult being imitated.

The terms "general idea" or "gross-framework idea" do not imply a generalization from a number of preceding experiences; rather, they imply a vague outline impression, a memory of some sort of preceding demonstration or observed performance. This outline impression guides the learners' attempts, and is not reflected in a smooth or polished performance; at first it usually results in just a crude approximation of that which they are trying to learn. Smooth and polished performance must await specific motivated practice, with performance being gradually adjusted from feedback of results.

This general idea of the action pattern might be strengthened by attention to some "etched" positions (not movements) in the pattern. These positions can serve as checkpoints for both presentation and performance. The gross idea of the initial or preparatory position for the act, of the arc and direction of the movement and of the final position in the act, might be sequentially imaged in a panoramic flow of the gross-framework idea through consciousness. In throwing, batting, stroking with a racket, and the like, etched positions might be (1) the side stance with the leverage arm (the one that holds the implement or ball) to the rear, (2) a general impression of the path of this acting arm as it moves, and (3) the swing through with the other side of the body taking the forward position. You can make your own "gross framework" for teaching a child to kick a football—catch or grasp it, step, drop it, and kick. These phases are aspects that should stand out as his attention diffuses over the whole act and moves ahead to the next aspect while he is performing the preceding one.

Students learn to notice the basic aspects of the movement pattern and to have them flow through in proper sequence, although the early stages may be marked by stops, awkward adjustments, errors both in precision of movement and in timing, and attempted corrections. In catching, hitting, or kicking a moving ball, a basic step is learning to anticipate the later position of the ball and to initiate movements in advance of the ball's arrival at the point of expected contact. It is assumed that through observation they have already achieved an image of the desired result against which to check their attempts. Postural adjustments for both cue reading and effective movement are to be learned. This learning procedure is chiefly the result of motivated practice and continual revision in terms of successive results. Much of the movement adjustment is made without the learners' own awareness of the exact changes made in the movement elements.

HOW SHOULD THE TEACHER IMPART THE GROSS-FRAMEWORK IDEA?

The method of giving beginners this general idea of the skill varies with the teacher and with the student. Demonstration has been the most successful method for the more apt learner and has been shown to be successful for the average learner as well if the skill is not too complex for his level of development. However, demonstration by itself is unlikely to be completely adequate with special groups such as low-skill learners, the very young, or the very old.

When working with such special groups, the teacher usually needs to introduce skills in very simple units. Manual manipulation, to assist in early efforts to perform the skill, will often serve as an effective supplement or even as a substitute for demonstration in "etching" the gross pattern in the minds of these special cases. Verbal explanation and description by the teacher appear to be the most commonly used methods of imparting the general idea, but their value appears to have been greatly exaggerated and their use generally overstressed.

Verbal Guidance [5]

Some experimental studies might help to clarify this point. Rivenes experimented with the learning of golf putting and of soccer kicking by complete novices. He used college students as subjects so that inadequate general vocabulary would be less likely to be a factor influencing the effectiveness of verbal presentations and simplified his vocabulary so that it seemed to include only words already in the subjects' current vocabulary.

Rivenes' control group was given demonstrations for the first four to five minutes of the first six practices, but no verbal guidance. His experimental group had exactly the same demonstrations, plus two to three minutes of carefully worked out verbal explanation and description accompanying the demonstration at each of the first six practices. The assumption was made that the two to three minutes of extra time for the verbal explanation given during the first six days of the experimental group's practice would not increase total learning time significantly. Rivenes measured learning rate, and retention after eight weeks without practice, for both the verbal and nonverbal groups. The only significant difference between the two groups in either learning rate or retention was in scores on a verbal written test in which the subjects tried to furnish verbal answers describing form and performance of the skill. The actual mean scores on physical performance, either in learning, or in retention after eight weeks without practice, were not significantly different. Mean time to learn to the criterion was slightly less for the nonverbal group and their scores were higher for retention, but the difference was so small as to be regarded as chance fluctuation.

Rivenes did find quite a significant correlation between scores on the verbal test and the rate of learning of the verbal-instruction group, but no such correlation for the nonverbal group. The fact that the scores of the two groups were not different in learning rate or retention indicates that the verbal group used a somewhat different, although not more efficient, learning procedure.[6]

Form

One problem the teacher must solve before trying to present the gross-framework idea of the skill has to do with form. Form is "the way to do it," the work method, the design of performance. In general, the teacher should use a form that has proved highly successful for past performers. Of course, a real problem arises here in the more complex skills because the experts tend to be characterized by diversity rather than uniformity of form.

Generally speaking, the teacher should use some relatively simple form with the beginner, yet one that employs sound mechanics and that is, if possible, somewhat adapted to the functional and structural characteristics of the specific learner. Fortunately, the learner will tend to adapt a gross-framework pattern to his or her own abilities by making adjustments in terms of ease and success. In fact, the focus on gross outline in imparting the general idea of the skill, instead of attention to precise detail, has the advantage of this greater probability of adaptation to the individual's structural and functional characteristics. Moreover, many demonstrations involve details and mannerisms peculiar to the specific demonstrator, and perhaps related to mediocre performance by the demonstrator. If the learner gets the general idea and is motivated to practice, he or she will gradually adjust performance to his or her own individuality as a result of feedback of practice results. In other words, the desire for most effective achievement of a purpose or goal causes a revision of responses following feedback of each performance result.

Once the beginner has the general idea and starts to practice, he or she will make many adjustments without consciousness of the precise movement selection made. Minor errors are unimportant at this stage because movements change as speeds change or as skill advances; and minor errors will tend to drop out. The polish of parts should be left to the advanced stages when the student will tend to fill in mentally the rest of the unit pattern. Only at this advanced stage does part practice have real meaning. At this stage the part becomes an overtly expressed bit of a mentally conceived whole.

Direction of Attention

To begin to understand this idea that much movement selection and integration go on below the level of conscious awareness, let us consider a few experimental approaches to teaching.

In 1931 Coleman Griffith blindfolded a group of beginning golfers for their first four weeks of a six-week session. He compared them with a similar group who took their early lessons in the normal manner and reported that those who had begun learning with sessions in which they were blindfolded were superior at the end.[7]

Frazier taught one group of beginners to serve a tennis ball in a completely dark indoor court for the first three-fourths of their experimental sessions, then brought them out to a regular court in daylight for the final sessions. The orientation these learners had received for their training in the dark area was a view of a brilliantly lighted loop film of the tennis serve. The balls were luminous, and the footline, net line, and racket frame were painted with luminous paint. She reported very slightly superior learning in her experimental group as compared to a control group taught outside in the daylight.[8]

Hoyt Sherman devised a method which accelerated the rate of learning of his beginning drawing classes at Ohio State University to such an extent that they learned in less than half the time required by groups taught by traditional methods. His experimental groups were placed in a completely dark room and each subject was placed at a desk on which were a large set of canvasses and adequate charcoal. The subjects were then given a 1/10-second exposure of a well-lighted picture which they were to draw. Following each exposure, they were again in complete darkness and were given one minute to sketch the figure they had just seen. Each day Sherman gave them twenty different figures to draw and twenty minutes (one minute per drawing) to sketch. He explained the success of this method of teaching by saying that he taught them to see by perceptual unity.[9]

In 1947 Berlin completed a study of the learning of a fine motor skill under what she called conditions of diffused attention. The skill was practiced by her various groups under the influence of different variables. The control group just practiced the skill. A second group was required to listen to various musical selections while practicing the skill. A third group had a series of additional activities to carry on simultaneously while practicing the skill. These extra activities included adding columns of numbers, reading a story, canceling misspelled words in a poem, and counting dots. After a considerable span of learning time, Berlin reversed the environmental and "distracting" situations of the second and third groups for a further series of lessons. She concluded:

Diffusing the learner's attention during the process of learning a fine motor skill after the orientation period is completed, is conducive to greater learning.[10]

In 1958 Cugini decided that Berlin's findings must surely be due to some error in experimental procedure. On the basis of this hypothesis,

Cugini undertook an experiment quite similar in design to Berlin's. However, Cugini changed the skill to three-ball juggling and increased the degree of "distraction." Her subjects recited the alphabet backward, spelled words backward, and solved arithmetic problems in addition, subtraction, mutliplication, and division while they were practicing juggling. Moreover, Cugini increased the difficulty of the mental problems to be solved as the experiment progressed. She rotated the groups so that group I had distractions during the first and third weeks, but group II had distractions only during the second week. In spite of her emphasis on the distractions, she was not able to obtain faster learning by her nondistracted group. She concluded that the distraction made no significant difference in the rate of learning.[11]

The studies of Berlin and Cugini are not completely comparable. Berlin used a fine motor skill and Cugini used a gross motor skill; moreover, Cugini increased the difficulty of the distracting task as the experiment continued. Perhaps the most important difference is that Berlin based her conclusions on 160 minutes of spaced practice whereas Cugini based her conclusions on only 72 minutes of spaced practice.

In those studies just cited in which early practices were conducted in the dark with blindfolds on the learners, or under so-called distracting conditions, we find a clue to the most effective direction of attention during the early stages of motor learning. Griffith thought that his procedure directed attention toward "feel" or kinesthetic perception; Sherman thought his procedure forced one to learn by "perceptual unity" —to see the whole image as a unit. Frazier did not try a hypothetical explanation. The "distraction" studies of Berlin and Cugini seem to have been designed to keep the focus of attention of the learner *off the movements,* although the general idea of the act remained at least in the periphery of consciousness and probably came into focus momentarily with great frequency. Apparently attention should be directed *away from the movements* and *toward the general idea* in the early stages of motor learning.

Two hypotheses have been suggested as reasons for the favorable effects of "inattention" on performance: (1) By attending to a muscular act, one is probably inhibiting the action of subliminal cues that are necessary for the integrations and adjustments in the act; and (2) consciousness cannot act on the basis of past experience that is in itself unconscious.[12]

Hellebrandt, after discussing the great importance of the proprioceptive system, says:

> Feedback from the muscles, tendons and joints appears to be a cunningly devised and exceedingly complex mechanism, a large share of which operates at levels below consciousness. Not only has automation come to in-

dustry. We now know that the machinery of the living body is equipped with its own servomechanisms. Its operation proceeds to a large extent without placing the slightest demand on the cerebral cortex. Innumerable mechanisms exist which are beyond the reach of the most astute physical therapist or teacher of physical education. Perhaps what we need most are techniques of motor learning that free the subcortical motor mechanisms from an oppressive domination of a stressed cortex. Starting from scratch, decorticated as it were, primitively integrated, we might then explore the wonders of that inherent, ancestral movement repertoire and use it as nature intended before encephalization produced its present degree of tension and inhibition.[13]

Hellebrandt's point about the great importance of proprioception in motor learning should not be divorced from her statement that its operation tends to occur below the level of conscious awareness. "Kinesthesis," "the feel of the movement," "a conscious muscle sense" are terms that have all been used extensively in the literature, many times with apparent assumption that such "sensing" in skill adjustment was a conscious, rationally directed type of learning. Experimental evidence does not support this viewpoint, although it does indicate the great value of proprioceptive sensing and adjustment.

Gallagher decided to study further the problem of the direction of attention.[14] He designed an experiment in which he taught three-ball juggling to beginners and took high-speed movies of their visual behavior during the various stages of learning. His assumption was that visual focus would be a fairly good index of the direction of attention. He also compared the visual behavior of those of high skill level with those of low skill level. Gallagher found that, as learning advanced, the subjects came more and more to a standard behavior of using a "distant stare" directed through the peak of the parabola of the path of the three juggled balls. The advanced-skill subjects had reduced vertical eye movements to zero and horizontal eye movements to nearly zero. Gallagher hypothesized that in the acquisition of the skill, the direction of attention gradually changed to only such visual cues to movement as were received from far-distant focus, relatively still eyes, and stimuli passing through the visual periphery. The movement patterns became largely automatic; that is, proprioceptively guided.[15]

The general idea of a motor performance, its outline or its plan of action, seems at first to be a largely conscious but rough symbolic outline of the action. As learning progresses, this outline is gradually transferred to the cerebellum and to motor-memory storage. The motor-memory plan or schema for action provides and guides action in response to recognized cues, individual intent, and momentary physiological state. As skill is developed to automatic performance, this monitoring results from the learned hierarchical organization and is released by memory-trace discharge, by proprioceptive guidance, or by both. When it is purely memory-trace discharge, it is open-loop action; that is, proprioceptive sensing has little or no effect. A fast memory-trace discharge may be released as an action unit without even proprioceptive guidance. G. A. Miller and his colleagues concluded: "A plan, either stored in or transferred to the cerebellum, would provide the roughed-in movement in advance of its actual execution." [16]

SHOULD WE FORCE HYPOTHETICALLY CORRECT BEHAVIOR ON THE NOVICE?

Another student followed up Gallagher's study and investigated the problem of whether or not forcing the novice to use this hypothetically correct visual behavior from the beginning of practice would accelerate her rate of learning (I say "her" because Miss Bush used only only female subjects). Bush's study produced some interesting data we are still puzzling over. She used only twenty novice subjects in her experimental group and twenty in her control group. They were equated on a one-ball "juggling-coordination test" that had been previously validated.

At all practices, her experimental group wore "blinders" that prevented vision below the horizontal level of the eye. The blinders were merely opaque material attached to the lower arc of eyeglass frames and fitted neatly beneath each eye. Both frames and material were light in weight and hence not annoying to the subject. Control group members underwent exactly the same practice regimen except that they had no artificial factor to force them into the hypothetically successful visual behavior—in other words, no "blinders." Both groups were started with two or three demonstrations of the juggling and a few verbal suggestions, but they had no further instruction during the succeeding practices.

Bush found no significant difference in the learning of her six best subjects in the respective groups. She says that the six fast learners in her control group quickly adopted the same pattern that the six fast learners in her experimental group were being forced to use. Five or six people at the bottom of the experimental group never learned to toss three balls in any juggling pattern so that they could make more than two to seven successive catches. Bush hypothesized that she had started these people with too complex a unit (three-ball juggling) for their level of motor-learning development.

The startling thing about her experiment was that no one of the remaining fourteen of her control group did any better than the poorest six in the experimental group. Although the experiment must be repeated, the number of subjects increased, and the total practice time lengthened before the conclusions can be more than hypotheses, Bush concluded somewhat as follows: (1) Apt students in a particular skill need little beyond the general idea of what the skill is, a desire to learn, and the opportunity to practice; (2) the very inept do not seem to learn much in spite of additional help; (3) the average student can progress rather steadily if provided with enough guidance and restriction to make the practice performances become attempts to approximate, at least grossly, the major aspects of the successful pattern.[17]

The reader should note that Bush's "restriction" was restriction of the visual field, not of movement. It is well known that the beginner and the expert differ in the cues observed. As learning progresses, the learner begins to react to fewer cues and to earlier-appearing cues. He also learns to ignore unimportant parts of the display. In Bush's experiment, there was a redirection of visual cues to be observed, and a stress on abbreviated-cue recognition—a recognition that seemingly permitted more rapid, and hence more effective, response continuities. It has not yet been established whether experimental devices such as that Bush used (to force attention to abbreviated-cue recognition, and perhaps to force nonobservance of irrelevant details of the display) speed up the learning of reaction to abbreviated, early-appearing cues.

Most of the experimental work on training in rapid observance of early-appearing cues has stressed speed practice with emphasis on shorter recognition time and more rapid response, with some augmented feedback as to what significant cues could be recognized earlier. The reduction of response time by the learning of autonomous, proprioceptively monitored response has already been mentioned, as has the effect of multimodality stimulus. Most of the experimental work on the speeding up of recognition rate has emphasized time stress instead of limitation and redirection of visual focus. There has been some work on the effect of attention focus on reception from a particular modality. If a complex discrimination is involved (more than the mere recognition of a light or sound signal), the direction of attention to one modality will slow the response to cues arriving in a different modality (by somewhere between sixty and seventy milliseconds).[18] So attention directed for a particular sense organ may be important in speed of a somewhat complex discrimination.

SHOULD WE LET THE LEARNER MAKE ERRORS?

Dr. John E. Anderson has said:

It is clear that errors are significant parts of the process of organizing a skill. In some degree the individual must be permitted to make his own errors in order that the learning process may go forward.[19]

You might think a moment about this statement, and then consider the experiment in which Bush forced novice subjects into the visual behavior they would use if they became proficient in the skill. It is a generally accepted principle that replacement of a less efficient performance habit by a more effective one is much more difficult after erroneous performance has persisted for some time. However, we do learn from our errors. It is from the feedback of results that we learn to avoid errors and adjust. Dr. Pearl Berlin, commenting in a lecture on the need for experience of error in order to discriminate the effective from the ineffective, said: "For example, one has to fall down to learn to ski but he does not have to break a leg."

Motivated learners try to readjust subsequent responses in attempts to improve after observing the results of previous trials. However, they sometimes profit from augmented feedback (teacher analysis of error and suggestion for improvement). Perhaps we should hypothesize that for the average or slow learner, failure to correct *major* errors early will retard the learning. The teacher should be alert to step in and correct a major error if it seems to persist after several trials. Violation of known principles of mechanics, such as using only the arm and not flexing the knees or trunk when throwing for distance or speed, are major errors because they deviate from the gross framework of the skill. The teacher should not, at this stage, correct supposed errors that do not deviate markedly from the gross pattern.

Correction of Persisting Errors

As the skill advances toward higher levels, the problem of persisting error arises. Such error is usually some variation in form that violates a basic mechanical principle, repeated until it begins to be a part of the automatized performance. Learners do not know what they are doing inefficiently, so they fail to adjust performance from the feedback of results. They continue the same inefficient aspect, try harder to succeed, but merely thrust the error deeper into the unconsciousness of automaticity. They begin to develop coverup, compensatory adjustments that produce low-level successes but handicap them for higher-level performance.

The tennis player who runs around his backhand, the baseball player who fails to shift his weight behind his throw and throws almost entirely with his arm, the hurdler who jumps over the hurdles, or the basketball player who always dribbles with a preferred hand (one side only) are examples of this problem. The error may be harder to analyze: it may involve a preparatory postural base with inadequate limb flexion, or disadvantageous position of the body's center of gravity over its base.

It may be a line of movement of the elbow that does not permit the most powerful push in shot putting or, in team games, habitual ball transfer to teammates in such a way as to retard their subsequent actions. It may be such a simple error as not putting the receiving hand at right angles to line of flight of the ball in the catching act—that is, trying instead to trap the ball between two hands extended parallel to the ball line of flight.

The teacher will need to bring the error to the conscious attention of the learner. Perhaps the teacher will need to demonstrate the erroneous performance in slow motion, then have the learner repeat it until he or she brings that part of the action to the awareness level of consciousness. Then the substitute part may be introduced into the total act. Once incorporated into the total pattern, the correction must then be practiced until it becomes a part of a new automatic performance.

EVALUATING METHODS

Berlin studied the effect of five different teaching methods on the rate of acquisition of a specific skill in golf, soccer, fencing, tennis, and lacrosse. She used a total of 111 college women divided into five groups. They were all given a general orientation to the five skills, then taught the five skills one at a time, with different instruction methods for each skill. The methods used after the general orientation were (1) demonstration plus practice, (2) trial and error practice only, (3) verbal instruction plus practice, (4) visual aids plus practice, and (5) a combination of the preceding four. The learning time for the trial and error group was entirely devoted to practice. In the other groups, some time was used for demonstrating, explaining, or showing movies. Berlin designed her experiment so that each method was tried out on each skill but with a different group as the method changed. Each group experienced all five methods; golf was taught to group I by demonstration and practice, to group II by trial and error only, to group III by verbal detail and practice, to group IV by visual aids and practice, and to group V by a combination of these methods. Then she compared the time it took each group to learn a skill under the respective methods, and ranked the methods as to effectiveness for most rapid learning per skill and for the five skills. The trial and error method proved to be the most efficient, and the combination of methods ranked second.[20] With respect to the verbal instruction method, Berlin commented:

Words have little meaning for the beginner in motor skills (such as these). It appears that the need for verbalization by the teacher is increased somewhat proportionately with the learner's increased experience in performing the skill. An adult learner may ask for verbal direction; an instructor might do well not to interfere with the learning process until such questions are raised or until interruption is deemed absolutely necessary.[21]

Several other studies have reported little value to verbal explanation as a means of giving the beginner the general idea of what to practice. It seems that the most effective methods are: show the act, then let the learner try it out; demonstrate again if necessary; point out major aspects; guide him or her manually if necessary; and let the person practice.

Methods with Exceptional Subjects

Dailey studied methods of teaching motor skills to the sensory handicapped (the deaf, the blind, and the deaf-blind), and then compared these methods with those used to teach (1) very young children, (2) senior citizens, and (3) low-skilled students at various educational levels. Except for skills that place great emphasis on balance, she found no retardation of motor skill learning due to deafness. Manual manipulation by the teacher and having the learner feel the movements of the demonstrator tended to be the best methods to give the blind the "general idea" of what to practice. To be effective, the manual manipulation must be a guiding, with the learner trying to move as guided. It must not be a passive, unconcerned submission to having one's limbs moved as the teacher wills.[22]

From what few data we have been able to gather so far, it is apparent that demonstration often needs the supplement of mechanical manipulation with infants or primary school children, and with low-skill students at any age, when they are trying to learn what seem to them to be complex skills. We have checked procedures among teachers who have had much experience with the teaching of very young children—for example, with Turner instructors who often start the children at gymnastics, and particularly tumbling, at the age of two or three—and have found wide use of manual manipulation but very little use of verbal description. As to advanced age, Berlin has made extensive use of manipulation in getting senior-citizen beginners oriented in their first lessons in swimming. Her subjects were in the sixth, seventh, and eighth decades of their lives.[23] Incidentally, she had great success in teaching them to swim.[24]

The Value of Verbal Teaching

When the skill is made up of a number of units the learner has already performed, perhaps of movement patterns already tied to verbal symbols, then verbal explanation is more successful and may be the quickest way to teach the skill. This is particularly so, it seems, if pictures or demonstrations of each act accompany the verbal description. Many motor tasks, even the army rifle assemblage, can be taught to large numbers of people more economically this way. The value of verbal explanation increases in many complex skills as learners get beyond the novice stage. The words now may have meaning in terms of past acts and their results—acts that may have become partially verbalized by the learners as they tied them into the gross pattern of their present skill.

In trying to evaluate the importance of verbal instruction in motor learning, we must take into account the nature of the skill, the nature of the specific learner, and the nature and purpose of the verbal instruction. Some skills are very difficult to describe verbally, so that directions for how to perform them are lacking in meaning; for example, pursuit-rotor skills and skills involving varying types of balance do not seem to lend themselves to "how to" verbal explanation. Moreover, some learners are better able to understand and follow verbal directions than are others. The vocabulary used to describe the skill may have little meaning for young children, for low-skilled persons, and even for the complete beginner in the particular skill. This latter point is what Sir W. G. Stimpson had in mind when he said, concerning the first lessons in golf: "Let the beginner shake himself down naturally before the ball and hit. Till he has done this for a good many days, no advice has either use or meaning." [25] As to the verbal instruction itself, we must distinguish between (1) directions for how to perform the skill, (2) explanations of why to perform the skill ·the stated way, (3) verbalizations that aim at focusing attention on results for more accurate feedback, and (4) verbalizations used for motivating purposes.

Individuals vary tremendously in their ways of learning. If the student cannot interpret the language into motor acts, or even into a general idea of what to do, the verbal instruction is ineffective. The explanation of "why" to do it the way directed can have no value in performance except as possible motivation, or perhaps as an understanding that leads to transfer to later similar situations. In commenting on the use of verbal instruction with the beginner, Ragsdale once said:

> In the beginning do not rely too much on words. . . . He will not understand the directions. He may be able to give you the meaning of every word used; he may be able to repeat the directions; but he has not connected the words with the movements of his hands and body. Directions are just empty words until the pupil has already learned something about the new task, until he has already developed a fair degree of skill. He must first build up a movement vocabulary before he can understand and profit by directions given in words.[26]

If the child can already see the results, as in the act of throwing at a target, for example, verbalization to aid feedback of results may be extraneous and even distracting if carried out while practice is continuing. As to verbalization for motivational purposes, the big problem is whether or not the teacher's words are really having a motivating effect and, if so, on which students.

If some knowledge is involved in the skill, then words may help, but skilled performance must be acquired through practice. When sequence continuities that are not highly integrated occur, words may help the student to link together successive acts. Renshaw and Postle, after experiments in motor learning with varying amounts of verbal instruction, concluded that language was favorable in maze tracing or in tasks where a sequence of levers was operated in a specific order, but

> beyond these limits and for other types of skills it may actually impede or hinder progress. The general case in which language inhibits is one in which . . . verbal habits cannot be made effective substitutes for direct sensory stimuli afforded by the task itself. The pursuitmeter, for example, can only be operated by the hands, not by the larynx.[27]

Fleishman and Parker studied the factors affecting retention and relearning of a perceptual-motor skill. The task was designed to simulate a complex skill (that of a pilot flying a radar intercept mission). Two groups differing in amount of verbal guidance were used as subjects. The experimenters concluded:

> The most important factor in retention is the *level* of proficiency achieved by the Ss [subjects] during initial learning. . . . The *type* of initial training [amount of verbal guidance] is unrelated to retention performance when proficiency level after original learning is held constant.[28]

Words may help the student at the more advanced level to focus attention on aspects he or she wishes to emphasize, although such emphasis is usually a direction of attention toward certain cue perceptions rather than toward the muscular activity itself. However, the advanced student may be helped by certain verbal guides to focus on a part of an act that needs polish or correction.

The habit of many performers of talking to themselves either aloud or subvocally during their own performances is so varied in use and effect that comment is of little value. Some seem to use some kind of verbalism as self-encouragement, some use verbal symbols as linking devices between skills in the unfolding panorama of a sport, and some merely use words as a sort of concomitant emotional outlet.

Teachers are very fond of verbal explanation. However, when talk interrupts needed practice time, *it may actually be a handicap to the learner.* Don't misunderstand this point. Students are quite individual in their methods of learning. Even beginners, especially those who have a background of experience in somewhat similar motor activities, may be accelerated in their learning by some verbal direction. However, this individual verbal guidance should be given in such a manner as not to reduce the practice time of that portion of the group which has the idea and the purpose and now needs chiefly the experience of trial and revision to improve. When John Dewey said, "We learn by doing," he could very well have meant any kind of learning. There is an old classroom maxim which states that "telling is not teaching." Both these statements are especially applicable in the motor-skill class.

MOVEMENT EDUCATION AND CREATIVITY

It would be a mistake to leave a chapter on methods in early stages of skill learning without discussing movement education and motor creativity. Movement education, as stated by its proponents, is new in character, innovative in design, and creative in scope. It proposes, through the use of exploratory and problem-solving experiences, to give the child "basic movements which underlie all skills." It proposes to experiment, invent, and explore the wide ranges of movement and its many untried possibilities. Moreover, its approach and method are supposed to stimulate creativity of response.[29]

Movement Education

Within recent years, movement education has been increasingly popular among certain groups of teachers. Movement education was started in England by a dance specialist from Germany, Rudolph Laban. It was designed to develop basic movements essential for later incorporation into higher units of dance performance. Laban's helper and successor, Meredith-Jones, expanded this type of program under the assumption that such "readiness training" would improve and accelerate the later learning of body control and sociomotor and recreational skills; that is, it would be an effective way to teach readiness for future movement demands. It was expected to develop coordination, kinesthesis, and general motor ability. One purpose was to develop in the child an understanding of movement. This so-called basic training was thought to be the best way to accelerate the future learning of various motor tasks.

"Experiencing the joy of moving," "exploration and problem-solving to develop understanding of movement," "movement experiences as ends in themselves," "analysis and discussion to provide a working movement vocabulary," and "analysis of movement elements as the basic step in skill analysis," are stated to be primary objectives of movement education. The movement educators talk about "space," "time," "force," and "flow" as the fundamental aspects into which all movement may be analyzed. In simple language, they are merely saying that, when we move, we do so in different directions, at different levels above base, at faster or slower rates, and with strong or light effort.

Children are stimulated by arranged environment and teacher suggestion (or command) to try out movements of all kinds according to the impulse or idea of the moment; for example, they get such suggestions from the teacher as "See how many ways you can get under, or over, that balance beam"; "See how well you can move all over the gymnasium floor without colliding with any of the various other members of the class who are doing the same"; "Move around with the body extended as high as you can" or "as close to the floor as you can make it"; "How many ways can you use this hoop?" The exercises involve stretching and flexing the body and limbs in all directions and planes, and varieties of ways of moving from place to place—crawling, hopping, rolling, somersaulting, and so on.

Certain hypotheses and questions perhaps should be considered in analyzing movement education: (1) Perhaps an environment that stimulates and permits "the joy of moving" is no more than what all healthy children experience, especially when they are turned loose in a well-equipped gymnasium or playground. The children then, of their own free will, begin to explore and try out various activities. (2) Some exploration is fun for children, but they soon introduce purposeful objectives into their activities. Movement as an end in itself is not enough. (3) Children are already problem solvers when they see an activity, get the gross-framework idea of the act, and then attempt to adjust their individual abilities to a performance approximation. Children seem to want to imitate much peer and adult activity; but a demonstration, an idea or example furnished them, may prevent much of the wasteful effort of pure trial and error. One hates to put children through frustrating experiences such as Thorndike's cat experienced in a cage when learning to press a pedal to get at its food. (4) The gross-framework idea is preferable to specific directions as to exact and precise ways for beginners to act. The evolving pattern of the act is then their own construction, their own creation. (5) Analysis and discussion, and attempts to verbalize the motor experiences, may actually retard the rate of skill learning. As Locke says:

Focusing on the part of feedback from movement which is available to conscious centers is of limited value in learning a complex skill. . . . The acquisition of motor skills is the gradual placement of control into automatic circuits to which consciousness is no longer adjunct. Any continuing stress on awareness defeats this process.[30]

The hypothesis of produced readiness, hence acceleration of future motor learning by the movement education program, implies that one can develop general movement ability, general coordination, and general movement patterns. In contrast to this hypothesis, much of the evidence available stresses the much greater value of specific training; that is, the specificity of transfer.

A motivation problem may arise in the so-called readiness programs. Children want, as rapidly as possible, to get into the games, the sports, and the purposeful activities of their older associates. They tend to find too little interest or purpose in a movement education program designed to be general preparation and readiness for future learnings. Gutteridge's statement about the lack of challenge and the boredom of some children's programs may be applicable here (Chapter 2).

There seems to be little experimental evidence to indicate a better base for future motor learning of those who have experienced the movement education program when compared to children from the traditional physical education program, or children from a sports and games program. Superiority of groups in dancing, ball playing, skating, swimming, or gymnastics seems to be specific to the training in these respective activities, even at the elementary grade level.

Certain principles seem to apply to the so-called basic training for future motor-skill learning. First, skills advance by integrating simpler patterns into larger and more complex units, and into relatively automatic hierarchies of activity. Second, transfer tends to be relatively specific; hence the simpler patterns, which later are used as subroutines in the larger and more complex hierarchical unit, should be close approximations to those that will fit into the larger and more complex unit. Third, certain basic categories of motor activity such as crawling and creeping, reaching and grasping, balancing, climbing, walking, and running, seem to be almost universal in the basic development of infants.[31] They develop in any normal, unrestricted child without any special training program.

Crawling, rolling, stooping, stretching, climbing, jumping, walking, skipping, gliding, dodging, doing cartwheels or somersaults, balancing over various small bases, throwing, and kicking are all relatively simple movement-pattern categories which preschool children tend to develop, and which may form building blocks or subroutines for higher units of motor skill. In Gutteridge's study [32] of nearly 2,000 young children (age twenty-four to eighty-three months), she found high development in most of the children by the age of seven years in climbing, jumping, sliding, tricycling, hopping, skipping, and galloping. Throwing, catching, and bouncing balls were skills of one-half to three-fourths of the children before the age of eight. This study was completed a generation ago, and has been corroborated by later study. As far as could be determined, Gutteridge's sample had not experienced a movement education program.

It seems to be true that

> The greater the variety of specific movements and skill patterns the child goes through in his early development, the more likely he is to possess the motor-movement equipment to form the base for the faster skill learning of the adult.[33]

However, the point must not be overlooked that the more nearly these activities approximate the simpler patterns and subroutines of the higher and more complex motor tasks, the greater will be the amount of transfer. Extensive training in early years (childhood), specializing only in gymnastics with apparatus, does not seem to help the teenager or young adult very much in the later learning of ball games, or vice versa. One of the criticisms hurled at the movement education programs is that many of the activities do not approximate closely enough the subroutines which are integrated into the hierarchies of later, more complex units and continuities of motor learning. Moreover, postponement of the age of trying out a more complex motor unit raises two problems. One is that the simpler patterns should be integrated into the higher units as soon as they become relatively automatic, if faster learning is desired. A second problem is that the extended practice of exploration, problem solving, analysis, and vocabulary development, and movement experience as an end in itself, may not be as interesting and challenging to children as attempts at participation with peers in the dances, games, and sports of their social milieu. As Locke says: "The fresh joy of a child's running is best preserved by doing it—not by talking about it." [34]

Some claims are made for more healthful personality development through early movement education than would occur through programs that are more competitive. A reverse claim is that the long-persisting self-analysis and introspection fostered in an attempt to develop "awareness of one's body and his self in space" may be less healthful mentally and emotionally than would be overt focus of attention on the activity. Two objections which one finds to movement education *beyond the primary grades* are (1) the specific nature of skill acquirement, and hence the low value of general readiness training; and (2) the inhibitory effect on motor learning of stress on conscious analysis (and accompanying intellectual content) in the early stages of skill development.

Some real advantages, however, do seem to have accrued from the spreading popularity of the movement education programs. One is the greater stress on activity programs for preschool and primary school children. Another is the attempt to keep the competitive element from discouraging the backward and slowly developing youngster. The very simplicity of many of the movement education programs may permit some success for slow-developing youngsters who would become greatly discouraged in the more competitive programs. However, this very aspect may decrease the interest of the more highly developed children.

There are now many types of programs called "movement education." Some seem to use simple activities that closely approximate what will be the component parts of later, more complex units of skill, and use them in play situations that have a high degree of intrinsic interest. These programs are not much different from what is often called a good "physical education" program. In addition, the very fact that the movement education program has impressed many people with its stated aims and objectives and its claims for basic training has led to much wider participation, and many more programs for children. The expansion of such programs into the higher grades and into secondary schools still needs much study before justification is established.

Creativity

We have said that skill learning is problem solving and construction, although it does not involve much mental analysis. Let us proceed, therefore, to a special aspect of construction, to what has been labeled creativity. Creativity has been defined as ability to produce something original; to invent or design something with a new form, value, usefulness, or something with original esthetic and artistic character. Uniqueness and variation from standard forms are descriptive terms used to characterize creative activity. Philipp defined motor creativity as the performance of a quantity of original movement patterns appropriate to a specific situation. Creativity does not seem to be a general trait, but rather is specific to particular field and activity.[35] Philipp found no significant correlation between Torrance's verbal and figural creativity tests [36] and Wyrick's Test of Motor Creativity. Wyrick defined motor creativity as ability to create both varied and unique motor responses to a stimulus. She combined both fluency and originality to get a creativity score, and found that the more original individuals also tended to be the most productive of varied responses— that is, more fluent.[37]

Motor creativity would not seem to differ in kind but only in degree from motor readjustment, rearrangement, and adaptation of simpler movement components into a higher hierarchical unit. In each case, it consists of the putting together of bits of former experiences in new arrangements. The degree to which the activity unit is a copy or imitation of a model, or is action under supervised guidance to attempt to reproduce a preestablished form and pattern of action, it is not considered original or creative.

Some of the writing on creativity seems to imply that the more bizarre and unusual the act is, the more likely it is to be called a creative expression; however, odd, eccentric, and extravagant acts are not usually highly desirable types of creativity. The analogy to creative imagination will perhaps illustrate the point. While ogres and monsters may be imagined and transcribed in myths, fairy tales, horror movies, and TV movies of creatures in outer space, this type of creative imagination has only limited use and value. Eccentric and grotesque movement patterns are often useful to the clown or comedian, but these also have only limited usage. Some of the movement education postures and movements may be useful in some types of dance but have little use elsewhere.

> Children, because they are less inhibited and regimented by custom and habit, will go through many unique sequences, making all types of faces, twisting the body in a hundred different forms and gyrations, rolling, hitching along, hopping, skipping, etc.[38]

Also beginners will often produce quite unique and original action patterns in their attempts at new activity, simply because they do not know what will serve their purposes. Sometimes they will try out unusual behaviors just to entertain themselves and to be different. Some studies have reported greater originality (creativeness) in those who have been less exposed to customary forms of performance in a particular society. Often this so-called creativeness is no more than responses based on quite different backgrounds poorly adapted to the purpose of the moment; or if the situation and impulse merely called for exploratory action, the so-called greater creativeness of those with different social backgrounds merely resulted from their putting together simple movement components they had acquired from those backgrounds.

Let me then propose certain hypotheses.

We do not know unless we know *something;* we cannot think unless we think *something.* Therefore, our thinking is limited to our background of knowledge. Creativity is no more than the putting together of bits of past experience in *new* arrangements; for example, my mythological eight-foot giant with only one eye, and that in the middle of his forehead, and with four arms instead of two, is original in construction, but the parts used were pulled out of my past experience (size, eye, location, arms).

In trying to transfer this hypothesis of reorganized component parts (previously experienced mentally but rearranged with much novelty) over to motor creativity, we run into difficulty. The individual's motor-movement experience by the time he is of school age is very great. Much of it is not available at the awareness level of consciousness; in fact, it may never have been. Yet the great quantity of varied childhood motor experience would seem to contain innumerable possibilities of motor components to be put together in new, original arrangements. How the individual can be stimulated to produce rearrangement and integration of novel patterns is another problem.

Perhaps novel rearrangement in the unconscious may occur in motor behavior in much the same manner as in creative imagination. Creative imagination has been described as consisting of three stages: saturation, incubation, and insight. Saturation means broad knowledge and intensive consideration of known facts and ideas about the specific problem. Incubation is a period of time to allow the various aspects of these data to become rearranged and restructured into new form in the unconscious. Insight is the emergence of some new idea into the awareness level of consciousness. New ideas, new plans, new schemes do seem to "pop up" in our minds when we have saturated ourselves with a problem and then let it incubate a while. A difference between mental and motor creativity may be that, in the latter, much change and novel behavior occurs with the individual noting only large, very evident gross factors in the change. It is true that mental design and planning of gross motor pattern and then overt trials may occur; but it is also true that overt trials with modification of results may occur without conscious planning and without mental awareness of what changes have occurred.

In actual life practice, original forms and styles of improved motor activity seem to come oftener from the advanced-skill person than from the beginner. The highly skilled person may possess a greater quantity of component motor parts to use in the synthesis of new patterns. Examples are the addition of the long run (by Wammerdam) in the pole vault, the "back of the ring" facing at the start of the shot put, and the multiple twists being added to gymnastic and diving skills. Forms may be created just to suit an individual—the "Fosbury flop" in the high jump, for example.

The inventor in science or industry is usually a specialist in one area. In that area, often quite specific, he or she usually has a tremendous background of specific facts about a problem before incubating the new arrangement or solution. This statement agrees with the earlier one that creativity is not a general trait. In motor creativity, worthwhile originality would seem more likely to result if the individual is equipped with as wide a background as possible of movement components and skills. But richness of background, in itself, is no guarantee of creativity. The individual must be willing and interested in trying out new patterns. We have tended too much to encourage exact imitation, precise patterns and regimented habits. Too much conformity and restriction will stifle some of the very creativity that adds so much joy to human activity; moreover, it will tend to stifle progress.

There is, perhaps, one aspect of creative ingenuity that is more pronounced in some individuals than in others (perhaps a hereditary factor), but we rarely seem to find great motor creativity without richness of motor-experience background. Creativity needs building blocks and purposes. It also needs great interest, devotion, and often encouragement. An atmosphere that fosters and stimulates creativity, rather than conformity and tradition, seems to help. Children, when not inhibited and stifled by adult control and prejudice, tend to be more exploratory and therefore creative. However, they need help to accumulate the extensive and varied simpler patterns to be used as component parts of new creations.

Certain characteristics of average beginners should be kept in mind. They are usually easily fatigued. They make many inappropriate extra movements and tend to become overstimulated, so that the energy spills over into surrounding musculature and produces interfering tensions. However, this variety and extensiveness of movement is also an advantage in that they more rapidly explore the possibilities of adapted response. Nevertheless, they may fall into basic errors in sound mechanics and persist in them so that, without help, their errors become obstacles to the achievement of their true potential.

SUMMARY

An important aspect of skill acquisition is learning to focus attention on earlier-appearing cues, and to abbreviate the number of cues and display details required for initiating appropriate action. This earlier, faster, abbreviated cue recognition permits response anticipation and well-timed, smooth flow of action. Preplanned action from motor memory, and proprioceptive monitoring when longer temporal continuity is involved, are aspects of the autonomous nature of skilled performance. Multimodal cues may speed up reaction time.

The gross-framework idea for starting the learner on a new motor performance may be imparted to the learner by (1) demonstration; (2) manual manipulation (but as a cooperative act); (3) verbal description; (4) movies, loop films, stick figures, or drawings; (5) feeling others perform the act combined with manual manipulation (for the blind); (6) by a combination of these methods.

Movement education is a type of program based on the hypothesis that innovative, exploratory, problem-solving techniques are best for teaching the child "the basic movements which underlie all skills." Such approaches are also hypothesized to be best for developing motor creativity in the child. Experimental data have not yet confirmed the superiority of the movement education approach in developing "basic readiness for future and more complex motor-skill learning." Creativity seems not to be a general trait but to be relatively specific to the particular area of incubation of any original constructions; it also seems partially dependent on the richness of experience in the specific area.

In trying to select a method of orienting the beginner, several points should be kept in mind:

1. Students are different and learn in many different ways.
2. The same student can, with practice and motivation, learn by several different methods.
3. Intelligence, experiential background, degree of motivation. age, functional and structural characteristics, and complexity of the skill all vary the effectiveness of method.
4. Teachers can often teach best by a method with which they are familiar, provided it is reasonably sound.

The following principles of method are a synthesis of experimental and empirically derived findings as to what works best for the majority of beginners.

1. Acquaint the student well with equipment and facilities, and introduce the new skills in unified acts large enough to make sense and to serve a purpose for the child.
2. Demonstrate; repeat at slower rate if further understanding is needed. Blackboard outlines and verbal explanations may not cause recall of sufficient cues from past experience. Follow the demonstration with learner practice.
3. Use closely integrated skill units for low-skilled beginners; for example, throwing, kicking, catching, striking.
4. Diffuse the attention over the total act, with higher levels of attention on the major features of the act.

5. Choose a design of performance, or form, in executing the activity that has proved successful with previous learners.
6. Use practice techniques that have proved successful in rapid learning for many preceding learners (short, spaced practices; warm-up with lead-up games, and so on).
7. Allow individuals enough leeway to adjust the form pattern to their peculiar structure and unique functional characteristics (different limb lengths, strengths, speeds, and so on).
8. Use constructive guidance rather than faultfinding in teaching the beginner. The free-flowing smoothness of automatic skill does not develop in a tense situation. The beginner needs normal tonus of his functioning musculature and relaxation in the antagonists.

DISCUSSION QUESTIONS

1. In imitation, does the child imitate the gross muscular patterns without thinking about the muscles involved?

2. Does the highly skilled performer of complex skills usually know exactly how he or she performs the skill?

3. Should beginners focus attention on the detailed movements of the act they are trying to learn?

4. Is there functioning at various levels of consciousness in learned motor-skill patterns?

5. Do the phrases "seeing with perceptual unity" (Hoyt Sherman) or "getting the gross-framework idea" imply that much of the detailed movement adjustment goes on below the level of conscious awareness?

6. Does the "gross-framework idea" represent an abstraction of major aspects and a generalization from many preceding experiences?

7. Should the instructor hold the beginner to the precise details of the recommended and demonstrated form?

8. Do the various experiments on sensory limitations (blindfolded, dark room while practicing, "distracting" mental activity during physical practice) indicate that the beginning learner should focus on the precise movements?

9. May focus of attention on, and voluntary conscious control of, movements of a learned act during the attempted performance interfere with unconscious proprioceptive cues that are basic to integrated, automatic performance?

10. Is conscious kinesthetic perception identical with proprioceptive facilitation?

11. Should we force hypothetically correct behavior on beginning learners in order to accelerate their learning rate?

12. Does learning to recognize correct cues and to make correct responses imply that learners must be allowed to make errors?

13. Does the constant error at the higher skill level tend to be a part of automatic performance?

14. Is verbal explanation the most successful way to give beginning learners the "general idea" of the skill to be learned?

15. Are there other reasons for the use of verbalization in motor learning besides its use in explanation of how to perform the act?

16. Has verbal explanation tended to be used too extensively in the teaching of motor skills?

17. Name the four major purposes of verbal instruction in motor-skill learning.

18. What are the changes in cue detected as motor learning progresses, and what effect do these changes have on response time?

19. Present your viewpoint and your reasoning regarding the hypothesis that certain basic movements underlie all motor skills.

20. Is the skill expert or the novice more likely to be creative in motor performances? Explain your answer.

NOTES

1. Charles W. Bowdlear, "An Experiment in Kinesthetic Learning," *American Physical Education Review*, 32, 2 (February 1927), 100.

2. Frederick C. Bartlett, "The Measurement of Human Skill," *British Medical Journal*, June 21, 1947, p. 877.

3. U. T. Place, "The Concept of Heed," *British Journal of Psychology*, 45 (November 1954), 247.

4. Bartlett, *op. cit.* Check also Polanyi's statements about "indefinable knowledge," Chapter 2.

5. See Polanyi's discussion of "indefinable knowledge," Chapter 2.

6. Richard Sven Rivenes, "Effect on Motor Skill Acquisition and Reten-

tion of Teaching by Demonstration With and Without Verbal Explanation." Unpublished master's thesis, Pennsylvania State University, 1961.

7. Coleman R. Griffith, "An Experiment on Learning to Drive a Golf Ball," *The Athletic Journal*, 11, 10 (June 1931), 11–13.

8. Vivian Frazier, "The Effects of Visual Limitations on the Rate of Learning of the Tennis Serve." Unpublished master's thesis, Pennsylvania State University, 1952.

9. Hoyt L. Sherman et al., *Drawing by Seeing* (New York: Hinds, Hayden and Eldredge, 1947).

10. Pearl Berlin, "An Experimental Study of the Learning of a Fine Motor Skill Under Conditions of Diffused Attention." Unpublished master's thesis, Pennsylvania State University, 1947, p. 182.

11. Elizabeth D. Cugini, "The Effect on Gross Motor Skill Attainment of Varying the Degree of Attention Focus During the Learning Process." Unpublished master's thesis, Pennsylvania State University, 1959.

12. See James Grier Miller, *Unconsciousness* (New York: Wiley, 1942), chap. VI, "Subliminal Unconsciousness."

13. Frances A. Hellebrandt, *Physiology of Motor Learning*. Condensation from a seminar presented at the University of Wisconsin on January 21, 1958, while serving as visiting lecturer in the Department of Physical Education for women. See *Cerebral Palsy Review*, 19, 4 (July–August 1958), 11.

14. James Dennis Gallagher, "A Study of Eye Movements and Visual Focus During the Learning of Juggling." Unpublished master's thesis, Pennsylvania State University, 1961.

15. Subjects learn to react to fewer cues and to earlier-appearing cues, and to ignore extraneous parts of the display.

16. G. A. Miller, et al., "Motor Skills and Habits," from chapter 6 in *Plans and the Structure of Behavior* (New York: Holt, Rinehart and Winston, 1960); reprinted in *Skills*, ed. David Legge (Baltimore: Penguin Books, 1970), p. 247.

17. Jone J. Bush, "The Effect of Motor Learning of Forcing Hypothetically Correct Visual Behavior on the Learner." Unpublished master's thesis, Pennsylvania State University, 1961.

18. See the discussion on Kristofferson's study in Chapter 3.

19. John E. Anderson, "Growth and Development Today: Implications for Physical Education." Paper presented at National Conference on Social Changes and Implications for Physical Education and Sports Recreation, Estes Park, Colorado, June 1958.

20. Note that each group was given a general idea or gross-framework idea of the skill in the orientation which preceded the introduction of the five method variables. Note also that the skills she used were basic and highly integrated skills chosen from each sport.

21. Pearl Berlin, "Effects of Varied Teaching Emphases During Early Learning on Acquisition of Selected Motor Skills." Unpublished doctoral dissertation, Pennsylvania State University, 1959, p. 196.

22. Jacqueline Dailey, "Methods in Motor Learning as Revealed Through a Study of the Sensory Handicapped." Unpublished master's thesis, Pennsylvania State University, 1961.

23. Here again it should be noted that the sixty- to eighty-year-olds wore ear plugs as a health factor; and in the water without their glasses, many could see none too well. These limiting factors seem to have required the use of manual manipulation to give them the "general idea" of what to do.

24. Pearl Berlin, "The Learning of Swimming by Senior Citizens." Research project cosponsored by the UAW Recreation Department and Wayne State University, Division of Health and Physical Education, October 20, 1960.

25. Sir W. G. Stimpson, *The Art of Golf,* 1887, cited by Mrs. Stewart Hanley in "The Sense of Feel in Golf," *Journal of Health, Physical Education, and Recreation,* 8, 6 (June 1937), 366.

26. Clarence E. Ragsdale, *Modern Psychologies and Education* (New York: Macmillan, 1932), p. 325.

27. Samuel Renshaw and Dorothy K. Postle, "Pursuit Learning Under Three Types of Instruction," *Journal of General Psychology,* 1, 2 (April 1928), 366–67.

28. Edwin A. Fleishman and James F. Parker, Jr., "Factors in the Retention and Relearning of Perceptual-Motor Skill," *Journal of Experimental Psychology,* 64, 3 (1962), 226.

29. Joan Tillotson, from an unpublished syllabus used in her Elementary Physical Education Workshop at Brigham Young University, 1968.

30. Lawrence F. Locke, "Movement Education—A Description and Critique," in *New Perspectives of Man in Action,* ed. Roscoe C. Brown and Bryant J. Cratty (Englewood Cliffs, N.J.: Prentice-Hall, 1969), p. 222.

31. The word "category" is used instead of "activity" because the muscular patterns involved in each performance named—crawling, creeping, climbing, balancing, walking, running, etc.—will vary from performance to performance; one climbs in various ways, changes balances for every postural or movement variation, strolls, meanders, or marches when walking, jogs or sprints when running, etc.

32. Mary V. Gutteridge, "A Study of Motor Achievements of Young Children," *Archives of Psychology,* No. 244 (October 1939).

33. John Lawther, "Movement Individuation, Motor Pattern Learning, and Creativity," in *Contemporary Psychology of Sport,* ed. Gerald S. Kenyon (Chicago: The Athlete Institute, 1970), p. 628.

34. Locke, *op. cit.,* p. 219.

35. Joan A. Philipp, "Comparison of Motor Creativity with Figural and Verbal Creativity, and Selected Motor Skills," *Research Quarterly,* 40, 1 (March 1969), 263–64.

36. Torrance Tests of Creative Thinking (Princeton, N.J.: Personnel Press, 1966).

37. Waneen Wyrick, "The Development of a Test of Motor Creativity," *Research Quarterly,* 39, 3 (October 1968), 756–65.

38. Lawther, *op. cit.,* p. 630.

Five

Motor Learning at Advanced Skill Levels

High-level skill response is chiefly preprogrammed motor-memory discharge and automatic, proprioceptively monitored action.

As a background for this chapter, the reader should refer to Hebb's statement about the nature of the learning of the half-grown or adult subject:

> . . . the subject is not learning now to make specific movements, but learning a relationship, an association, between perceived environmental events. This makes adult learning primarily perceptual. . . .
>
> Learning at maturity concerns patterns and events whose parts at least are familiar and which already have a number of other associations. . . .[1]

Preceding chapters have discussed abbreviation of the cues needed for perception, learning to recognize earlier-appearing cues, motor-memory storage and preprogrammed release of motor action, and automatic, proprioceptive monitoring of temporally linked subskills functioning within larger and more complex units. The learner's problems are selective attention, early cue reception and prediction, automatic response release, and proprioceptively guided readjustment to feedback from ongoing action. Learning at the adult level is faster because there is wide utilization of the previously established repertoire of movement patterns. In other words, there is a difference because already available basic body control and simpler individuated movement patterns can be adapted to the new purpose.

A distinction should be made here between the learner who has a wide background of simpler skills that may transfer and the individual who arrives at adolescence or even adulthood with relatively little experience in vigorous physical skills. The latter at best will have to resort to many of the slower processes of childhood motor-skill learning. Granting differences in backgrounds and aptitudes of various skill learners, we still have great differences in the learning process of individual learners as they advance from the beginning to the more advanced levels of skill learning.

The throwing, striking, catching, and kicking acts of adolescents who have experienced a variety of vigorous physical activities during their developing years have already developed considerable adaptability. They adapt throwing acts to stones, sticks, balls, disci, or even trout lines. They have had innumerable experiences in throwing with different distances, different backgrounds of the target, and different implements to be projected. They have kicked many things before being introduced to the game of soccer. They gradually adjust their background of throwing to the game of basketball and throw to a teammate or toward the basket. They already have many running, jumping, and change-of-direction acts in their repertoires. Those that seem to be similar to the needs for new purposes are adapted and then refined to fit more precisely into the new skill.

As the skill develops to higher levels, it gradually becomes generalized; that is, adapted to varying backgrounds, variations in implements, different playing surfaces, differing opponents, changing weather conditions, and so on. A highly developed skill is so generalized that the performer makes the movement adjustments to varying conditions automatically, for the most part, as he or she attends to the cues for action. High skill level means generalization. Think of the relative impossibility of frequent success in kicking for the goal in a soccer game or shooting for a basket in a basketball game without this generalization. Distances, angles, body positions, postural base, physiological efficiency in function all vary, but the highly skilled athlete usually adjusts to these factors automatically in terms of the situation cues. His or her attention is on the precise cues to guide action, but not on the action itself.

At the higher performance levels, motor patterns for performing the same act become, to a considerable degree, individualistic; no two persons perform them exactly alike. We acquire motor patterns but we have our own characteristic habit styles. Our walking gait, our characteristic posture, even our highly integrated sport skills are personal and individual habits. However, we need to use caution about the meaning of the word "habit," for it does not imply rigid inflexibility of behavior. The exigencies of the situation, variation in cues and in precise body or object position, degree of fatigue, immediately previous active musculature, even the whim of the moment are all factors in variation in our *automatic* bodily performance. This statement is applicable although the end results are successful and seem to indicate the same performance.

USE OF VARIOUS MUSCLES FOR THE SAME ACTION

We speak, throw, kick, strike, or write with our minds on the cue to response and, at times, on the idea of result. We let the body take over the act while we focus on the cues. In fact, we are often focusing ahead for the next cues while the body reacts to those already perceived. Moreover, the desired result of any particular kind of act tends to be approximately the same but the muscle pattern used to achieve it varies. Our gross motor acts—opening a door, throwing a ball, pushing an object —are goal-oriented but may be performed by various combinations of our musculature; yet they are performed with the complete automaticity of action we ordinarily think of as habit repetition. Actually this point is taken for granted in achieving high levels in competitive sports. The irradiation of high stimulus (high motivation) causes variations in performance and the tapping of unprobed synergistic aids. The higher-level learner develops many motor equivalents for performing the same skill so he can change the pattern to offset fatigue or to meet variations in the situation.

The excellent soccer player passes the ball with either foot or with the head, and with innumerable variations in type of pass used and, therefore, in the precise muscle patterns. The highly skilled basketball player is expected to shoot with either hand from many different angles, from different heights of release, from different distances, using different arcs. The assumption is made that, at the higher levels, different body acts are available and will be utilized as the cues of the situation stimulate them. Moreover, the successive sport skills, once developed to be utilized in the unfolding panorama of a game, are closely associated units but are not habituated into an invariable sequence. Cues from the environment cause sudden changes in the sequential order. The catching and throwing acts are often combined into what seems to be a unified, highly integrated, total response. The action seems to be an automatic response to the cues of the situation. Yet a slight change in cues, a playback from the developing situation, will cause a substitution of different parts in the total act, and a readjusted act that, in itself often seems also to be a "habit" pattern.

Remember that skills are not specific to the muscles which first acquire them, and that movement patterns but not muscles are represented in the cortex. In other words, our idea at the moment may stimulate a movement pattern, through the cortex, but the muscles that carry out the act vary from performance to performance.[2] Actually the same skill, once learned, may often be performed in gross pattern by completely different musculature. The fact that movement patterns rather than muscles are represented in the cortex often tends to be overlooked in the analysis of motor skills. The movement pattern utilized to achieve a goal is constructed over whatever happens to be the postural base of the moment. The tonic discharge of every muscle in the postural system is influenced by different impulses from every other muscle. Any movement pattern is therefore related to the axes of the body and to gravity.[3] Excitations from proprioceptors and distance receptors (vision, hearing, touch) interact and continually affect the postural base. This principle may be overlooked by those who try to stereotype the pattern for achieving a particular goal.

Handwriting can be done with reasonable legibility with chief reliance on either arm or finger movements. Writing on a blackboard does not involve the same muscle movements as writing on manuscript paper at a desk. Almost any literate adult can write legibly with his or her nonpreferred hand; the writing can also be approximated in inverted or reversed form, or even when the subject is blindfolded. Lashley's explanation is that the associative linkage is not of specific movements but of direction of movements; that is, of space coordinates.[4] Once knowing the space relations of the movements to write the letter *a*, say, I can then write the *a* with the right or left hand, or write it in an inverted or reversed position. I can spell a word backward by visualizing the space relations of the letters, then running through them in reverse space relationship. Let the reader try this out on a familiar four- or five-letter word. Lashley's example of trying to play a melody backward is perhaps a more graphic example. He says he must first visualize the music spatially, then strike the keys in reverse order.

It has long been well established that practice of one part of the body in performing a skilled act increases the ability of the bilaterally symmetrical part to perform the same act. This effect has been called "cross education." Practice also seems to improve ability in other parts of the body that are not bilaterally symmetrical with the part exercised in the practice. With regard to the first type, in a study with adults attempting to write with the nonpreferred hand, Thorndike reported:

> . . . the adult starts in writing with the wrong hand with nearly as great facility as the child of eight or nine has in writing with the right hand after two years of schooling.[5]

In 1949 Joanne Black attempted to determine the degree to which the skill of handwriting could be performed by other body parts not bilaterally symmetrical. Her subjects practiced writing with a short pencil held between the molar teeth, and later with the pencil held between the large toe and the adjoining toe of the nonpreferred foot. She measured the quality of the "handwriting" (better called cursive writing in this case) by use of the Ayres handwriting scale, and the quantity by counting the number of letters written in each two-minute practice session. Black used practices of two minutes per day for each type of writing. She had her subjects practice ten days, or a total of twenty minutes of practice for the head writing and a total of twenty minutes for the foot writing.

At the very first practice with the pencil gripped in the teeth, 17 percent wrote legibly. After ten practices (a total of twenty minutes), all subjects wrote legibly with the pencil gripped between the molar teeth. In the foot writing, none of her subjects wrote legibly on the first trial, but 83 percent were writing legibly during the nineteenth and twentieth minutes of practice.[6]

In 1960 Frances Williams did a follow-up study of script writing with various body parts. Using herself as a subject, she practiced cursive writing with the pencil gripped by the teeth, taped to her elbow, taped to her knee, and gripped between her toes. She practiced only two minutes per practice period but practiced twice a day, five days a week for two weeks (a total of forty minutes of practice per method). After completing the two weeks of head writing, she started with elbow writing the next week and continued for two weeks; and so on for knee and then foot in that order. Williams makes no comment about whether or not the sequential types of practice affected each other.

Her legibility ratings on the Ayres handwriting scale were phenomenal—from a beginning rating of 30 on the first practice of head writing to a rating of 90 (highest rating on the scale) by the thirty-ninth and fortieth minutes. She was almost equally successful in elbow writing but achieved maximum score four practices earlier. Knee writing was legible when she first started and improved in quality rating from 20 (at the first minute) to 40 by the fourteenth practice. The quality did not improve in the last six practices. Her foot writing rose only to a quality rating of 30 in forty minutes of practice, and did not reach minimum acceptable legibility (rating of 20) until the thirteenth and fourteenth minutes of practice.[7]

Although based on only one individual, this follow-up study indicates two points: (1) Other nonsymmetrical body parts may take over a skill and perform it successfully with very little practice (note her head writing in particular); and (2) individuals vary greatly in relative rapidity of adaptability of particular body parts to the performance of skills learned originally by use of quite different body parts. (Williams was much better than most of Black's subjects in her head writing but did not achieve the level of the average of Black's subjects in foot writing.)

Examples of skills performed by musculature not used in the original learning practices are numerous among adults, especially in rehabilitation hospitals. Patients who have lost limbs seem to be able to approximate previously learned skills, at least in gross pattern, with very little additional practice of the new body part used; and they seem to refine the performance rapidly, providing there is no serious brain or spinal cord injury. One extreme example is the Hugarian pistol shooting champion, Karoly Takacs, who lost his preferred arm and then won the world pistol shooting championship one year later, using his other arm.[8]

While performance of a skill by other body parts tends at first to be more awkward and clumsy, the rapid acquisition of more precise performance by the new part indicates that much of the gross-framework pattern has been programmed into the computer of the individual's neuromuscular system, and not just as an automatic-action pattern attached to the specific muscles that did the overt performance in the first acquisition of the skill. However, only the gross-framework idea seems to be carried at the level of conscious awareness. The adaptability of the new body part to the performance of the skill indicates a great amount of proprioceptive facilitation that is not registered at the awareness level. Such ready adaptability seems to occur only when the skill has previously attained a high level. As in all learning of any great degree, motivation to use the new body part is basic to its effective adaptation.

Variation in the various muscle actions within one skill in consecutive successful performances has been demonstrated in electromyographic studies. This adaptability of the human body is indeed fortunate because identical situations in which exact repetition is desirable are unlikely to occur—not that one could repeat exactly the same muscle act even if one wanted to, as is well demonstrated by a person's inability to duplicate exactly his own signature in longhand writing. Identity of signature is considered a proof of forgery (tracing) when such signatures are challenged in court.

MORE EFFICIENCY, HIGHER MOTIVATION

More advanced students in a particular skill are likely to be conditioned so that early fatigue is not a handicap to longer practice, and hence to more learning. Not only are they in better physical condition for that particular skill performance, but their relative adaptation to the skill has eliminated many gross, inappropriate movements wasteful of energy. They have adjusted their emotional state so that too much energy is not wasted in tenseness and spillover of energy into antagonistic musculature. They have probably developed a bit more of whatever strengths and endurances are needed for the skill; hence they have more energy and waste less of it in inefficient action. If highly motivated, they can effectively subject themselves to long, grueling, and persisting efforts with intent to improve.

VERBALIZATION

At higher skill levels words may have meaning in certain aspects of the skill—as a means of tying together sequential simpler skills, as a means of tying specific cues to specific responses, and as a means of learning which acts and what variations of previous acts are appropriate for present purposes. Verbal descriptions or explanations, by a teacher or from articles written by experts, may be meaningful and helpful. Highly skilled persons often have verbal symbols attached to the simpler units or aspects of motor patterns; hence they can profit from verbal direction emphasizing cues for readjustments and refinements indicated by the feedback of results. They now understand in movement pattern what it means to "shorten or lengthen a backswing," "choke up on the bat," "keep a wide base and flexed knees," "keep the ball about knee height for the batter on the outside (or inside) corner of the plate," and so on. They have developed, to some extent, a skill vocabulary.

The highly skilled individual often uses words as

1. An emotional outlet—expression of joy or disappointment
2. A means of self-motivation—he talks to himself and perhaps tries to "pep himself up"
3. A means of mental practice—things to stress, errors to avoid
4. A help in recalling sequential order of skill units, and aspects to emphasize
5. An aspect of his particular retention pattern

The instructor often uses words in an attempt to

1. Give the learner the gross-framework idea of the motor skill
2. Bring a certain cue under attention focus
3. Suggest correction of error in a subskill, and augment feedback

Sometimes the instructor wants to explain why the individual should try to adhere to a certain form, or why a particular type of practice seems to produce better results. Motivation is, of course, a common purpose of many verbal expressions by the instructor.

It should be noted that effective skill vocabulary is almost entirely devoted to the general idea of the act, to the gross framework or some aspect of the framework, and rarely to specific muscle contraction. We think about lengthening or decreasing the arc of swing in striking actions, of kicking with the foreleg and foot in soccer, or snapping the wrist in handball or badminton, and so on. Highly skilled performers often have verbal symbols for aspects of the gross framework to which they wish to attend; for example, the peak of the lob directly above the net (in tennis), when the server is driving her deep and then rushing the net. Perhaps she says to herself, "Lob if he drives me real deep for the return stroke"; or "sideline placement if I can play closer and play the ball on the rise."

MENTAL IMAGERY

The performer may have a partial image of his own intended act as he prepares to make it; that is, the pitcher in baseball says he has an image of the path of the ball across the plate as he intends it to go. He sees in his mind's eye, for example, the ball breaking down and out over the outside corner of the plate at about knee height; he has this image of the ball path while he performs the act. Of course, the ball does not always go where he planned.

Warren's *Dictionary of Psychology* defines an image as follows:

> An image is an experience which reproduces or copies in part, and with some degree of sensory realism, a previous perceptual experience in the absence of the original sensory stimulation.

The amount of such imagery in motor learning and performance is still uncertain. It does seem from experimental evidence that focus on the goal (consciously conceived) is a common procedure and also the most effective one. However, that a clear visual image of a successful performance of the act, as a guide to performance, is necessary or even highly advantageous is not borne out by experiment.[9]

Petro tested a group of subjects on vividness of mental imagery, then had them learn a novel motor skill. He concluded, as a result of his findings, that vivid mental imagery was no advantage in fine motor-skill learning. He found no type of imagery superior to any other (visual, auditory, kinesthetic), and found no correlation between either vividness or the type of imagery and the amount of motor learning within a specified series of practices.[10]

Petro used the same type of *subjective* imagery tests as had customarily been used by psychologists in the past, and his measures of learning were somewhat questionable. He used inverted, reversed script writing with the nonpreferred hand as his skill, and then used only a quality score as his measure of learning (rated on the Ayres handwriting scale). Nevertheless, he stressed speed of writing in his directions to his subjects, and omitted a quantitative measure in his total learning score.

A year later Moody did an imagery study in an attempt to determine the relationship, if any, of imagery differences to levels of ability and experience in motor skills. Moody devised visual imagery tests of an objective nature. Her first test presented geometric figures, and then, soon after, the same figures mixed among similar figures. The subjects were scored on ability to identify from memory the precise figures they had seen before. Her second test was a series of filmed acts selected from sport and physical education activities. A few moments later the subjects were shown the same acts mixed among rather similar acts, and were asked to identify the acts seen previously. Her third test was similar to the second in its use of films, but subjects were expected to write verbal answers to certain verbal questions about details of the act, as remembered some moments after the brief film exposure.

Moody used female subjects divided into four categories: (1) young, active physical education faculty women; (2) senior majors in physical education; (3) freshman majors in physical education; and (4) freshman nonmajors (students in other curriculums). She assumed discreteness of her subjects after (1) selection at widely divergent experience levels, (2) various tests, and (3) a motor-skill learning experince in which relative scores were recorded. Her findings were as follows:

1. No difference among the respective groups in ability to recognize previously presented complex geometric forms.
2. No difference in ability to recognize previously presented motor acts.
3. A difference in answering verbal questions that demanded recall of details of previously presented motor-skill acts; three groups, the majors at each level and the teachers, all did significantly better than the one group of nonmajors. The differences among the three groups in physical education were nonsignificant.[11]

The reader should note that it was in verbal response only, and not in visual identification, that the difference occurred. Recall does seem to be tied more closely to verbal symbols than to visual images. However, these majors and faculty in physical education could be assumed to have progressed far enough in many types of motor learning to have a skill vocabulary. Perhaps, also, these experiments are a further indication that many important variables affecting motor learning and retention are at the proprioceptive, nonawareness level of behavior. At least, visual imagery does not seem to be a very important variable at the advanced level of motor skill learning.

OTHER ASPECTS OF ADVANCED-SKILL PERFORMANCE

We tend to get more enjoyment out of performing a skill in which we have already developed some ability. Moreover, we tend to develop higher levels in those skills toward which we have strong motivation. The problems of motivation, emotion, and psychological aspects of competition will be discussed at greater length later. It is sufficient to say here that at the higher skill level, subjects are usually more strongly motivated to excel; hence they drive themselves nearer to their true potential. In other words, what they ordinarily think and feel to be their best performance (their psychological limit) approaches closer and closer to their true potential (their physiological limit).

Several other aspects change at the higher levels. Individuals learn faster cue recognition from early-appearing and abbreviated cues. They undergo a great reduction in number of external cues necessary to guide action. The cues are already tied to motor-memory programs and to proprioceptive automation. Experience has produced familiarity, anticipation, and expectancy, all of which make faster and more precise response possible. At this expert stage, the variability of form among individuals is very great, especially in the open skills, because of difference in size and lever length; in strengths, speeds, and endurances; and in background. The introduction of conscious attention to movements that are already automatic slows and disrupts smooth, fluid performance.

Performance Rate

Because promptness of action is often so important in skill performance, a short summary should be included here about factors that directly affect performance rate. The old hypothesis (single channel theory) was that, during reaction time to one stimulus, there could be no start of reaction to a second stimulus even after proprioceptive monitoring had been developed. Recent research has indicated that this hypothesis is not quite exact. If the second stimulus arrives relatively early during the reaction time (RT_1), the second overt response is not delayed the two full reaction times (RT_1 plus RT_2). However, the complexity of the movement response to RT_1 affects the amount of delay to the response to S_2. Also, response to S_2 can occur more quickly if there is no response to S_1. An additional factor is the finding that a movement under way can be increased in rate without a full reaction time delay.[12]

Speed of response is increased by learning practice, by changing the response from exteroceptive monitoring to proprioceptive monitoring, by anticipation and expectancy. Multimodal stimuli have been found to produce faster responses than single-sense stimuli.[13] Finally, reaction and movement time are both subject to the individual differences in capabilities to learn and perform.

Distractions

Learners at the high skill level are often less subject to distractions, particularly in team games. They have been negatively adapted by the many attempts of crowds and opponents at distraction, and hence they learn to ignore, and perhaps not even consciously hear, much of such vociferous behavior. They can concentrate on what they are doing without letting extraneous stimuli have much effect on performance. The fact that so much of the performance is already automatized helps many an athlete carry on in spite of others' attempts at distraction. He or she has developed the ability to concentrate on cue perception for the activity to such an extent that many of the irrelevant and extraneous stimuli from the environment, which often distract the beginner, are not stimuli at all to him or her. In fact, he or she does not consciously see or hear them. In some sports in which it is customary to protect the competitor from outside noise or distraction—tennis, and especially golf, for example—even the expert player often lacks such negative adaptation. He or she may object to noise or movement while concentrating on a stroke.

Some learners will develop this type of negative adaptation to an environmental situation so that they can concentrate on their reading or lesson assignments in spite of conversation, a radio playing, or other activity in the immediate environment. Many a parent has to speak more than once to a child if the child in engrossed in a book, some play activity, or even television. Sometimes the child may be intentionally ignoring the parent, but often the parent's voice really does not enter the child's field of consciousness because he or she is so deeply absorbed in the activity of the moment. This type of absorption in the activity tends to develop as part of higher-level skill.

Effectiveness of
"Part Drill"

At the higher levels of skill, individuals can spend practice time very efficiently in polishing weak spots in performance. The polish of these parts is, at this stage, much more effective with respect to rate of learning because it is not "part drill." The "part" is now a meaningful act because the learners see its significance in the total pattern, and fill in the rest of the pattern mentally while overtly performing the part. They are, for example, overtly practicing only a pivot, but mentally the pivot is the footwork on the double play pattern by the second baseman, the reverse around the post man in basketball, or the sharp change of direction to be ready for the next stroke in tennis after returning an opponent's placement down a side line. Learners may also carry out the total pattern overtly but with attention focused on one special aspect they wish to change in some manner. The rest of the act is carried out more or less automatically while they attend to the one part.

The Constant Error and Its Correction

The "constant error" that creeps in now and then in performance at the higher skill levels is corrected in somewhat the same manner. The "constant error" is an inefficiency that has crept into the performance of a more highly skilled performer who is unaware of the exact nature of the error. As mentioned earlier, the attention is focused on the error (by teacher demonstration of the error, by a film showing the error in slow motion, by a rehearsal of the error under attention focus by the learner). The steps in correcting performance of the advanced person who is working inefficiently because of a constant error are as follows:

1. Have learner rehearse or practice performance of the error itself, with focus of attention on the error.
2. Have learner rehearse the act with the correction inserted.
3. Practice the modification (the correction) together with the total act until the modification becomes united into the automatic-action response of the total act.

Sometimes this process of correcting a constant error seems to the learner very much like starting again at the beginning. However, if these steps are followed, the relearning of the changed pattern is much faster than the original learning of the former pattern. Much of the old pattern does not have to be learned, and attention can be focused on the aspect to be corrected until it too becomes automatic action. This last step of practicing until the correction becomes automatic is very important; otherwise, the performer will revert to the former pattern under the stress of competitive performance.

SELF-ANALYSIS AND INDIVIDUALITY

Learners at the higher levels of skill can often profit from self-analysis through films and photographs of performance; they can then experiment with form and work methods. The strong motives, the persisting, grueling practice with intent to improve that characterize many learners at the higher skill levels cause these individuals to experiment, to try out and adopt variations in form, training, and practice regimens. The individual learner is more likely to make modifications in terms of structure, function, and personality. Individual differences among learners increase at these higher performance levels.

A teacher or coach who is an expert in the field, especially one who is well trained in mechanical analysis, may be quite helpful to the learner in guiding self-observation. However, the teacher who has training in the applied physics of body mechanics but little experience in the skill itself is often likely to overlook certain variables that have to do with the learner's individuality—for example, the running form of Bob Hayes, the fastest dash man in the world from 1964 to 1966, an Olympic champion, and later a professional football player. Slow-motion pictures of his fastest races revealed a somewhat wider base, an extreme bunch start, and a bit of lateral body sway during his performances. Questions about this form were raised among some of the academically trained body-mechanics "experts" who viewed the pictures. The expert coaches who handle men and women of Olympic caliber are very careful to allow individual adjustments by athletes who have already reached higher skill levels, even though such adjustments vary widely from commonly advocated practices.

The self-analysis and attention to part movements of the total act is often a valuable part of the practice procedure at advanced levels, but this process must be completed and the attention directed away from part-movement focus when peak performance in competition is expected. Here the attention must again be back on *cues* to what adjustments to make, the strategy of the situation, and so on, but not on the specific movements. The body must now be trained to respond automatically to the cues the performer is trying his best to catch and turn over to the body automatism for performance. Some of these cues will cause feedback readjustments in action patterns already under way. Perception of the cue flows into automatic response but, as soon as a cue is perceived, the attention focus moves ahead to try to catch the next appropriate cue.

Mental Rehearsals

At the advanced levels of skill learning, mental rehearsals between practices seem to be advantageous in several ways. First, they serve as a review of the learner's former procedures, practices, and results and therefore as a means for planning more effective succeeding practices and performances. Second, they tend to prevent retroactive inhibition; that is, the increase of forgetting, or at least the lowering of performance level as a result of the influence of intervening activities between the practice and performance sessions. The athlete who never thinks of the sport except when he or she arrives on the field or court is a problem for many a coach. Such an athlete seems to need much additional review and stimulation, and still never seems to perform up to potential. Of course, it may be that a part of the lowered efficiency is just a lower degree of motivation toward peak performance. Perhaps he or she has not gotten ready mentally and emotionally for peak performance.

Learners who are rehearsing their activities mentally during intervals between physical practices will consider experiments in form and procedure and their respective results. Such mental rehearsal, and the underlying concern for higher levels of performance, occasionally bring forth new ideas which, tried out in practice, produce an improvement. In other words, this underlying concern tends to incubate ideas for modifications or changes that occasionally prove quite valuable as an aid to better performance. This incubation is the process mentioned earlier as the intermediate step in creative imagination.

The following are some purposes for which mental practice is advocated:

1. To prevent retroactive inhibition
2. Review procedures, successes, failures, get new ideas of what to try
3. To plan more precisely the next practice—work methods, designs of performance, points to emphasize
4. To institute a proper (or better) mental set for the learning at the next practice
5. To supplement physical practice—to act as a review when more physical practice is impossible, or unwise because of overfatigue; to accelerate learning at the advanced levels and aid retention

We might safely assume that mental practice is often a valuable supplement to physical practice; that its effectiveness will vary with the nature of the skill being practiced; and that it will tend to be more effective as the learner moves out of the novice stage.

Last-Minute Skill Review

The individual at any skill level will tend to fluctuate in levels of performance. At the high skill level, learners tend to practice not only longer but also more frequently than beginners. Their purpose is now not merely to improve, but also to decrease the amount of fluctuation in performance. Moreover, at the high skill levels, much practice and constant polish is essential just to preserve the level attained. Such learners not only practice daily, but review skills for each performance by a precontest rehearsal; they insist on a few strokes (or throws) of review after any rest interval, if such review is permitted (five "warm-up" pitches at the start of each inning in baseball, for example). This precontest review is ordinarily called a warming-up procedure, but it is more than that. Muscular warmth and body flexibility are important, but so are the fine adjustments within the skill itself, which seem to profit from this last-minute review.

SUMMARY

The following statements attempt to summarize present thinking and evidence with regard to the acquisition of high levels of skill.

1. Advanced motor-skill learning emphasizes perception of what to do, and much of the basic movement adjustment is transferable from previous experience. The integration of movement patterns is largely bodily adjustment below the focus of conscious attention. The attention is focused on cues to what to do, and the bodily adaptations are gradually acquired from feedback of results and proprioceptive adjustments. The amount of transfer, and hence rate of attaining higher levels, is much less for learners who rank low in phsyical activity backgrounds.

2. Motor skills become generalized as learners advance to the higher levels; that is, the skills become more and more adaptable to variation in the performance situation and environment.

3. The most efficient form, work method, and practice procedure tend to vary with the individual. Within the same individual, design of performance and precise muscle contractions continually vary even though the overt act is successful and achieves what seems to be an identical result. At higher levels, the motor skill does not rest only in the muscles used in acquiring it but may be performed, at least in gross pattern, by use of other body parts.

4. Learners at the higher skill levels are somewhat conditioned for that skill and hence less easily fatigued; they make fewer inappropriate movements, and have less spillover of energy to muscles antagonistic to the performing muscles (less overtenseness). They therefore have more energy to spend in learning practice and in performance.

5. They begin to acquire a skill vocabulary that helps (a) in understanding instruction, (b) in clarifying the skill framework, (c) in tying together smaller units which are not highly integrated, (d) in mental planning and rehearsal, and (e) in retention.

6. Learning rate and retention of the skill do not seem to be dependent on ability to retain vivid, conscious mental images of the desired performance.

7. Higher motivation at the higher skill levels decreases the distance between what individuals think or feel they can do (psychological limit) and what they are actually able to do (physiological limit).

8. At the higher levels, subjects learn to recognize cues for action more quickly, and to need fewer cues to release appropriate action.

9. Learners often become negatively adapted to extraneous stimuli—that is, less easily distracted.

10. Drill on parts to polish certain weaknesses is now whole learning because individuals fill in mentally the rest of the act as they practice the part; hence part drill is meaningful and conducive to more rapid learning.

11. Serious errors at advanced levels tend to be constant errors, with the performer unaware of their exact nature. They have to be brought to the level of conscious awareness, a correct part substituted, and the new part practiced within the whole unit until it becomes a part of automatic performance.

12. Self-analysis during practice, with instructor help and mechanical aids, often accelerates improvement at the higher levels. Any changes following such analysis must be tried out experimentally in practice; and any modifications in performance that prove valuable must be automatized before being utilized in situations demanding peak performance.

13. Better results seem to be obtained when highly skilled and conscientious performers are allowed considerable leeway in form adjustments to suit their individuality.

14. Learners at the higher skill levels can profit more from mental rehearsal between practices—to review former procedures and results, to plan subsequent practices accordingly, and to prevent forgetting or lapses in mental alertness.

15. Performers at higher levels need physically to review performance frequently not only in an attempt to improve, but also just to maintain this higher level once it has been reached. Moreover, they find it helpful to review skills just before a competitive performance. These last moments of review practice seem to decrease downward fluctuation and add the final polish needed for a precise performance.

DISCUSSION QUESTIONS

1. Does the very nature of the learning of the adult differ from that of the young child?

2. Is the versatile athlete's ready adaptability to the learning of a new skill merely evidence of another specific aptitude?

3. May rate of motor-skill learning at adulthood be increased by quantity and breadth of motor-skill experience during childhood and adolescence?

4. Are high-level performances of motor skills quite precise in exact duplication of movements each time they are performed?

5. Can the highly skilled performer successfully execute what seems to be the same skilled act—scoring a goal, hitting the baseball, volleying the opponent's return—in many different ways?

6. Does the retention of a motor skill, once it is acquired, rest only in the musculature that practiced the skill?

7. Are the tension of the highly skilled athlete and of the novice equally likely to spill over into the antagonistic musculature during exacting performance?

8. Does the motor-skill learner tend to introduce verbal cues into motor-learning patterns?

9. Is skill vocabulary largely limited to gross-framework symbolism?

10. Is visual imagery essential for high motor-skill development?

11. Do psychological limits tend to inhibit the individual from achieving his or her true potential?

12. In general, is the highly skilled athlete more easy to distract during performance than the individual at a lower skill level?

13. Is part drill more effective at advanced skill levels?

14. Is the constant error of the highly skilled performer usually an unconscious error?

15. Do individual differences in form decrease among performers as they become more highly skilled?

16. Should the teacher or coach change the form of superior performers who seem to be violating certain basic mechanical principles?

17. Is mental rehearsal between physical practices often valuable at the high skill level?

18. Should the last few minutes of the practice of the skills, just before an important contest, be eliminated lest they "take the edge off" the individual's performance in the contest?

NOTES

1. D. O. Hebb, *The Organization of Behavior* (New York: Science Editions, 1961), pp. 156, 127.

2. Consult, for example, F. A. Hellebrandt's discussion of this principle in "The Physiology of Motor Learning," reprinted in Howard S. Slusher and Aileene S. Lockhart's *Anthology of Contemporary Readings* (Dubuque, Iowa: Brown, 1968), p. 92. Original is in *Cerebral Palsy Review*, July–August, 1958.

3. K. S. Lashley, "The Problem of Serial Order Behavior," in *Skills*, ed. David Legge (Baltimore: Penguin Books, 1970), p. 36.

4. Lashley, *op. cit.*, p. 35. R. S. Woodworth noted this retention of direc-

tion of movements and of locations in space in his article, "The Accuracy of Voluntary Movement," *Psychological Review*, 2, Whole No. 13 (1899), 3.

5. Edward L. Thorndike, Elsie O. Bregman, J. W. Tilton, and Ella Woodward, *Adult Learning* (New York: Macmillan, 1928), p. 38.

6. Joanne Black, "An Experimental Study of the Learning of a Fine Motor Skill." Unpublished master's thesis, Pennsylvania State University, 1949.

7. Frances Irene Williams, "Specificity of Motor Pattern Learning as Determined by Performance of Cursive Writing by Head and Jaw, Elbow, Knee, and Foot Muscles." Unpublished master of education problem, College of Health and Physical Education, Pennsylvania State University, 1960.

8. Ernst Jokl, *The Clinical Physiology of Physical Fitness and Rehabilitation* (Springfield, Ill.: Charles C Thomas, 1958), pp. 88–90.

9. "Consciously conceived" does not necessarily imply imagery. Much of the adult's thinking seems to involve chiefly verbal symbolism.

10. Ronald J. Petro, "The Effects of Imagery on the Learning of a Novel Motor Skill." Unpublished master of science thesis, Pennsylvania State University, 1964.

11. Dorothy L. Moody, "Imagery Differences Among Women of Varying Levels of Experience, Interests, and Abilities in Motor Skills." Unpublished doctoral dissertation, Pennsylvania State University, 1965.

12. See L. T. R. Williams, "Psychological Refractoriness of Two Serial Motor Responses," *Research Quarterly*, 44, 1 (March 1973), 24–33, and earlier studies cited in this article.

13. See J. R. Swink, "Intersensory Comparisons of Reaction Times Using an Electropulse Tactile Stimulus," *Human Factors*, 8 (1966), 143–45; and W. J. Wargo et al., *Human Operator Response Speed, Frequency, and Flexibility* (Santa Monica, Calif.: Report No. NAS 12–103 by Dunlap Associates for Electronic Research Center, NASA).

Six

Practice and Factors Affecting Its Influence on Motor Learning

Practice merely sets the stage—for improvement, for deterioration, or for automation of mediocrity.

In the learning of motor skills, practice sets the stage for other factors to take effect, but practice in itself is no guarantee of improvement. Although it is true that we sometimes learn without any intent to learn,[1] desire to learn is almost a necessity for significant progress. We practice handwriting most of our lives, yet our handwriting has probably long since ceased to improve, and may gradually have become somewhat less legible. Moreover, mere practice for entertainment or recreation does not tend to stimulate much improvement. In fact, if we are satisfied to perform without striving to improve, we are unlikely even to maintain whatever level we have already achieved. In competitive performance, practice against inferior, unchallenging opponents may cause deterioration of performance or, at best, habituation in mediocre performance. Moreover, even practice with intent to improve may not produce observable learning in certain cases, such as those involving inefficient forms, a constant error, or even the approach to a high skill level. If the skill is such that knowledge of results is difficult to determine, the subject, unguided in making adjustments, may learn little or nothing. The effect of precise knowledge of results and feedback for adjustment will be discussed later.

EMPHASIS

In the early learning stages, practice on wholes, meaningful units, and gross-act approximations, *not* practice on relatively isolated and less meaningful parts, gets better results. For example, in the tennis serve, a gross-framework idea (imparted by films or demonstration, or both) should be followed by attempts to execute a serve, rather than separate analyses and practices of the grip, then the foot positioning, the trunk rotation, the racket swing, and the ball toss. For the advanced learner, occasional drill on a single isolated aspect may be needed and valuable, but such isolated drills are whole learning for her because she now fills in the rest of the complex skill mentally while practicing in isolation, but overtly, a special aspect of the more complex unit.

The specific purpose of a practice will determine the methods and emphases of that practice. Assuming that skill learning (not recreation or social experience) is the major objective, the aspect for particular emphasis will determine the nature of the practice. If speed and accuracy are both basic factors in the skill, the early emphasis should be on both, with perhaps slightly greater emphasis on speed because accuracy is specific to the speed practiced. Regarding the best methods for speed skill training, Crossman says that visual or verbal instruction are of use for putting the best methods into the repertoire but that "for selection, systematic practice under pressure for speed is probably the only effective way." [2]

The feedback or knowledge of results of skill performance should be visual and perhaps quantitatively precise in verbal description. The augmented feedback (instructor direct or indirect guidance) should be as closely adapted to individual needs as is possible, although group instruction is often the only possible approach when one is attempting to teach large classes.

Much practice at high skill levels is done to maintain the level, with little expectation of improvement. In academic areas, practice beyond immediate ability to respond correctly is called overlearning and drill, and is done to ensure greater retention over longer periods of time. Besides the establishment of the skill (retention), the use of this practice beyond the stage at which successful performance has been achieved has an additional purpose, although the difference may be more qualitative than quantitative. This additional purpose is the one discussed earlier under "generalization." In motor skills of a complex nature, much practice is essential to increase the adaptability of the skill to the innumerable changes in environment, in opponents, in courts, fields, equipment, and even in the subject's own physiological condition. It takes practice in many situations to generalize the skill so that automatic performance results in spite of varying environmental cues. Highly skilled action, although automatic and proprioceptively guided, is not stereotyped action. Automatic adaptation to the situation of the moment is the result of the acquired generalization of response so essential for upper levels of skilled performances.

FREQUENCY
AND DURATION

Let us assume that the level of a skill is far enough below the individual's potential that he has much to learn before reaching that potential; let us further assume that the individual is motivated to practice toward improvement. Several questions now arise about the practice itself: How long should the individual practice without a rest interval? How long should the rest interval between practices be? The answers to these questions vary with (1) the age of the learner; (2) the complexity and the strenuousness of the skill; (3) the specific purpose of the particular practice; (4) the level of learning already attained; (5) the experiential background of the learner; and (6) total environmental conditions, including other demands and distractions, activity between practices, and other factors.

With regard to the first of these, the age of the learner, span of attention for effective practice on one skill seems to be shorter for children than for older persons. As to the second point, complexity and strenuousness, fatigue limits the effectiveness of long practice sessions, and complexity involves the problem of reactive inhibition—trying to cover too great a scope and to persist too long will cause some interference and confusion. The third point, specific purpose, refers to the immediate objective of the practice; that is, whether the immediate purpose is a quick overview of the complex skill for an impending performance, intense polish of a weak aspect, correction of a constant error, development of additional speed or additional endurance in certain aspects of the skill, or some other aim. As to the fourth point, the level of learning already attained, fatigue is likely to be more of a problem at lower levels, as is span of time during which the learner can concentrate on and be motivated toward the practice. As was mentioned in the last chapter, longer practices and often greater interest characterize high-level performers.

The fifth point, experiential background of the learner, concerns variations in physical condition, in applicable simpler skills, and in length of time the person can concentrate on and remain motivated toward the practice. The variable of "experiential background of transferable skills" is the one that has not been taken into account in some recent studies claiming the learning of motor skills entirely by mental practice. The value of mental practice seems to increase somewhat as greater heights and varieties of skill are acquired.

Finally, many factors are included in the category of total environmental conditions. The serious academic student, for example, cannot devote as much time to effective practice as the nonschool amateur or the professional. Weather and temperature may be limiting factors in length of effective practice.

Length of Practice

Although there have been numerous studies on the most effective length of practice periods, many have been done on laboratory apparatus such as pursuit rotors, mirror drawing or star tracing apparatus, chain assembling, and reaction time apparatus. In general, the time span of such studies, both of practice and of intervening rest periods, is relatively short. To just what extent we should apply the findings of laboratory studies of these fine motor skills to the gross and complex activities of physical education is difficult to say. The findings of several of these studies will be presented briefly.

Henshaw and Holman,[3] using various groups and varying the lengths of practice on a chain assembly skill, concluded that extending the daily training period beyond a certain length had no apparent effect on the amount of learning. From experiments with mirror tracing, Harmon and Oxendine [4] reported that the relatively longer practices were superior in the first three practices. Riopelle,[5] in a learning study involving complex reaction time, reported increasing superiority of shorter daily practices over longer ones as the experiment was continued. Oxendine,[6] in a mirror tracing experiment, reported that a constant practice length was superior to increasingly longer and increasingly shorter practice sessions.

In pursuit-rotor learning studies, Duncan [7] reported that shorter practice sessions produced more learning in spite of less total practice time. Denny, Frisbey, and Weaver [8] reported that distributed practices produced more learning than the massing of practices. Travis,[9] experimenting with various practice lengths, concluded that the last half of the longer practices was wasted time. Ammons and Willig [10] concluded that longer practice sessions led to poorer performance.

A few older studies attempted to throw light on specific public school problems. Fowler D. Brooks [11] reported a study of improvement in the skill of handwriting involving 184 pupils in three schools. The time span for the study was four and a half months. The pupils in one school practiced handwriting fifty minutes each week; those in the second school practiced seventy-five minutes each week; and those in the third school practiced one hundred minutes each week. Brooks reported that the fifty minutes per week gave as good results as the other two longer practice schedules.

Pyle [12] ran an experiment on the learning of typewriting by nine women and one man, seniors and graduate students in college. Five subjects practiced ten half-hour periods per day with a half-hour rest between practices. They continued this schedule for nine days. The other five subjects practiced two half-hours per day with the same rest interval between their two practices. They continued this schedule for forty-five days. Each group had a total of forty-five hours of practice. Pyle reported that he found no significant difference in the amount of learning from these respective practice schedules. (The reader should note the age of Pyle's subjects.)

Pyle [13] also reported another study in which he had four subjects practice transcription of a new alphabet. He had them practicing daily, but varied the length of practice as follows: (1) fifteen minutes; (2) thirty minutes; (3) forty-five minutes; and (4) one hour. He reported that the subject practicing only thirty minutes per day was the most successful in spite of the differences in total practice times. (The reader should note the size of the sample.) In the second part of his experiment, he had three subjects practice half-hour sessions with rest intervals, but massed into one day. One subject practiced a total of five hours, a second practiced six, and the third practiced six and a half hours. The fourth subject practiced only four spaced half-hour periods that day. Pyle reported that this last subject, practicing only a total of two hours, achieved almost as much as the other subjects who worked most of the day.

The distinction is not always made in the experimental literature between the length of the practice sessions and the closeness with which practices are clustered in the time schdule. Some experimenters call long sessions "massed practice," whereas others use this term to refer to a series of sessions with relatively short rest periods between. The length of any one session touches on the problem of how long the subject can continue practicing advantageously as far as improvement (learning, not just performance) is concerned. Excess fatigue, persistence of interest level, and environmental or social demands on the subject must not be overlooked in planning practice length.

We may synthesize available evidence on practice length as follows:

1. In early stages of gross motor-skill learning, relatively short practice sessions are more profitable in terms of minutes of practice. This finding may merely be a result of degree of interest and low level of physical condition. Extra length added to practice sessions for beginners seems to produce no more learning. Children in particular seem to obtain no profit from the additional time in the longer practice sessions. In some types of skills, adults may increase frequency and length of practices without apparent loss in amount of learning in total minutes of practice time. Moreover, the additional hours of practice (in shorter calendar time) permit an earlier date

of mastery. Practices can be too short or too long and only experience with the particular skill and learner will indicate the most profitable length.

2. Constant lengths of practice sessions have been reported to produce more learning than regular increases or regular decreases in length of succeeding sessions.

3. Short interspersed rest periods within the practice session seem to increase the amount of learning—perhaps a factor in interest and enthusiasm, or a reactive-inhibition avoidance factor.

4. Adults who are in need of acquiring the skill in a short time can practice profitably many hours per day if it is not an activity that demands great physical effort and much fatigue in the muscles employed. At times one cannot afford to postpone the desired learning-level caused by short, well-distributed practices. One may not have the time to spread the practice over several weeks or months.

Distribution of Practice

Length and frequency of rest periods also affect learning rates. A few experiments on frequency and distribution will be presented.

In studies utilizing the pursuit rotor, Irion [14] found superiority of learning when rest intervals were interspersed within the practice. Hilgard and Smith [15] reported that distributed practice was consistently better than massed practice. Doré and Hilgard [16] reported that the massing of practice was a greater disadvantage in later practices than in the first few. From two studies, Ammons [17] reported that approximately one to two minutes between trials was the most effective rest interval, and that massing produced as much learning as five-minute rests between trials.

Franklin and Brozek,[18] in an experiment involving gross bodily reaction time and pattern tracing, reported that strictly regulated practice was not absolutely necessary, and that intensive training could be undertaken without loss of effectiveness. Tsao,[19] using mirror drawing as the skill, reported that no advantage resulted from distribution of practice in the early stages, and that massing produced more of a disadvantage later on. Nance,[20] using as the skill a complex coordination task, reported distributed practice to be best for both paced and unpaced work. Kientzle,[21] using inverted writing as the skill, reported distributed practice to be superior, both with earlier and later practices. Ryan,[22] using a balance skill on a stabilometer, reported a detrimental effect from massing practice.

Massey,[23] using the tracing of a six-sided star as the skill, distributed the practices of her three groups as follows: Monday, Wednesday, and Friday for fifteen practices; Monday through Friday for twenty-five practices; and practices twice on the first day, then once on days 2, 3, 5,

8, 13, 21, and 34, for a total of nine practices. She found no difference in the three groups at their respective ninth practice sessions. At the end of the experiment her Monday through Friday group was slightly better than her Monday, Wednesday, and Friday group. She says the summation plan of the third group takes too much time for learning.

Harmon and Miller [24] reported somewhat different findings from those of Massey. They used the skill of billiards with four groups practicing as follows: daily for nine days; three days per week for three weeks; once per week for nine weeks; and once on days 1, 2, 5, 8, 13, 21, 34, and 55. They report that the only significant superiority among the various practice distributions occurred in the last distribution, and it did not appear until the sixth practice.

Knapp and Dixon [25] completed a practice distribution study with seventy college senior men as subjects, using the skill of three-ball juggling. This study was later replicated with high school students by Knapp, Dixon, and Lazier.[26] One group practiced five minutes daily and the other group practiced fifteen minutes every other day. The subjects practiced until they could make 100 successive catches. For the college men, one minute of practice in the daily session was the equivalent of 1.8 minutes of the longer, alternate day practice session. The findings with the high school groups were similar (one minute was equivalent to 1.78 minutes). Cozens,[27] in a study of class work in track and field, reported that he found three practices per week of one hour each, extending over an entire school year, to be better than six practices per week of one hour each for one semester.

Stull [28] completed studies on quantity and distribution of practice using swimming and bowling as skills. He measured skill in swimming by speed tests and by the number of strokes learned. His groups in both swimming and bowling were able to develop as much skill in three weeks of six practices per week as the other groups were able to develop in six weeks of three practices per week. For endurance swimming (long distance), he found different results. The three times per week practices produced as much ability in endurance swimming as the six sessions per week. It should be noted that Stull started in each case with novice subjects.

Scott [29] reported that four days per week were better than two or three in learning swimming. Niemeyer [30] reported that thirty minutes of practice, three times per week, were superior to sixty minutes, twice per week, in teaching swimming, badminton, and volleyball. (Note that the twice per week groups also had thirty more minutes of practice per week.)

Young [31] reported a study of archery and badminton in which groups that practiced four days per week for six weeks were compared with groups practicing two days per week for twelve weeks. She reported that the more concentrated practice was best for archery and the more widely dispersed practice best for badminton.

Whitley reviewed three theses on gross motor learning, completed at the University of California at Berkeley, which showed no superiority in learning by distributed practice over the learning by massed practice (Graw, Osterollo, and Parker), and one study (Caplan) that found more learning with distributed practice.[32] In his own study, Whitley found no difference between distributed and massed practice in the amount learned. Stelmach reported the same finding (no difference in learning) and stated that learning a motor task is a function of the number of trials and is independent of conditions of practice distribution.[33]

Whether the learning of motor skills should be conducted under distributed or massed practice conditions depends on various factors. A rather common practice in school and sport situations for the learning of motor skills has been to employ daily or triweekly practice periods of relatively short duration. Even shorter practice periods are often employed in public schools when the practices are arranged to occur twice daily. The decrement in learning because of massing of practice is slight and perhaps insignificant in most cases. When interest can be maintained, when outside factors do not interfere, and when extreme bodily fatigue does not occur, massing of practice seems equally effective (assuming the number of practice trials is the same). The massed practice has the additional advantage of reaching higher skill levels sooner.

This need for an early achievement date may be met in certain types of activities by practices more than once a day, providing there are sufficient rest intervals. With children, the shorter practice periods seem to hold more interest and challenge. Various other distributions with increasingly longer rest intervals have been tried. The factor of how soon the learner wants the higher level of skill to be available (need and motivation) seems to be a more significant factor than the massing or distributing of practice.

EFFECTS OF FATIGUE

A number of studies have dealt with the effects of fatigue on performance and on learning. Somewhat conflicting results have been reported. Several studies reported deleterious effects on performance but not on learning.[34] In general, extreme fatigue decreases the number of repetitions and the proficiency of performance during practice sessions. If the motor skill to be learned employs muscle movements closely related or identical to those highly fatigued by immediately preceding exercise, the deleterious effect seems to occur in learning as well as in performance. However, even mild delay between fatiguing exercise and the practice of the skill to be learned seems to allow enough time for recovery so that the learning is not significantly affected. Often the effect of fatiguing effort wears off very quickly during the less intense effort of the skill being practiced in the designed experiments.

Benson [35] found fatigue impaired performance on the speed component of a jumping task. The task was a hopping-and-stepping continuity through a set pattern designated by thirty-two painted footprints. The subjects had exercised on a bicycle ergometer until heart rate reached 180 beats per minute and then continued the fatiguing exercise two additional minutes. Each jumping exercise was started within five seconds after the subject left the bicycle ergometer. The accuracy score on the jumping (measured in decrease in misses of the painted footprints on which the subject was trying to land) actually improved more significantly for the fatigued group than for the nonfatigued control group. In the second part of Benson's experiment, he had subjects practice three-ball juggling when fatigued in the same manner. His fatigued subjects learned juggling significantly faster than his nonfatigued control group.

Godwin and Schmidt [36] performed an experiment involving an action of rotating a handle around an axle 327 degrees, than immediately reversing the same movement and following this with an eleven-inch movement of striking a barrier to the right. The fatiguing exercise immediately preceding each such learning trial was the rotation of a friction-type arm ergometer through the same dimension and orientation as the learning task. This fatiguing task involved the attempt to turn the crank at a rate of sixty revolutions per minute against heavy resistance. The subjects continued the fatiguing exercising for two minutes even though they could not maintain the sixty revolutions-per-minute rate. Godwin and Schmidt found that a sufficiently severe fatigue task would impair learning.

Godwin and Schmidt report another study [37] which seems to indicate that it is more beneficial to practice in a nonfatigued state even though the task is to be performed later in the fatigued condition; that is, one does not prepare oneself to perform better in a fatigued state by conducting previous practice in the fatigued state. This preliminary hypothesis does not quite seem to parallel Henry's report on specificity versus generality in learning motor skills.[38] In regard to this theory, we should recall Hellebrandt's statement that individuals in a fatigued state change their muscle patterns; that is, revert to more primitive and basic movement patterns.[39] The muscle units employed in what seems to be the same gross motor act are known to vary somewhat, depending on relative degrees of fatigue of the respective muscle units. Bartlett says: "Movements become less precise and accurate as fatigue increases and skill performance is marked by a progressive lowering of standards of performance." [40]

One of the problems of fatigue studies is the fact that muscles used in the same skill may vary considerably, yet preserve equal levels of performance of the same gross motor task. Studies of the preservation of equal competence of certain industrial workers in spite of advancing age are additional examples of variation in muscle pattern to execute the same skill equally successfully even in long, continued effort. It would seem that the effect of degree of fatigue on learning is a very complex problem, depending on type of activity, level of skill, aspect of learning to be measured, degree and specificity of the fatigued area, and the possibility of rapid recovery from fatigue effects during the learning exercise.

MENTAL PRACTICE

Mental practice was discussed briefly in the preceding chapter with regard to learning at high skill levels. Many contradictory findings have been reported on the value of mental practice. Part of the confusion arises over the use of highly unreliable tests. Another point of confusion is the definition of motor learning. If the so-called skill is just an easy succession of simpler skills already learned by the subjects, they often can arrange the order mentally, then put them together in a gross approximation of the pattern by physical performance. This type of procedure is not much different from reading the directions and then putting together some new household appliance or toy; nor is it different from the army's teaching of rifle assembly from projected sound films. This "thinking through" is to a great extent a verbal process. We do this kind of learning when we find our way across a strange city from verbal directions and street names. It is somewhat akin to maze learning, the experiments in which have been largely omitted from this text. As Hilgard states: "The maze is sometimes included as a skill, but its motor aspects are in fact subordinate to the serial learning of choices, often learned verbally." [41]

Vandell, Davis, and Clugston [42] reported that mental practice was almost as effective as physical practice (using the skills of dart throwing and foul shooting). Twining [43] reported 137 percent improvement from physical practice and 36 percent from mental practice in ring tossing. Halverson [44] reported improvement with both mental and physical practice, but she says that "the mental practice was not as effective as the actual practice." Verdelle Clark [45] reports mental practice to be much more effective at the advanced skill levels than at beginning levels, whereas physical practice is quite superior for the novice groups.

Jones [46] reported that he was able to obtain suitable performance of the "hockswing upstart" in gymnastics without physical practice or demonstration. His subjects were provided with written descriptions of the act, a reading of the descriptions plus mechanical analysis by the instructor, and mental practice by the students; but they observed no physical demonstration and did no physical practice. He reported that 56.67 percent of his subjects were able to perform the skill at the first physical trial. Jones says:

> It is possible for male university students without previous experience to learn gross body skills of a gymnastic nature by a learning procedure involving only the reading of a mechanical analysis and mental practice of the skill.[47]

But Jones reports no test at the start of the experiment, so we cannot be certain that his groups were complete novices in gymnastic skill background.

Trussel concluded that mental practice was not effective if the subjects had had no experience in performing the novel skill.[48] Corbin concluded that mental practice must be based on real experience.[49] Phipps and Morehouse decided that the effectiveness of mental practice is specific to the skill and is more pronounced in simpler skills.[50] This last conclusion would seem to imply that previous physical experience had included many of the subroutines of the skill showing much progress with mental practices. Oxendine concludes:

> Time which might be profitably devoted to mental practice appears to be dependent on the nature of the task; *i.e.*, its complexity, familiarity, and whether the learner has the physical abilities to perform.[51]

RETENTION AND REMINISCENCE

Retention is the degree of persistence of learning over periods of no practice. It is the opposite of forgetting. It is of necessity measured by performance, but performance is only an approximation. Various factors affect performance—warm-up decrement, reactive inhibition, degree of interest, physiological fluctuation, and so on.

Reminiscence is usually defined as significant improvement in performance after periods of no physical (overt) practice, and often after a considerable lapse of time (See Fox and Lamb's study below). One explanation of this phenomenon is that the performance is lower than the learning would permit because of mental fatigue or boredom, especially from long practices, and that this inhibiting factor disappears after a period of no activity.[52] Another hypothesis is that certain types of learning may *set* more firmly with time, perhaps because the more successful responses have had more repetitions in the practice periods than the less successful. The less successful (errors) are therefore forgotten sooner and interfere less at the later performance. Perhaps a more common explanation is that mental practice has occurred since the last overt practice.

Eysenck [53] reports that when the skill involved in the pursuit rotor had been well developed (ten weeks' span of time during which fifty practices were conducted), it was retained to a high degree after one year of no practice. He found no relationship between the final learning score and the retention score after one year.

Ammons et al.[54] reported a study of long-term retention of a perceptual-motor skill. The skill was a sequential manipulation of a series of controls on a compensatory pursuit task. He used twenty-two groups of male college students, ranging in age from twenty to thirty-six. Some of his subjects were trained to a moderate and some to a high degree of skill. His various no-practice intervals ranged from one minute to two years. He reported that a greater proportion of proficiency was lost by groups receiving less training. In a study of motivational factors in gross motor-skill learning, Sparks [55] used high school boys as subjects and volleyball as the skill. Sparks reported that the type of verbal incentive experienced during the learning significantly affected the retention of the skill, although he found no significant difference on group scores at the end of the learning period.

In a study involving the skill of bouncing a basketball from the foul line into the basket, Singer [56] reported that distributed practice was better for immediate acquisition but massed practice better for ultimate retention. Fleishman and Parker,[57] on a highly complex tracking test, reported that the most important factor in retention was the level of proficiency achieved during initial learning, and that long retention was unrelated to the distribution of the practice in the original learning. They tested their subjects at various intervals over twenty-four months.

Fox and Lamb [58] completed a retention study with seventh-grade youngsters as subjects, using softball throwing and batting as the skills. They reported that tests after five weeks of no practice (following the learning period) revealed no significant gain or loss, but that tests given over a range of seventeen to twenty-two weeks after the completion of the learning period revealed a really significant gain. Fox and Young [59] reported, from a study involving the skills of badminton, that improvement had occurred (reminiscence) after six and after nine weeks of no practice in the wall-volley skill but not in the short-serve skill. Purdy and Lockhart [60] reported a study of retention of five novel gross motor skills by thirty-six college women after nine to fifteen months of no practice. They concluded that the fast learners are better retainers than the slow learners.

Baer's doctorate at Johns Hopkins [61] was a study of relationship of rate of learning to retention in certain motor skills. His skills were ball catching in a cup, card sorting, and a soccer dropkick. For the first two skills the subjects all practiced until they had learned to a certain level, although it took them varying amounts of time to reach this level. For the soccer dropkick, the subjects were just given equal opportunity to learn (the same amount of practice time). He measured the first two groups after six weeks of no further practice and the soccer groups after nine weeks of no practice. He reported a slight but insignificantly higher retention by the fast learners in each case if recall (first raw score on first trial of relearning) or relearning (number of trials needed to relearn the skill to previous level) were the measures of retention used. However, if the savings method of measuring retention was used (number of trials required for learning compared to number of trials required for relearning), the slow learners were significantly better than the fast learners in retention.

Bender [62] completed a study of the relationship of learning rate and retention, using three skills: field hockey juggle skill, volleyball wall-volley skill, and a badminton wall-volley skill. She measured the retention of her various groups after three lengths of no-practice intervals (69 days, 120 days, and 197 days). She reported that the loss method of measuring retention (raw score on last trial of learning minus raw score on first trial of relearning) and the size of the raw score of the first relearning trial (absolute retention) both indicated better retention by the fast learner. However, if the measure was the difference in number of trials to learn and the number of trials to relearn (the so-called savings method), the slow learner was superior. Perhaps certain specific statements will clarify these points.

Although fast learners may forget more than slow learners, they have learned so much more that they are still superior to the slow learners in total amount retained; that is, they are still superior in the skill after the extended no-practice interval. However, the slow learner needs relatively more trials to learn than to relearn to the former level. Bender also reported an increase in individual differences of subjects with increase of practice except at the high skill level; at that level, this difference seems to decrease again.[63]

PART AND
WHOLE LEARNING

Some of the differences in reported results of studies of whole and part learning are due to differences in definition of the terms. Let us first agree on a definition of terms. Gates defines a whole as a "definitely segregated, independent pattern which possesses unity, coherence and meaning in itself above that implied by its parts." He says that an aggregation of items without systematic relation, either spatial, temporal, or ideational, even though repeated as a unit (such as nonsense syllables), does not constitute a whole. A part is "an element in a total situation which is essential to the meaning as a whole but which loses its peculiar meaning when isolated from the whole." [64] The whole method of learning is the practice of going through the entire activity each time and using as many of the whole repetitions as are necessary to acquire adequate performance. The part method is the learning of the individual elements of the whole, then learning to combine them into proper serial order.

There are various approaches to the part learning method. In the so-called *pure* part method, each part is mastered separately before going on to the next. After all parts are mastered, they are then put together as a whole. However, this last step usually involves a considerable amount of learning before the parts become linked into a unit of automatic action. Sometimes this integration into a unit takes more time to learn than was necessary to learn all the individual separated parts. Moreover, sometimes a part learned separately does not quite fit, and a constant error persists in the performance of the large unit. The *progressive* part method involves the learning of part one; next the learning of part two; next the combining of parts one and two; next the learning of part three; then the combining of parts one and two with part three, and so on.

Some subjects seem to learn better by the part method simply because they are accustomed to learning by it. There may be more delay in immediate success when they start with the whole unit, whereas some success soon becomes apparent when they start with the part. The required span of attention is of necessity longer when one goes through the entire act each time. Moreover, the teacher may be accustomed to teach the activity by a particular method (part or whole), and may be better at teaching by the method with which he or she is familiar. On the other hand, the activity to be learned may be a closely knit unit and hence easier to learn by the whole method; or it may be a complex and loosely organized aggregation of units. This latter type is often best learned by breaking it up into simpler units.

It should be remembered that many team games are not wholes. They are loosely organized aggregations of skills that can be put together in various orders as the game unfolds. Shooting, passing and catching, rebounding, dribbling, and so on, can be classified as some of the simpler wholes that make up the game of basketball. These wholes are then developed into higher units of play patterns. One of the difficulties of the part method, with its isolated development of parts or subwholes, is that the parts may be developed in isolation in such a way that they do not fit precisely into the unit of higher complexity. Many a boy has learned to dribble as an isolated skill and then has had trouble using his dribble effectively in the game because he watches the ball while dribbing. He misses cues for assists, dribbles into clustered opponents and loses the ball, or even fails to realize when he has a good scoring opportunity.

An old study of Beeby [65] illustrates this last point. Beeby was interested in discovering if a movement pattern, when divided into a number of simpler movements, still represents exactly the same movements with exactly the same relation to each other as they have when performed in the whole combination. In his experiment he used a wooden mazelike apparatus and a stylus. His conclusions were that the constituent movements performed as parts were essentially different from what they were in the whole unit; hence he concluded that the whole method of learning was preferable.

A generation ago Grace McGeoch [66] made an analysis of thirty studies of the relative efficiency of the whole and part methods in learning and retention. She concluded that these studies did not justify any generalization regarding the superiority of any methods, and that the absolute and relative efficiencies of any given method are the complex result of the pattern of experimental conditions in which many factors are differentially and reciprocally effective. She listed the nature of the learner and the nature of the material to be learned as basic factors. McGeoch's viewpoint was endorsed by Gates many years later. Gates stated that "the most effective method of learning depends, first, on the degree of meaningfulness, difficulty, and length of the material and, second, upon such factors as the individual's intelligence, age, background of experience, and characteristic methods of study." [67]

Studies of whole and part methods have used mazes, typewriting, mirror drawing, piano playing, puzzle solving, card sorting, and other activities as material to be learned. The experiments mentioned below, except for Brown's with the piano, will be only those dealing directly with gross bodily activities.

Brown [68] did several studies of methods used in learning to play the piano. In one she concluded that learning to play a score with both hands at the same time was more efficient than the method of first learning by each hand separately. In another experiment [69] she used three different scores. The first was practiced from beginning to end until it was mastered; the second score was divided into units, each unit was practiced until learned, and then the units were combined; the third score was learned by first practicing from beginning to end, and then devoting special practice to those measures in which there were errors. Brown concluded that the whole method was the most efficient except with the difficult scores. With them it ranked second, but the pure part method ranked last in each case. Shay [70] equated two groups of freshman male students, then taught the upstart on the horizontal bar to one group by the progressive part method, and to the other group by the whole method. In the first method, the skill was divided into the swing, arch of the body, flexion of the thighs, and extension of the thighs. Shay reported that the whole method was superior, and that it gave smoother timing and continuity.

Knapp and Dixon [71] used the skill of three-ball juggling in a study of the efficiency of the whole and part methods. Their learning criterion was 100 successive catches in three-ball juggling. They used seventeen matched pairs of college seniors in one group and twelve matched pairs in another. In each group half the subjects used only the whole method of practice. The other half in the first group used what the experimenters called the part-whole method. They followed a fairly rigid pattern of practice, starting in each practice with one ball, next progressing to two balls, and, in several practices progressing to three. The other half of the second group was left free to choose its own method of practice. The experimenters did not find a difference that was significant at the 5 percent level, but they did conclude that (1) subjects using the whole method tended to attain the criterion most rapidly; and (2) the initial accuracy attained by the subjects using the part-whole method did not have transfer value.

McGuigan and MacCaslin,[72] and later McGuigan alone,[73] conducted studies of whole and part methods in the learning of rifle marksmanship, using army basic training men as subjects. They used 148 men in the first experiment and 200 in the second. The experimenters concluded that the whole method was better than the part method in slow fire for all subjects, but only for those of above-average intelligence in the sustained fire approaches. In a doctoral study at Indiana University, O'Donnell [74] experimented with whole and part methods in the teaching of tennis. She found only slight differences, but what she found tended to favor the whole method, based on forehand performance and on scores made on the Dyer backboard test.

Theunissen,[75] also in a doctoral study at Indiana, compared whole and part methods in the teaching of golf. His two groups of twenty-four subjects were equated on a "general motor ability test" that raises some question. His groups had ten weeks of indoor instruction and were finally measured by their scores on eighteen holes of play. He states that the group taught by the whole method had a significantly lower mean. Niemeyer [76] conducted a study of 366 students in three activities: swimming, volleyball, and badminton. Two classes in each were taught by the part method and two by the whole method. Niemeyer states:

> The swimming results showed that the students in the whole method group learned to swim sooner, farther, and faster than those in the part method group; moreover, they showed better form. . . .
>
> The performances in badminton indicated that overall learning was not significantly affected by the different methods used. . . .
>
> The performance results in volleyball indicated that the part method was significantly better than the whole method in early, late, and overall learning or improvement.[77]

Lewellen [78] completed a study of whole and part methods in the teaching of swimming to 104 children, ages seven and a half to nine and a half. For his part method he used the Red Cross progressive part method. In his whole method he says the total activity was presented to the pupil from the beginning of the learning process. "Practice on any unit by the learner was carried out only as he attempted the total stroke pattern." Lewellen reported that the whole method was superior to the Red Cross method in developing proper form and distance skill. Godlasky [79] compared two groups of college men learning to swim, one group starting with the dog paddle, then later progressing to the crawl stroke; and the other group starting in immediately with the crawl stroke. He found no difference in learning rates by the two procedures.

In the comparison of swimming and volleyball, part of the difference has been hypothesized to be a difference in variety of movements involved in the latter, and the greater need for constant exteroceptive cue reception in volleyball. It could be also that more, and perhaps some finer, skills are combined in the hierarchies of volleyball skills. It has also been proposed that many of the movements of swimming are more primitive, grosser and more basic in the development of locomotion in man, and hence easier to combine into an integrated unit.

Perhaps we should summarize this whole-part discussion by saying that, generally speaking, learners should start with a whole or subwhole, but at least a unit that has meaning for them. The unit should be as large as they can perceive in its gross framework. If the unit is too simple, it does not challenge them and their interest will flag. If the unit is too difficult, if they persist and persist without evidence of success, they get discouraged and quit. They may even build up an emotional block against the activity, as many children have done after repeated failure in a situation. The teacher may make an error in the size of a unit if he tries to start students off as he would those of high skill backgrounds. On the other hand, the grade school teacher who is weak in physical-skill performance but is assigned the task of teaching physical education in the self-contained classroom, tends to make the opposite error. She introduces her students to activities at too low a level, activities that lack any challenge for active youngsters. Gutteridge [80] found this lack of challenge even in nursery school and kindergarten. After an extensive study, she reported that children in the second and third year of nursery school and kindergarten were often unchallenged and bored by the apparatus and equipment.

The unit for learning should be meaningful and should be taught in as close conformity to its applicable use as possible, with application in more complex hierarchies clarified as soon as practical. When the skill is too difficult and too long, it will need to be broken down into smaller segments, but these segments should be integrated units and should have meaning in themselves. Complex games, for example, need to be broken into smaller units for faster learning, then integrated into more complex hierarchies for more sophisticated use. The so-called polish of parts of the more advanced performer is never "part learning" because he sees the part in its total pattern while he is polishing it, and he does his readjusting in terms of what will fit best in the whole activity.

Learning is more meaningful, and therefore more economical, if it can be intimately linked with its application. This statement is not meant to oppose specific drills or part-method teaching, but to emphasize the fact that students learn an activity more rapidly if they see the need for it. Organization of the parts into the whole pattern must be a conscious goal even while the student is focusing on parts. Even for part polish, when the size of the unit is not too great, it may be advisable to practice the whole while keeping in mind the specific part that needs particular attention. The student is thereby etching in the details of the configuration. The part emphasized receives continual correction from the stress of the whole dynamic pattern.

Understanding of use aids retention, but in motor skills there is no meaningful understanding until the skill unit is used in the context of the purposeful action. There are all kinds of throws, kicks, dribbles, pivots, dance steps, and strokes. What variation or type to use depends on the situation. The individual has not learned the meaning of the motor unit until he knows the adjustment to use in the phase of the activity panorama in which he is trying to act appropriately. The real test of any learning is the ability to use that learning, when needed, in the appropriate situation. The importance of early experiencing of the motor act in the game, the dance, or the stunt for which it was developed is apparent. This application refines the learning and facilitates its retention. We remember more easily what we have used successfully.

KNOWLEDGE OF RESULTS

Knowledge of how effective one's performance is becoming as it occurs, of precisely what variations are less successful, and of just what the result of the performance was seems to be basic to learning. Little or no learning takes place without knowledge of results of performance. Bilodeau and Bilodeau stated in a recent summary of studies concerning the importance of knowledge of results: "Studies of feedback or knowledge of results show it to be the strongest, most important variable controlling performance and learning." [81] Wolfle states in his summary of research on knowledge of results that "laboratory studies are unequivocal in emphasizing the importance of giving a subject as specific and as immediate information as possible concerning the outcome of his efforts." [82]

Several basic principles about the effect of knowledge of results on the stimulation of learning have been established:

1. Learning is proportionally greater as the quality, exactness, and precision of this playback of knowledge of results increases.[83]
2. When knowledge of results is not available, learners often can improve to some extent by setting up their own criteria from past experience, to help them subjectively approximate their results.[84]
3. With a delay of knowledge of results, performance declines.[85]
4. Performance deteriorates when knowledge of results is withdrawn.[86]
5. Continuous and complete knowledge of results fosters much greater learning than discontinuous and incomplete knowledge of results.[87]
6. Precise supplemental aids (graphs, films of action, etc.), which provide more precise knowledge or make apparent the differences between the learner's performance and those of better performers, seem to increase learning.[88]
7. Feedback of incorrect information retards learning in direct proportion to the amount of misinformation.[89]

KNOWLEDGE OF MECHANICAL PRINCIPLES

Almost all the studies of the value of a knowledge of mechanical principles as an aid to motor-skill learning have used beginners as subjects. Judd [90] compared two groups, one given and the other not given an explanation of the law of refraction, in their rate of learning to hit a target under water with darts. He reported no difference in the groups at the first depth experienced, regardless of knowledge of the mechanical principle; but he noted a superiority of the group with the knowledge of light refraction when the depth of the target was changed. Hendrickson and Schroeder [91] used an air gun instead of darts, but otherwise their experiment was about the same in design as Judd's. They reported that the groups with an explanation of light refraction were superior both at the first target depth on which they practiced and when the depth of the target was changed.

Frey [92] studied the relative effectiveness of a group given an elaborate analysis of reasons for specific forms compared with a control group without such elaborate analysis in the teaching of tennis, volleyball, and rhythms. She concluded that the differences in learning by the two methods were negligible. Colville [93] selected three principles of mechanics pertinent to certain common motor skills and three motor skills that utilized these principles. For each skill she used an experimental group which was taught to understand and apply the principle, and a control group taught without direct reference to the principle. She found no difference in learning in her respective groups. She then tried the respective groups on other activities in which the principles were applicable, and again found no significant difference in performance levels. Cobane [94] tried somewhat the same type of experiment in the teaching of tennis. She reported no difference in skill performance by the respective groups.

Nessler, after a study of methods adapted to the teaching of low-skilled college women, made the following statement about the value of knowledge of mechanical principles:

> Skill learning for the poorly skilled is not analytical. A knowledge of mechanical principles may be helpful in analyzing the complete act, but does not seem to aid the poorly skilled in his performance. Poorly-skilled students are interested in the mechanical principles related to skill learning, but are unable to incorporate this theoretical knowledge into their performance of these motor skills.[95]

Broer [96] reported greater success with a group that had been taught simplified mechanics prior to the teaching of volleyball, basketball, and softball than with the control group, which had no prior instruction in the simplified mechanics. Her subjects were two classes of seventh-grade girls.

Coleman found that experience in a basic skills course (emphasizing application of mechanical principles) prior to a bowling course produced no significant difference in bowling success from that of a group without such a basic skills course.[97] Burdeshaw et al. reported that a preceding basic skills course (emphasizing application of mechanical principles) did not produce any superiority in badminton to that of a group without such a preceding basic skills course.[98] These results are both in disagreement with the findings of Broer reported above.

In a master's thesis at the University of Maryland, Barrett[99] reported, with respect to the teaching of mechanical principles as a part of instruction in swimming, that *subjective ratings in form* indicated superiority of the group with the knowledge of mechanical principles. Halverson[100] reported in her master's study at the University of Wisconsin that knowledge of mechanical principles seemed to produce no superiority over a control group without such knowledge (the skill was one-handed shooting in basketball).

Perhaps a word of evaluation of this problem should be added here. Knowledge and understanding of the mechanical principles of the skill to be learned may not accelerate the learning of the skill for beginners. If much time is spent on theoretical explanation with consequent loss of physical practice time, the teaching procedure might well be questioned. On the other hand, a knowledge of mechanical principles may have some motivating value. Moreover, majors in the field of physical education will need such knowledge to guide their own selection of practice form and method for their future pupils. The experimental literature does not cover the value of mechanical analysis for the advanced student, but empirical evidence seems to indicate somewhat greater value at the higher skill levels.

The following considerations should be taken into account when deciding whether or not to include knowledge of mechanical principles as a basic part of early motor-skill learning:

1. It may not be of significant value to the beginner in motor-skill acquisition.
2. It may later help in transfer to another skill.
3. It may waste necessary physical practice time (in verbal explanation and analysis) and thereby actually retard the rate of skill learning.
4. It may be motivational, at times, if it arouses learner's interest.
5. It is valuable for prospective teachers to know mechanical principles so that they can use appropriate teaching form and procedure with future students (so they can augment feedback).

MOVING PICTURES, LOOP FILMS

There have been a number of studies of the value of moving pictures and loop films in the teaching of motor skills. Only a brief summary will be presented here. First, they are of real value in giving the learner the general idea of the action pattern if the teacher is not completely competent at demonstration. Moreover, they may add to the learner's motivation. Second, slow-motion pictures will sometimes reveal the precise form when the act itself cannot be performed in slow motion as a demonstration device. The live slow-motion demonstration actually incorporates different movement patterns from those used in acts that must be performed rapidly to be functional in normal performance. Third, moving pictures of the learner may help him discover constant errors, and may be quite helpful in form analysis at high skill levels. Moreover, comparison of the learner's performance with the performance of experts may be an added and valuable supplement to the knowledge of his own results. Fourth, time that might better be utilized in physical practice is sometimes wasted in showing moving pictures. Fifth, knowledge of precise results of individual performance in many team games is very difficult to obtain other than by postgame movie analysis, yet such knowledge is essential for rapid learning. However, the films may need to be analyzed by an expert teacher, and material abtracted, synthesized, and then pointed out to the learner. Finally, the extensive use of film, paralleling the teaching and practice of a motor skill with beginners, is of questionable value.

Mention perhaps should be made here of new devices that give instant playback television recordings of performances. When available, these instruments make possible the great advantage to learning discussed above in the section on knowledge of results.

SUMMARY

In skill learning, practice sets the stage for other factors to take effect but in itself is no guarantee of improvement. Practice on the whole unit seems to produce faster learning than part-practice in motor skills if the skill is not long and complex. One of the problems of part-practice in motor skills is that the part learned may not be formed to fit precisely into the whole skill. When a complex skill is divided and learned in separate units, much learning still remains before these simple units can be combined for highly-skilled performance. There are too many variables in motor-skill learning to permit an over-all generalization with regard to the effectiveness of whole and part methods. It is perhaps safe to assume that the learners should start with a whole or subwhole, but at least a unit that has both meaning and challenge to them.

The specific purpose of the practice will determine methods and emphasis of that practice—speed, accuracy, maintenance or generalization of the skill. Precise knowledge of results fosters and is almost essential for rapid learning. Short, frequent practices seem more effective in early stages, particularly for complex and strenuous skills. Adults and those of advanced skill seem to suffer no decrement in learning rate from longer and more concentrated practices. Generally speaking, intervals between practices should be relatively short (a day or less) unless the practices are extremely fatiguing. Practice while fatigued tends to impair performance but does not always retard learning rate. Practice while in a nonfatigued state even seems to be of more value for learning to perform, later, in a fatigued state. The type of activity, the level of skill, the aspect of learning to be measured, the degree and specificity of the fatigued area, and the rate of recovery all seem to vary the effect of fatigue on learning rate.

Mental practice seems to be of more value in simple skills or in skills in which the individuals have already acquired the simpler units of the skill hierarchy. The value of mental practice tends to increase with the level of the skill.

Reminiscence (improvement during nonpractice intervals) does seem to occur at times and may be due to mental practice, to greater retention of successful tries over those unsuccessful therefore less often repeated attempts, to increase of interest at next practice, or even to a longer time for a pattern to "set".

Fast learners tend to retain more than slow learners simply because they have learned more, although the slower learners may have somewhat better retention of the amount they did learn.

An analytical knowledge of the mechanical principles of the motor skill may help in later transfer to a similar skill, often seems to be of value for self-analysis and improvement of performance at the advanced skill levels, and is a valuable aid to teachers of motor skills. Such analysis tends to be of little or no advantage for specific skill acquisition by beginners.

Moving pictures and loop films may help beginners to get the general idea of a skill. They permit the individuals to see their own performances and compare them with expert performances; hence, they guide revision and improvement. Although movies and tapes may furnish guides when needed, they can not replace physical practice as the major factor in motor-skill learning.

DISCUSSION QUESTIONS

1. Why is practice in itself no assurance of skill learning?
2. Practice at high skill levels is essential just to maintain the high level. Explain why.

3. Explain why one should not attempt to keep all conditions constant in the practice of open skills.

4. Does the length of practice for most effective learning vary with the skill being practiced? Give examples.

5. Does the length of practice for most effective learning vary with the level of learning? Illustrate by example.

6. Do individuals vary in length of practice sessions most effective for their learning, assuming approximately the same individual skill levels?

7. Why are short, frequent practices more common for the skill learning of elementary school students?

8. Explain why the adult often finds it advantageous to use quite long practice sessions.

9. In general, is daily (or five times per week) practice superior to two or three times per week when total practice time is held constant?

10. Can motor skills completely novel to the learner be learned without physical practice?

11. Explain why mental practice tends to be more valuable at advanced skill levels.

12. Does the slow learner need proportionately fewer relearning trials than the fast learner to achieve his posttraining test score, after a relatively long no-practice interval?

13. Do fast learners retain a greater percentage of what they have learned than slow learners after a long no-practice interval?

14. Is a complex game (hockey, soccer, football, tennis) a whole?

15. Are the teacher, the learner, and the skill itself all variables that affect the relative effectiveness of the whole as compared to the part method?

16. What determines the most appropriate size of the motor-skill unit with which you begin your skill teaching?

17. Does meaning in motor skills imply ability to describe the skill verbally?

18. Is knowledge of results essential for significant progress in skill learning? Why is this more than just a motivational factor?

19. Does the time taken from physical practice to develop an intellectual understanding of the mechanical principles of the skill tend to decrease total time needed to acquire the skill?

20. What aspects of motor learning are sometimes accelerated by showing movies of his or her own performance to the individual?

NOTES

1. Refer back to latent learning, Chapter 3.

2. E. R. F. W. Crossman, "A Theory of the Acquisition of Speed-Skill," *Ergonomics,* 2 (1959), 153–66. See also *Skills,* ed. David Legge (Baltimore: Penguin Books, 1970), p. 293.

3. Edna M. Henshaw and P. G. Holman, "A Note on Over-Training," *British Journal of Psychology,* 20, 4 (April 1930), 333–35.

4. John M. Harmon and Joseph B. Oxendine, "Effects of Different Lengths of Practice in Learning a Motor Skill," *Research Quarterly,* 32, 1, Part 1 (March 1961), 34–41.

5. Arthur J. Riopelle, "Psychomotor Performance and Distribution of Practice," *Journal of Experimental Psychology,* 40, 3 (June 1950), 390–95.

6. Joseph B. Oxendine, "Effect of Progressively Changing Practice Schedules on the Learning of a Motor Skill," *Research Quarterly,* 36, 3 (October 1965), 307–15.

7. Carl B. Duncan, "The Effect of Unequal Amounts of Practice on Motor Learning Before and After Rest," *Journal of Experimental Psychology,* 42, 4 (October 1951), 257–64.

8. M. Ray Denny, Norman Frisbey, and John Weaver, Jr., "Rotary Pursuit Performance Under Alternate Conditions of Distributed and Massed Practice," *Journal of Experimental Psychology,* 49, 1 (January 1955), 48–54.

9. Roland C. Travis, "Length of the Practice Period and Efficiency in Motor Learning," *Journal of Experimental Psychology,* 24, 3 (March 1939), 339–45.

10. Roy B. Ammons and Leslie Willig, "Acquisition of Motor Skill: IV. Effects of Repeated Periods of Massed Practice," *Journal of Experimental Psychology,* 51, 2 (February 1956), 118–26.

11. Fowler D. Brooks, "Time Assignment and Rate of Improvement in Handwriting," *Journal of Educational Psychology,* 10, 7 (September 1919), 350–53.

12. W. H. Pyle, "Concentrated versus Distributed Practice," *Journal of Educational Psychology,* 5, 5 (May 1914), 247–58.

13. W. H. Pyle, "Economical Learning," *Journal of Educational Psychology,* 4, 3 (March 1913), 148–58.

14. Arthur L. Irion, "Reminiscence in Pursuit-rotor Learning as a Func-

tion of Length of Rest and of Amount of Pre-rest Practice," *Journal of Experimental Psychology*, 39, 4 (August 1949), 492–99.

15. Ernest R. Hilgard and M. B. Smith, "Distributed Practice in Motor Learning: Score Changes Within and Between Daily Sessions," *Journal of Experimental Psychology*, 30 (February 1942), 136–46.

16. Leon R. Doré and Ernest R. Hilgard, "Spaced Practice as a Test of Snoddy's Two Processes in Mental Growth," *Journal of Experimental Psychology*, 23, 4 (October 1938), 359–74.

17. Robert B. Ammons, "Acquisition of Motor Skill: III. Effects of Initially Distributed Practice on Rotary Pursuit Performance," *Journal of Experimental Psychology*, 40, 6 (December 1950), 777–87; and "Effect of Distribution of Practice on Rotary Pursuit Hits," *Journal of Experimental Psychology*, 41, 1 (January 1951), 17–22.

18. Joseph C. Franklin and Josef Brozek, "The Relation Between Distribution of Practice and Learning Efficiency in Psychomotor Performance," *Journal of Experimental Psychology*. 37, 1 (February 1947), 16–24.

19. J. C. Tsao, "Shifting of Distribution of Practice in Mirror Drawing," *Journal of Experimental Psychology*, 40, 5 (October 1950), 639–42.

20. Roy D. Nance, "The Effects of Pacing and Distribution on Intercorrelations of Motor Abilities," *Journal of Experimental Psychology*, 37, 6 (December 1947), 459–72.

21. Mary J. Kientzle, "Properties of Learning Curves Under Varied Distributions of Practice," *Journal of Experimental Psychology*, 36 (June 1946), 187–211.

22. E. Dean Ryan, "Prerest and Postrest Performance on the Stabilometer as a Function of Distribution of Practice," *Research Quarterly*, 36, 2 (May 1965), 197–204.

23. Dorothy M. Massey, "The Significance of Interpolated Time Intervals on Motor Learning," *Research Quarterly*, 30, 2 (May 1959), 189–201.

24. John M. Harmon and Arthur E. Miller, "Time Patterns in Motor Learning," *Research Quarterly*, 21, 3 (October 1950), 182–87.

25. Clyde G. Knapp and W. Robert Dixon, "Learning to Juggle: I. A study to Determine the Effect of Two Different Distributions of Practice on Learning Efficiency," *Research Quarterly*, 21, 3 (October 1950), 331–36.

26. Clyde G. Knapp, W. Robert Dixon, and Murney Lazier, "Learning to Juggle: III. A Study of Performance by Two Different Age Groups," *Research Quarterly*, 29, 1 (March 1958), 32–36.

27. Frederick W. Cozens. "A Comparative Study of Two Methods of Teaching Class Work in Track and Field Events," *Research Quarterly*, 2, 4 (December 1931), 75–79.

28. G. Alan Stull, "Relationship of Quantity and Distribution of Practice to Endurance, Speed, and Skill Development by Beginners." Unpublished doctoral dissertation, Pennsylvania State University, 1961.

29. M. Gladys Scott, "Learning Rate of Beginning Swimmers," *Research Quarterly*, 36, 1 (March 1954), 91–99.

30. Roy K. Niemeyer, "Part versus Whole Methods and Massed versus Distributed Practice in the Learning of Selected Large Muscle Activities," *62nd Proceedings of the College Physical Education Association*, New York, December 28–30, 1958 (Washington, D.C.: The American Association for Health, Physical Education, and Recreation, 1959), pp. 122–25.

31. Olive G. Young, "Rate of Learning in Relation to Spacing of Practice Periods in Archery and Badminton," *Research Quarterly*, 25, 2 (May 1954), 231–43.

32. Jim D. Whitley, "Effects of Practice Distribution on Learning a Fine Motor Task," *Research Quarterly*, 40, 4 (December 1970), 577, 581–82.

33. George E. Stelmach, "Efficiency of Motor Learning as a Function of Intertrial Rest," *Research Quarterly*, 40 (1969), 198–202.

34. R. B. Alderman, "Influence of Local Fatigue on Speed and Accuracy in Motor Learning," *Research Quarterly*, 36 (1965), 131–40. D. W. Bartz and L. E. Smith, "Effect of Moderate Exercise on the Performance and Learning of a Gross Motor Skill," *Perceptual and Motor Skills*, 31 (1970), 187–90. A. V. Carron, "Physical Fatigue and Motor Learning," *Research Quarterly*, 40 (1969), 682–96. W. Phillips, "Effect of Physical Fatigue on Two Motor Learning Tasks." Unpublished doctoral dissertation, University of California, Berkeley, 1962.

35. David W. Benson, "Influence of Imposed Fatigue on Learning a Jumping and a Juggling Task," *Research Quarterly*, 39, 2 (May 1968), 351–57.

36. Margaret A. Godwin and Richard A. Schmidt, "Muscular Fatigue and Learning a Discrete Motor Skill," *Research Quarterly*, 42, 4 (1971), 374–81.

37. M. L. Barnett, D. Ross, B. Todd, and R. A. Schmidt, unpublished manuscript, Motor Behavior Laboratory, Department of Physical Education, University of Michigan, 1971.

38. Franklin Henry, "Specificity vs. Generality in Learning Motor Skills," *Proceedings of the College Physical Education Association*, 59 (1956), 68–75.

39. Frances Hellebrandt et al., "Tonic Neck Reflexes in Exercise of Stress in Man," *American Journal of Physical Medicine*, 35 (1956), 144–49.

40. F. C. Bartlett, "Fatigue Following Highly Skilled Work," *Proceedings of the Royal Society*, 131 (1943), 248–57. See also Legge, *op. cit.*, p. 301.

41. Ernest R. Hilgard, "Methods and Procedures in the Study of Learning," in *Handbook of Experimental Psychology*, ed. S. S. Stevens (New York: Wiley, 1951), chap. 15, p. 536.

42. Roland A. Vandell, Robert A. Davis, and Herbert A. Clugston, "The

Function of Mental Practice in the Acquisition of Motor Skills," *Journal of General Psychology*, 39, 2 (October 1943), 243–50.

43. Wilbur E. Twining, "Mental Practice and Physical Practice in Learning a Motor Skill," *Research Quarterly*, 20, 4 (December 1949), 432–35.

44. Lolas Elizabeth Halverson, "A Comparison of Three Methods of Teaching Motor Skills." Unpublished master's thesis, University of Wisconsin, 1949.

45. L. Verdelle Clark, "Effect of Mental Practice on the Development of a Certain Motor Skill," *Research Quarterly*, 31, 4, Part 1 (December 1960), 560–69.

46. John Gerald Jones, "Motor Learning Without Demonstration of Physical Practice, Under Two Conditions of Mental Practice," *Research Quarterly*, 36, 3 (October 1965), 270–81.

47. *Ibid.*, p. 275.

48. Ella M. Trussel, "Mental Practice as a Factor in the Learning of a Complex Motor Skill." Unpublished doctoral dissertation, University of California, Berkeley, 1958.

49. Charles C. Corbin, "The Effects of Covert Rehearsal on the Development of a Complex Motor Skill," *Journal of General Psychology*, 76 (April 1967), 143–50.

50. Stephen J. Phipps and Chauncey A. Morehouse, "Effects of Mental Practice on the Acquisition of Motor Skills of Varied Difficulty," *Research Quarterly*, 40, 4 (December 1969), 773–78.

51. Joseph B. Oxendine, "Effect of Mental and Physical Practice on the Learning of Three Motor Skills," *Research Quarterly*, 40, 4 (December 1969), 755–63.

52. Jim D. Whitley, "Effects of Practice Distribution on Learning a Fine Motor Task," *Research Quarterly*, 41, 4 (December 1970), 580.

53. S. B. G. Eysenck, "Retention of a Well-developed Motor Skill After One Year," *Journal of General Psychology*, 63, 2 (October 1960), 267–73.

54. R. B. Ammons, R. G. Farr, E. Bloch, E. Neuman, M. Dey, R. Marion, and C. H. Ammons, "Long-term Retention of Perceptual-Motor Skills," *Journal of Experimental Psychology*, 55, 4 (April 1958), 318–28.

55. Jack Leon Sparks, "Relative Effects of Various Incentives on Learning and Retention of a Gross Motor Skill." Unpublished master's thesis, Pennsylvania State University, 1963.

56. Robert N. Singer, "Massed and Distributed Practice Effects on the Acquisition and Rentention of a Novel Basketball Skill," *Research Quarterly*, 36, 1 (March 1965), 68–77.

57. Edwin A. Fleishman and James F. Parker, "Factors in the Retention and Relearning of Perceptual-Motor Skill," *Journal of Experimental Psychology*, 64, 3 (September 1962), 215–26.

58. Margaret G. Fox and Ethel Lamb, "Improvement During a Nonprac-

tice Period in a Selected Physical Education Activity," *Research Quarterly*, 33, 3 (October 1962), 381–85.

59. Margaret G. Fox and Vera P. Young, "Effect of Reminiscence on Learning Selected Badminton Skills," *Research Quarterly*, 33, 3 (October 1962), 386–94.

60. Bonnie J. Purdy and Aileene Lockhart, "Retention and Relearning of Gross Motor Skills After Long Periods of No Practice," *Research Quarterly*, 33, 2 (May 1962), 265–72.

61. Reuben A. Baer, "The Relationship Between the Rate of Learning and Retention in Several Motor Activities." Unpublished doctoral dissertation, Johns Hopkins University, 1940.

62. Eileen Koper Bender, "The Relationship Between Rate of Learning and Retention of Certain Sensorimotor Skills." Unpublished master's thesis, Pennsylvania State University, 1961.

63. Many experiments in motor learning make this same error of comparing difference in absolute scores at various levels; yet it is evident, for example, that an improvement of one-tenth of a second in the 100-yard dash from 12 seconds to 11.9 seconds does not represent the same improvement as the change from 10 seconds to 9.9 seconds. In archery, an inch closer at the outer edge of the target does not represent the same improvement as an inch closer within the last three inches of the target center. Such improvements, although numerically the same (in Bender's case, less), may very well represent even greater degrees of mastery at high level of skill than at earlier stages.

64. A. I. Gates et al., *Educational Psychology*, 2nd ed. (New York: Macmillan, 1953), pp. 371–72.

65. C. E. Beeby, "An Experimental Investigation into the Simultaneous Constituents in an Act of Skill," *British Journal of Psychology*, 20, 4 (April 1930), 336–53.

66. Grace O. McGeoch, "Whole-Part Problem," *Psychological Bulletin*, 28, 10 (December 1931), 713–39.

67. Gates, *op. cit.*, p. 374.

68. Roberta W. Brown, "A Comparison of the 'Whole,' 'Part,' and 'Combination' Methods of Learning Piano Music," *Journal of Experimental Psychology*, 11, 3 (June 1928), 235–47.

69. Roberta W. Brown, "The Relation Between Two Methods of Learning Piano Music," *Journal of Experimental Psychology*, 16 (June 1933), 435–41.

70. Clayton T. Shay, "The Progressive-Part versus the Whole Method of Learning Motor Skills," *Research Quarterly*, 5, 4 (December 1934), 62–67.

71. Clyde G. Knapp and W. Robert Dixon, "Learning to Juggle: II. A Study of Whole and Part Methods," *Research Quarterly*, 22, 4 (December 1952), 398–401.

72. F. J. McGuigan and Eugene F. MacCaslin, "Whole and Part Methods in Learning a Perceptual Motor Skill," *American Journal of Psychology*, 48, 4 (December 1955), 658–61.

73. F. J. McGuigan, "Variation of Whole-Part Methods of Learning," *Journal of Educational Psychology*, 51, 4 (August 1960), 213–16.

74. Doris J. O'Donnell, "The Relative Effectiveness of Three Methods of Teaching Beginning Tennis to College Women." Unpublished doctoral dissertation, Indiana University, 1956.

75. William Theunissen, " 'Part'-Teaching and 'Whole'-Teaching of Beginning Group-Golf Classes for Male College Students." Unpublished doctoral dissertation, Indiana University, 1955.

76. Niemeyer, *op. cit.*

77. *Ibid.,* pp. 123–24.

78. John O. Lewellen, "A Comparative Study of Two Methods of Teaching Beginning Swimming." Unpublished doctoral dissertation, Stanford University, 1951.

79. Charles A. Godlasky, "An Experimental Study to Determine the Relative Effectiveness of Two Methods of Teaching the Crawl Stroke in Swimming." Unpublished master's thesis, Pennsylvania State University, 1955.

80. Mary V. Gutteridge, "A Study of Motor Achievements of Young Children," *Archives of Psychology*, No. 244 (May 1939).

81. Edward A. Bilodeau and Ina McD. Bilodeau, "Motor-Skills Learning," *Annual Review of Psychology*, 12 (1961), 250.

82. Dael Wolfle, "Factors Determining the Effectiveness of Training," in Stevens, *op. cit.*

83. Margery H. Trowbridge and H. Cason, "An Experimental Study of Thorndike's Theory of Learning," *Journal of General Psychology*, 7, 2 (1932), 245–58. See also summary of recent studies by Jack A. Adams in *Journal of Motor Behavior*, 3, 2 (June 1971), 130ff.

84. William F. Brook and L. Norvell, "The Will to Learn: An Experimental Study of Incentives in Learning," *Pedagogical Seminary*, 29, 4 (December 1922), 305–62; Clay C. Ross, "The Influence upon Achievement of a Knowledge of Progress," *Journal of Educational Psychology*, 24 (1933), 609–19; Harold Seashore and A. Bavelas, "The Functioning of Knowledge of Results in Thorndike's Line-Drawing Experiment," *Psychological Review*, 48, 2 (March 1941), 155–64; Trowbridge and Cason, *op. cit.*

85. George W. Angell, "The Effect of Immediate Knowledge of Quiz Results on Final Examination Scores in Freshmen Chemistry," *Journal of Educational Research*, 42, 5 (January 1949), 391–94; Irving Lorge and E. L. Thorndike, "The Influence of Delay in the After-Effect of a Connection," *Journal of Experimental Psychology*, 18, 2 (April 1935), 186–94; F. G. McGuigan, Frances Crockett, and Carolyn Bolton, "The

Effect of Knowledge of Results Before and After a Response," *Journal of General Psychology*, 63, 1 (1960), 51–55; Irving J. Saltzman, F. H. Canfer, and J. Greenspoon, "Delay of Reward and Human Motor Learning," *Psychological Reports*, 1, 3 (September 1955), 139–42; F. V. Taylor, "Simplifying the Controller's Task Through Display Quickening," *Occupational Psychology*, 31, 2 (April 1957), 120–25.

86. S. J. MacPherson, V. Dees, and G. C. Grindley, "The Effect of Knowledge of Results on Learning and Performance: II. Some Characteristics of Very Simple Skills," *Quarterly Journal of Experimental Psychology*, 1 (1948), 68–78.

87. David S. Abbey and P. A. Cowan, "Incomplete Visual Feedback and Performance on the Toronto Complex Coordinator," *Perceptual and Motor Skills*, 11, 1 (August 1960), 43–45; Maynard W. Shelly, "Learning with Reduced Feedback Information," *Journal of Experimental Psychology*, 62, 3 (September 1961), 209–22.

88. John Annett, "Learning a Pressure Under Conditions of Immediate and Delayed Knowledge of Results," *Quarterly Journal of Experimental Psychology*, 11, 1 (February 1959), 3–15; Maxwell L. Howell, "Use of Force-time Graphs for Performance Analysis in Facilitating Motor Learning," *Research Quarterly*. 27, 1 (March 1956), 12–22; Lawrence G. Lindahl, "Movement Analysis as an Industrial Training Method," *Journal of Applied Psychology*, 29, 6 (December 1945), 420–36.

89. Robert E. Morin, "Factors Influencing Rate and Extent of Learning in the Presence of Misinformative Feedback," *Journal of Experimental Psychology*, 49, 5 (May 1955), 343–51.

90. Charles H. Judd, "Practice Without Knowledge of Results," *Psychological Review Monograph Supplements*, 7, 1, Whole No. 29 (March 1905), 185–98.

91. Gordon Hendrickson and William H. Schroeder, "Transfer of Training in Learning to Hit a Submerged Target," *Journal of Educational Psychology*, 32, 3 (March 1941), 205–13.

92. Bernice Frey, "A Study of Teaching Procedures in Selected Physical Education Activities for College Women of Low Motor Ability." Unpublished doctoral dissertation, State University of Iowa, 1947.

93. Frances M. Colville, "The Learning of Motor Skills as Influenced by Knowledge of Mechanical Principles," *Journal of Educational Psychology*, 48, 6 (October 1957), 321–37.

94. Edith Cobane, "A Comparison of Two Methods of Teaching Selected Motor Skills." Unpublished doctoral dissertation, Syracuse University, 1959.

95. Joan Nessler, "An Experimental Study of Methods Adapted to Teaching Low-skilled Freshman Women in Physical Education." Unpublished doctoral dissertation, Pennsylvania State University, 1961, p. 148.

96. Marion R. Broer, "Effectiveness of a General Basic Skills Curriculum for Junior High School Girls," *Research Quarterly*, 29, 4 (December 1958), 379–88.

97. Dorothy M. Coleman, "The Effect of a Unit of Movement Education upon the Level of Achievement of the Specialized Skill of Bowling." Unpublished doctoral dissertation, Texas Woman's University, 1967.

98. Dorothy Burdeshaw, Jane E. Spragens, and Patricia A. Weis, "Evaluation of General Versus Specific Instruction of Badminton Skills to Women of Low Motor Ability," *Research Quarterly*, 41, 4 (December 1970), 472–77.

99. Mildred E. Barrett, "A Study of the Effect of the Knowledge of Mechanical Principles on Learning Specific Swimming Strokes." Unpublished master's thesis, University of Maryland, 1957.

100. Halverson, *op. cit.*

Seven

Motivation, Emotion, and Stress

> One only learns to tolerate stress, to perform adequately in spite of stress, by practice under stressful conditions; but the degree of stress must be tempered to the individual's developing tolerance.

The terms "motivation," "emotion," and "stress" are used with such a variety of meanings or shades of meaning in the literature that our discussion must of necessity start with some differentiation. Stress is often used to describe physiological imbalance, although some writers talk about psychological stress, by which they seem to mean feelings and emotions. The synonyms "activation" and "arousal" are terms commonly used to indicate response to stimuli. Activation is perhaps best considered as a state of arousal that may occur along a continuum from mild or lethargic response to extreme or near maximum response, with increasing degrees of physiological and psychological imbalances accompanying the increase in arousal. Degrees of motivation could perhaps be used to describe this continuity, although the upper degrees of arousal are often catalogued as emotional reactions. However, Duffy has implied that any attempt to distinguish between nonemotional and emotional behavior is unnecessary because the latter state merely represents greater intensity of motivation.[1]

The physiological imbalances are usually called stresses, although the term stress is more often used only for the relatively higher degrees of imbalance and attempts to restore balance and equanimity. Cofer and Appley[2] characterize stress as being more extreme than an ordinary motivated state; an implied threat is subjectively perceived, and there is perhaps harmful ego involvement. The stronger physiological reactions are a type of defense reaction.

169

MOTIVATION

Let us then define motivation as a state of "being aroused" to action —aroused from passivity or calmness to restlessness, to a degree of dissatisfaction or disturbance, and then to directed, purposeful acts. This state of arousal to action, this disurbance of homeostasis, may result from some internal organic or psychic need. Hunger, thirst, tissue injury, and sex are commonly listed as primary motivations. These needs become conditioned or directed through learning into purposes or desires to obtain something or escape from something. The *motive* is then the desire for a specific object or goal, or the desire to escape from a situation or environment.

Individuals are activated by many motives—not only those commonly recognized, such as desires for food and water, but also many derived or learned motives, such as desire for money, praise, social status, security, self-respect. They get to want to finish a job, once started; or perhaps they take pride in their workmanship or in personal appearance. They seem to have a basic need to express their potentialities and to react to their environment.

Some human motivations, perhaps what we mean by psychic rather than organic needs, have to do with our apparent need to be active and to explore and manipulate our environment. These motives are not only almost universal in the human species but are also characteristic of much animal behavior. Much of this type of activity has been characterized as play. As Huisinga says:

> This intensity of, and absorption in play finds no explanation in biological analysis. . . . The fun of playing resists all analysis, all logical interpretation. . . . Here we have to do with an absolutely primary category of life, familiar to everyone at a glance right down to the animal level. . . . Since the reality of play extends beyond the sphere of human life it cannot have its foundations in any rational nexus, because this could limit it to mankind. . . . In culture we find play as a given magnitude existing before culture itself existed, accompanying it and pervading it from the earliest beginnings right up to the phase of civilization we are now living in.[3]

A continuance of a quiescent state is annoying to the healthy human, who seeks activity. As Cannon says, the individual seems to seek imbalance through activity.[4]

It must not be assumed that these psychic needs are the products of learning, although the direction of their expression in activity involves learning. For example, our need for affiliation with some of our own kind seems to be inborn. Complete and extended isolation is a serious punishment for the normal human being. Even many animal species display a need for affection, seeking physical contact and cuddling very early in the infant stage. In a famous study by Harlow and Zimmerman,[5] monkeys were raised with two fake mothers, one fabricated from terrycloth and one from wire; they came to prefer the cloth mother although their feeding was administered through the wire mother. The experimenters say:

> These data make it obvious that contact comfort is a variable of critical importance in the development of affectional responsiveness to the surrogate mother, and that nursing appears to play a negligible role. With increasing age and opportunity to learn, an infant fed from a lactating wire mother does not become more responsive to her as would be predicted from a derived-drive theory, but instead becomes increasingly more responsive to its non-lactating cloth mother.[6]

Motivating conditions tend to focus attention and behavior on goal-related aspects of the situation; that is, the motive tends to direct the persistent though variable activity and to determine the type of responses made. With increase in strength of motive, there is a corresponding increase in energy expended.

The evidence is somewhat conflicting as to the effect of strength of motivation on learning, but at times the rate of learning seems to increase with increase in stimulus. The increase may result from nothing other than the set to learn, the greater attention, and the greater variety in trial attempts. However, there is a peak of strength of effective stimulus for each individual, after which the learning curve seems to drop in many types of complex learning. Along the continuum of motivation from mild through strong stimuli with the more generalized resultants (emotional accompaniment), we tend to have more action, more varied action, and often improved performance up to the individual's particular tolerance, then a drop in performance efficiency, and finally complete failure of effective performance. However, various factors affect the shape of the curve: [7]

1. Previous experience and learning, hence degree of automatic response
2. Complexity of the appropriate response
3. Earlier associated learnings and conditionings
4. Various need states of the individual
5. A generic factor (such as trait anxiety, although attempts to measure trait anxiety have not been very successful).

Incentives

Incentives are external stimuli the individual likes, wants, desires to obtain. They are devices to get people to do tasks irrespective of any satisfaction inherent in the doing of the work itself. If they are really incentives to the individual, they increase performance of the goal-directed activity. Industry uses bonuses, promised raises in salary, public recognition, or piece-work payments as incentives. The ego satisfaction of the employee is at times more important to him or her than money and security. The ego involvement of the worker crops up frequently in attempts at settlement of strikes in industry. Ego involvement is any treatment that affects the worker's (or learner's) status in his social group or society, his self-pride, prestige, and self-estimation. To some teachers a raise in professional rank is very important even though it does not include a raise in salary; conversely, some teachers have different goals and would prefer to have the raise in salary even if it meant a lower professional status.

Common incentives used by teachers to stimulate students are praise and reproof, promise of reward, prizes, better grades, rivalry and competition, and ego involvement. They use these devices in attempts to stir the students to greater activity. It is clear that one must be active to learn; hence one must have some drive and must attend to the learning situation. One must have a set toward learning.

EMOTION

The upper levels of arousal seem to be accompanied by feeling tones that occur as higher degrees of motivation begin to produce more generalized chemical and physiological reactions. (1) The stimuli, (2) the feeling tones, and (3) certain responses become patterned through learning into what we ordinarily call forms of *emotional expression*. For example, punishment or failure may produce conditioning of many neutral but associated stimuli so that any similar situation produces anxiety and worry. The anxiety and worry feelings are types of emotion. The chemical and physiological changes produced by anxiety and worry (or by any other emotion feeling, such as irritation and anger) are the body's attempts to restore normal homeostasis. They are the efforts we call stress. Disturbance of homeostasis, and therefore stress, may also be caused by many other stimuli besides those catalogued as emotional; for example, cold, heat, disease, tissue injury, and heavy physical effort.

Milder degrees of emotional stimulation tend to improve performance and hasten learning. When the learning reaches more advanced levels and much of it is already automatized, a higher degree of emotion can be experienced without loss in performance efficiency and, at times, even with an improvement in performance. However, the nature of the individual, previous experience with emotional stimuli, and subsequent success or failure will affect efficiency of action under strong stimuli. Actually, evpression of emotion develops into specific patterns, both in motor expression and in neural action. Emotional behavior in the mature adult often has acquired adjusted responses so that it is only distinguishable from ordinary motivated action by intensity, vigor, and degree of concern. However, it may also have acquired nonadaptive and antisocial responses in the emotionally immature adult. There are some cases on record of performance of feats beyond normal powers after extreme visceral upheaval in the presence of an emergency situation. These are probably not nearly as frequent as cases of inferior performance or even of complete inhibition of adjusted action.

Vaughan [8] presents the view that it takes an upsetting experience such as the disparagement of one's ability at the unkind hands of another to remove the inhibitions that circumvent one's expansion; that no one knows how much he can do until he is driven by some excitement to extend himself. Emerson says in his essay "Compensation":

> Our strength grows out of our weakness. The indignation which arms itself with secret forces does not awaken until we are pricked and stung and sorely assailed.

Changes with Increased Intensity of Stimulation

Any activity implies drive or motive, but only those involving strong feeling tones, more extensive glandular and visceral reactions, and activity of the parasympathetic division of the autonomic nervous system are classified as emotional. Let us assume varying degrees of stimulation, varying degrees of need, and varying degrees of equanimity or homeostasis. Under the mild stimuli of everyday living, we may make habit response or learned adjustments without extreme physiological reactions or strong conscious feelings of pleasure or pain, joy or sorrow, excitement or boredom. We may get up in the morning, eat breakfast, and go about routine duties without experiencing stimuli strong enough to activate to any appreciable degree the parasympathetic system and the endocrine glands. Our digestion proceeds while we go about the other activities of daily living. We respond to the regular rhythm of organic needs, hunger and thirst, at suitable intervals; and to task responsibilities, family duties, and social obligations by adjustment patterns already learned or easy to construct from our background of experience.

If we use the term emotion, let us think of it as a word used to describe the conscious feeling tones accompanying the higher levels of activation—perhaps from the mild feelings that only slightly disturb the tempo of ordinary living (and that accompany the milder increases in physiological disequilibrium) to the extremes of vigorous and violent feelings and reactions. We have a continuum from mild anxiety to extreme fear; from gentle affection to passionate love; from mild annoyance to violent anger. The term emotion is commonly used to describe the heightened feeling tone that accompanies stronger stimulus and subsequent disequilibrium, a greater upheaval than what we speak of as ordinary motivation. Our mild hunger motivated us to eat breakfast.

When we are strongly activated through deprivation, serious ego involvement, or threat, we begin to experience deep feeling tones (emotion) and an accompaniment of extensive autonomic, glandular, and visceral reactions; higher tonicity in the smooth muscles; more blood flow into the skeletal musculature; extra energy release, and so on. Hunger is often blocked out and digestion may be halted. Even fatigue may be vitiated to some degree. Resulting higher tension in the musculature may make us quicker to respond and more active. However, with very strong stimuli, the greater tension in the musculature may spill over into the antagonists and hinder rather than facilitate appropriate and rapid responses. Whether or not the stronger activation improves performance is a complex problem. Degree of automaticity of the appropriate responses, complexity of those responses, and various conflicting needs and drives are all part of the adjustment problem. Research has not yet established whether or not very strong arousal facilitates learning, although some experimental evidence seems to indicate that retention of learning improves with practice under higher arousal.[9]

Emotion, a Subjective Feeling

Some writers who continue to label high arousal as emotion call the extensive physiological changes themselves the emotion; but for our purposes we shall consider the greatly heightened feelings and sensations, of which we are aware at the conscious level, as the emotion. Perhaps the reader has experienced a near-miss situation in a car in which automatic responses on steering wheel and brake have extricated him or her from what might very well have been a tragic accident. The motor-memory discharge of the brake-press act occurred so rapidly that conscious awareness could occur only after the highly automated motor act. The emergency responses being over, the situation is normal again in an instant except that, afterward, we begin to feel a surge of emotion, the fear that accompanies the stirred-up state from the sudden very strong stimulus. The feelings we experience under very strong stimulation are apparently a conscious accompaniment of certain deeply stirred physiological states; but whether or not they are always the results of the physiological disturbance is another question. Perhaps the emotionally stimulating situation initiates both the neurological pattern we feel as emotion and the physiological disturbances; that is, perhaps they are concomitant occurrences, and perhaps each reinforces the other. Long ago William James said:

My theory . . . *is that the bodily changes follow directly the perception of the exciting fact, and that our feeling of the same changes as they occur IS the emotion.*[10]

Let us assume that the rather extensive bodily changes, both chemical and physiological, which we shall list in more detail a little later, *may be* the stimuli for the psychological effect we experience consciously and label an emotion. But we must not overlook the fact that mental states can also initiate extensive physiological changes. Daily irritations on the job may run up blood pressure and stop digestion. Anxiety and worry are purported to be causal factors in stomach ulcers. On the other hand, play, games, and joyous physical activity are advocated for mental health—a form of catharsis to restore emotional normality, equanimity, and equilibrium.

STRESS

The term stress has been used extensively in the literature, especially after the publication of the work of Hans Selye.[11] Selye presents stress as disturbance of normal homeostasis, an effort to achieve equilibrium after homeostatic balance has been upset. The effort involves action of the parasympathetic division of the autonomic nervous system, and extensive visceral and glandular activity. The stimuli that cause stress (stressors) may come from physiological or psychological needs or deprivations, or from environmental conditions. Selye divides the stages of reaction to stressors into the alarm stage, the resistance stage, and the stage of exhaustion. He defines stress as the process involving nonspecifically induced changes within the biologic system. The body is said to be experiencing stress when it undergoes any stimulus strong enough to cause some activation of sections of the autonomic nervous system, glandular reactions, and various bodily adjustments for increased effort. Selye states that the resistance stage involves secretions of glandular hormones and formation of conditioned reflexes as defense reactions.

The term stress is used to describe bodily conditions in the adjustment to physical effort, to fatigue, and to tissue injury and resistance to disease or harmful poisons. It is also often used to describe the stirred-up states of the organism that James felt to be the precursors of the conscious feeling called emotion.

Lundervold,[12] using electromyographic records, reported wider muscle use with: (1) fatigue, (2) stress or stronger stimulus, and (3) greater speed. Each of these three factors also produced more tension in the antagonists. Training produced higher speed with less muscular activity, according to the electromyographic records. Unpleasant feelings increased the muscular and vascular work. Favorable psychic factors seemed to tend to postpone fatigue. Hellebrandt, in commenting on the usefulness of certain automatic reactions that emerge under stress, says:

> The irradiation associated with extreme stress is so wide-spread that a willed movement limited to a single appendicular joint may evoke action potentials in muscles located in all four extremities, the head and neck, and the trunk. These seem to us to be orderly and wholly integrated total patterns of response. Observing them we get the impression that they are the obligatory concomitants of very severe stress, and the only way in which the highest threshold motor units of the muscle subjected to direct training can be activated. These are the motor units held in reserve and called upon when truly maximum effort is demanded—when you rush into a burning house and perform some phenomenal feat of strength, or when you break the 4-minute mile, or swing your paralyzed legs across a street in the time-span of the green light that gives you the right of way.[13]

The reader will need to use caution in interpreting the literature with respect to stress and emotion, for the terms seem at times to be used interchangeably. In fact, some of the texts have called the deep visceral and glandular changes from strong stimuli emotion. The definition is unimportant as long as the reader is not confused about whether he is considering physiological and chemical changes, or conscious feeling patterns accompanying such changes. Actually, under what would normally be an emotionally stimulating situation, animals show behavior symptoms that seem to be their typical, overt, emotional-pattern reactions *even after their cortices are removed.*

We have used the conscious aspect, the feeling tones, to define emotion in this chapter in order to attempt to distinguish between emotion and certain types of stress. The strong stimuli that cause extensive disequilibrium, internal upset, and a stirred-up physiological state do not need to be emotional in the common usage of the term (intense feeling stimuli). Toxic substances, illness, or tissue injury may also cause extensive chemical and physiological changes in the body. A common psychological product of stress is what is usually called anxiety (or degrees of that state, which ranges from mild worry to fear, if you prefer other terminology).

Physiological and Chemical Changes

Perhaps it would be well to mention again several of the kinds of chemical and physiological changes that seem to precede or accompany the subjective feelings which we have called emotion. When the parasympathetic division of the autonomic nervous system is strongly stimulated, we have a cooperative inhibition effect in the cranial and the sacral divisions. There is stimulus to the smooth muscles and the ductless glands. Digestion is stopped. There is contraction of the arteries that feed the blood to the alimentary canal, and the blood is forced out into the skeletal musculature and into the body's peripheral blood vessels. Blood pressure often increases, saliva flow decreases, perspiration increases, body temperature changes, the heart and respiration rates increase, there is much glandular activity including the release of adrenin into the bloodstream, some changes in blood chemistry including a release of more sugar into the blood, and a speeding up of the coagulation time of the blood.

With higher blood pressure, chemical changes in the blood, faster and stronger heartbeat, and faster breathing, osmosis is faster, food and oxygen reach the cells sooner, and waste products are carried away faster; that is, more energy is available for effort and less fatigue occurs. The body makes these adjustments to emergency conditions, but the direction of these extra powers for performance depends on the individual's ability to adjust and control their expression. Here previous conditioning and learning experience play important roles.

EXPERIMENTAL STUDIES: AN OVERVIEW

Experimental studies in the fields of motivation, emotion, and stress suffer from several weaknesses. For one thing, we can only measure change in performance and then hypothesize that the change was due to the additional factor introduced into the experimental situation. But the experimenter is also a variable. As we can well remember from our own school experiences, praise or reproof from one teacher might have a much different effect than the same treatment from a different teacher. The kind of instruction and the social conditions surrounding the total experimental environment may also affect results.

Moreover, the effectiveness of the stimulus may very well vary with the level of learning already attained. The previous degree of success or failure of the subjects may affect the results. Both age and intelligence of the subjects may be variables. If there is great ego involvement by some subjects, anxiety over failure may have disruptive effects. Introspective, questionnaire, and projective techniques are at best very subjective measures. When such procedures are not used to measure emotion, some measure is usually taken indirectly by measurement of certain body changes; however, most of the physiological responses so measured are affected by too many other variables to be sure indices of degree of emotional arousal.

In an old but frequently cited study of competitive bicycle riding, Triplett [14] stated in 1897: "From the above facts re: the laboratory races, we infer that bodily presence of another contestant participating simultaneously in the race serves to liberate latent energy not ordinarily available." Competition and rivalry are common variables used in motivational studies. In a study of very young children, Greenburg [15] found some competition occurring in the activities of children between the ages of three and four in their various play activities and in their various efforts to achieve recognition or dominance in a situation. There was a gradual increase of competition with age, so that competition had become extensive between the ages of six and seven. Mehran K. Thompson says of competition:

> Competition and rivalry satisfy basic needs in the individual and the race. We speak of competitive games and often refer to the game of life as such, for, from the cradle to the grave, we are competing for something or other. Competition and rivalry are rooted in the *élan vital,* the evolutionary urge. They constitute the push in the struggle to survive and the desire for supremacy. Competition runs all through life. A man must compete for the means of livelihood, for his social position, for his friends, in fact, for everything which is worth-while. Civilized society has not eliminated rivalry; on the contrary, it has extended the field from the purely physical and biological to the intellectual, social, moral, and spiritual. . . .

> The object is to utilize the advantages and avoid the pitfalls (in the use of competition to motivate school learning.) The advantages are: (1) it provides zest and meaning to life; (2) it is positive and satisfies a basic urge; (3) it builds up morale and ego-maximization; (4) it stimulates growth, development, and maturation; (5) it could lead to self-improvement, for competition can be used against oneself as well as against others. The chief danger is that if competition is too keen, the individual is likely to suffer defeat, frustration, and possible demoralization. [16]

INDIVIDUAL VARIABILITY IN REACTION

Gerwitz and Baer [17] experimented with children in a simple motor-skill "game." Each subject of one group was isolated for twenty minutes before he started the skill. A second group went directly to the experiment. A third group was "satiated" on the way to the experimental situation by extremely solicitous and approving comments and actions on the part of the experimenter. All were praised during performance. The "deprived" subjects, those who had been isolated, were superior in acquiring and performing the skill; the group that went directly to the experiment ranked second; and the "satiated" group, the group that had had extensive praise preceding the experiment, did the poorest.

One difficulty in trying to measure degree of motivational arousal is the fact that individuals vary widely in specific behavioral and specific physiological reactions. The same stressors may disturb one subject greatly but leave another unconcerned. Moreover, the same stimuli, assuming equal stress on the individuals measured, will cause different degrees of physiological and behavioral reactions in the respective individuals. As Lacey and Lacey propose,[18] each subject has his own method of adapting or responding to a stressful situation. As indices of arousal, the palm perspiration print and the GSR measures are good examples of individual variation. Sensitivity of sweat glands to activation is known to vary widely among individuals. It has been suggested that this inaccuracy of attempts to measure arousal by behavioral and physiological indices might be partly corrected by using a composite of several different measures (physiological and behavioral) as the arousal index.[19]

We have already listed several factors that affect an individual's degree of arousal and type of response to a specific motivational situation —previous experience with the same or similar situations, *trait* anxiety (admittedly difficult to measure), level of learning and degree of response automation, conflicting needs and drives, complexity of the appropriate responses, and so on. Almost any experimenter who has dealt with groups of considerable size has found great individual variability in effects. This variability is often not stressed because conclusions are drawn from group means and their differences. Two studies will be mentioned in which attention has been focused on variability. In other experiments the reader can note the same phenomenon upon examination of the data.

Birger Johnson [20] compared bicycle ergometer work by junior high school boys under a combination of incentives. His incentives were a competitive situation plus urging and encouragement during the exercise trials. His measures of reaction to "emotional stimulation" were changes in heart rate and blood pressure. He states that the reactions of these adolescents were very variable and that acute adjustments in heart rate and blood pressure indicated greater effort but not necessarily greater total work output. Some boys were able to do more work under the motivating conditions, while others were not, in spite of physiological indications of greater effort being exerted. Rexroad [21] concluded, after finding a great variety of results from electric shock in continuous multiple-choice reactions with college students, that electric shock punishment had three effects: (1) disruptive, (2) incentive, (3) instructive.

STRESS EFFECTS AND LEVELS OF LEARNING

The Hullian-Spence drive theory proposes that habit strength (various habits elicited by the situation) and drive strength (a factor including all the various need states) jointly determine response strength. Whether performance will be facilitated or deterred by high drive will depend upon the relative strength of the competing response tendencies. Highly anxious subjects will do better on simple tasks, but those with low anxiety are superior to the highly anxious on the complex skills.[22] In two studies by Runquist and Ross, and Runquist and Spence on simple conditioned-response learning, the level of arousal was estimated from galvanic skin conductance, pulse rate, respiration rate, and EMG or ECG recordings. The high-arousal scores, classified as "emotionally responsive," showed superior learning performances.[23] In various studies of simple task learning,[24] performances of subjects with higher anxiety drives have been reported to be superior to those of less anxious subjects. In more complex learning, individuals with a higher level of drive (anxiety) have been reported to do more poorly in the early stages but actually better than those with a lower level at late stages of learning.

Carron [25] reported a study of stabilometer learning in which the subjects were first scored on the Taylor Manifest Anxiety Scale. They were then divided into three groups: the high scorers on the MAS, the low scorers on the MAS, and a control group of twenty from the low anxious and twenty from the high anxious. During the early learning the two experimental groups, the high- and the low-anxious groups, were administered mild electric shocks during the practices. This situational stress affected the highly anxious group adversely but did not affect the low-anxious group's performance. When electric shock stress was introduced late in the progress of learning, both high- and low-anxious groups did less well. However, after the late shock stress was removed, both groups which had received electric shock during practices (high and low MAS scorers) did better than the control group.

Stennett studied effects on performance of auditory tracking under various types of incentives and various levels of arousal as indicated by palmar skin conductance and EMG readings. He reported best performance to occur at intermediate levels of arousal.[26] Ryan reported,[27] from a study of effects of a shock stressor on performance, that performance was impaired early in the learning, but late in the learning no such impairment occurred. In an earlier study,[28] Ryan reported that the difficulty of the task and the proficiency of the individual determined the stress effect. In a stabilometer learning experiment, Ryan measured arousal of the subjects in relation to effectiveness of performance. He reported that higher arousal groups had a superior performance to that of the low-arousal groups; and that arousal, as measured by skin conductance, precedes performance.[29]

Birch [30] studied the effects of the variation in the strength of the stimulus on ability of chimpanzees to solve a motor problem in order to get food. The lengths of food deprivation were 2, 6, 12, 24, 36, and 48 hours. Birch reported poor results with low levels and high levels of motivation. When the motivation was low, the animals were easily distracted and tended to deviate into non-goal-directed behavior. Under intense motivation, the animals concentrated on the goal but shut out features of the situation that were essential to success. Those animals working under intermediate conditions of motivational intensity were more successful. Their behavior was goal-directed but adequately flexible to permit solution of the problem.

Fleishman [31] reported, from a study using a simulator of manipulation of airplane controls as the skill and strong verbal exhortation as the incentive, that only the better half of the motivated group did better than the control group. Lazarus and Deese "found some evidence which led them to believe that emotional stress induced early in the learning process, before skills have been well organized, produced a detrimental effect on learning, while stress induced later in learning produced a slightly facilitating effect." [32] Craig [33] experimented with achievement in a perceptual-motor task under two conditions—normal reaction and action forced within a limited time. Generally, higher mean scores were achieved under the time-limit situation.

Matarazzo et al.[34] conducted a study to investigate the hypothesis that anxiety, as an acquired drive, would facilitate learning up to a point, but beyond this level increased anxiety would hinder learning. They used the Taylor Manifest Anxiety Scale and classified subjects into four groups on a scale of increasing anxiety level. The four groups then were put through a maze-learning experience. The time required to learn by the respective groups supported their hypothesis.

Ulrich [35] studied the effects of emotional stress on two groups of college women, one experienced and the other inexperienced in varsity type sports. The stress situations were anticipations of different types of experience. For the experienced group, they were anticipated participation in (1) a class basketball game, (2) an intramural game, (3) an interschool game, (4) a written test in one of their regular courses, and (5) attendance at a game of some importance to them. Then half of each group participated in the anticipated event and the other half was denied participation. However, the anticipated and actual *interschool* experience was omitted as a stressor for the inexperienced group.

Ulrich used changes in pulse and respiration rates and a blood count (of eosinophils) as her measures of degrees of stress. She reported that the inexperienced group had greater stress scores than the experienced in all situations involving basketball; that the experienced group revealed stress scores significant at the 1 percent level only in the anticipated test and the anticipated interschool contest situations, with higher stress scores being recorded in the former. For the inexperienced group, the differential levels of stress significant at the 1 percent level were, in descending order: anticipation of written test, of intramural contest, and of class contest. For the poststressor situation (after participation or denial of participation), the experienced group that was not permitted to participate registered higher stress scores than those who participated. For the inexperienced group, the reverse was true; those who did participate registered higher stress scores than those who were not permitted to participate. Ulrich hypothesizes that the threshold of stress may be raised by experience in the stressor situation.

Mitchem and Tuttle [36] studied the effects on static neuromuscular tremor magnitude of (1) graded bouts of exercise of differing strenuousness, (2) students' anticipation of a final written examination, and (3) wide age differences. They reported that neuromuscular tremor magnitude varied directly with the strenuousness of the exercise. They also reported that anticipation of the examination increased tremor, and that tremor was greater after sixty years than it was in adolescence.

Chase,[37] after experimenting with incentives for children of two to eight years, reported that praise was more effective than no motivation but that reward was more effective than praise. Leuba,[38] experimenting with fifth-grade children, found little effect from praise, and got best results from a combination of rivalry, praise, a chocolate bar, and social recognition. Abel,[39] working with fifth- and sixth-grade boys, reported that praise was superior to no motivation but that a reward of one cent per trial was superior to praise. (This was forty years ago, when a penny would buy something for a child.) She also reported that praise seemed to lose its effectiveness as an incentive over a period of time.

Forlano [40] tested the effect of various motivating conditions on the performance of sixth-grade pupils in a cancellation test. His conditions were: (1) individual improvement goal, (2) class improvement goal, (3) team improvement (class competing with class), and (4) team improvement (boys competing against girls). He reported significant superiority over base trials in two of the situations, self-improvement and team improvement with boys competing against girls. Note that in the Birger Johnson study cited earlier, the junior high school boys actually did less well under competitive stress. Note also the similarity of Forlano's strongest motivating factors to those noted by Strong in the discussion that follows.

Hartrick [41] studied the effects of self-competition, reward, audience, and a nonmotivated situation on work output on a bicycle ergometer. He found significant increase in work output under the motivating situations but no significant group differences in the effects of the respective motivating conditions. He used male college undergraduates as subjects. Ryan [42] tested the effects of three different incentives on hand dynamometer scores of four groups (including a control group) of male university students. The incentives he used were: (1) verbal encouragement, (2) knowledge of past results plus sight of scoring dial while performing, (3) threat and application of electric shock for failing to improve on each trial. The control group was merely told to make a maximum effort. Ryan reported finding no significant differences among the four groups under the respective conditions. He suggests that if the subjects understand that maximum effort is to be exerted in strength testing, no additional incentive is necessary.

Strong [43] studied the relation of motivation to performance on physical performance tests. He used 434 boys and girls from the sixth grade. His experiment included both experimental and control groups and six "motivating methods": (1) competition with classmate of equal ability; (2) competition with one's own record in an attempt to improve; (3) equal group (team) competition; (4) competition within classes to set class record; (5) competition with classmate of markedly different ability; (6) level of aspiration—with knowledge of his past record, the subject was urged to set a new goal, then encouraged to reach it. Strong concluded that the validity of the measures of "physical fitness tests" is dependent on the motivating conditions under which they are administered. He found that level of aspiration and team competition were the most effective of the six motivating conditions, and that the types of motivation used were more effective with boys than with girls in performance on fitness tests.

Laird [44] reported that when intense and personal "razzing" was given to college men taking a series of motor tests, their steadiness diminished but fatigue also diminished. Lakie [45] attempted a study to determine the relationship of task difficulty, personality traits, and motivation. He reported that the success-motivated individual seemed to do better on complex skills than the individual motivated to avoid failure. He concluded that, to obtain better performance, the emphasis should be on what to do, not what not to do—that the direction of attention should be toward positive acts rather than on acts to avoid. Within limits, strong arousal seemed to improve neurological and endocrine integration for competitive performance.

Bayton and Conley,[46] in a study of effects of success and failure stress on a manipulation task, reported that the failure stimulus was very effective after initial success, but produced inferior performance after initial failure; that is, previous success or failure determine the nature of the later response to failure. Ulrich and Burke [47] found no difference in work output on a bicycle ergometer under success and failure stressors, although these scores were significantly higher (1 percent level and 5 percent level, respectively) than the earlier "base" trials. However, the physiological measures indicated more expenditure of energy under failure stress.

Sparks [48] experimented with adolescent boys in the learning of an overhand volleyball serve for a three-week training period. He used a praised group, a praised and criticized group, a criticized group, and a control group. Sparks reported no significant difference in group scores measured at termination of training but significant differences in later retention. All three "motivated" groups did better than the control group. The "praise and criticism" group did better on these retention tests than any of the other groups. The praised group did not differ significantly from the criticized group.

Gates and Rissland [49] used college students in a three-hole motor coordination test and a color-naming test, with encouragement and discouragement as the respective motivating conditions. They concluded that some comment was better than none, and that the poor performer was more likely to be unfavorably affected by discouragement and reproof than the more proficient one. Gilchrist [50] had his college students repeat an English examination with half praised for their success on the first test and the other half reproved for doing so poorly. The two groups were actually equal. On the second trial, the praised group showed a very significant improvement but the reproved group did no better, and in some cases worse, than on the first trial.

Johanson [51] reported from an experiment that when the subjects were informed of previous reaction time immediately before a trial, simple reaction time was reduced about 6 percent; but a mild shock administered when the reaction time was slow was more than twice as effective in reducing reaction time. Bunch [52] reported that subjects learning a maze under the threat of electric shock learned with 50 percent fewer trials than the control group, 30 percent fewer errors, and in 30 percent less time. Average time per trial indicated however, that the subjects receiving shock responded more cautiously. Henry [53] found that motivating the subjects with electric shock whenever reaction or movement time was slower than the subject's average had a significant effect on speeding up the reaction or movement. Howell [54] reported that the tension caused by the use of electric shock produced an improvement in total time of motor response. Munro [55] used electric shock to motivate subjects when their speed of movement was slow. This motivation speeded up their movement time and the amount of improvement transferred to a second movement pattern; the improvement persisted for several weeks.

PERSONALITY AS RELATED TO DRIVE STRENGTH, LEARNING, AND PERFORMANCE

The Matazarro et al.[56] study mentioned earlier is really concerned with an acquired personality trait, and whether or not the effect of the motivational stressor changes with particular aspects of personality. In the Sparks study mentioned earlier,[57] no relationship was found between scores on the California Personality Index and rate of learning or retention while subjected to various motivational devices. France [58] found no relationship between scores on the Minnesota Multiphasic Personality Inventory and physical performance scores in three events, the hop-step-and-jump, the agility run, and pull-ups.

Walters [59] made an analysis of changes in social adjustment of "motivated" and "nonmotivated" groups during a seven-week bowling course. Her social adjustment measure was the Cowell Personal Distance Ballot. Both groups improved in social adjustment over the seven weeks, but the "motivated" group improved significantly more than the "nonmotivated" group. I am of the opinion that the term "nonmotivated" is a little strong for a group of bowlers who are improving and who received "the usual commendation of exceptional skill or good progress." However, this is a minor point in a study that demonstrates the value of stronger motivation in developing this greater degree of social adjustment. The individuals in the "motivated" group were provided with several additional incentive conditions, such as remaining on the same team, having scores posted, receiving publicity as team winners, and having the losers treat the winners.

A personality factor purported to affect behavior is what is called trait anxiety.[60] Martens says: ". . . anxiety is generally regarded as a product of stress and a mediator of its influence on behavior." [61] Anxiety is a state of uneasiness, worry, apprehension, psychic tension. Spielberger says that *trait* anxiety

. . . predisposes an individual to perceive a wide range of objectively nondangerous circumstances as threatening, and to respond to these with state anxiety reactions disproportionate in intensity to the magnitude of the objective danger.[62]

The distinction made in the literature between *trait* and *state* anxiety is that the former tends to be a stable, behavioral disposition while the latter is a situational and transitory state which fluctuates with time and situation. In popular language, a person supposedly possessing trait anxiety would be what is commonly called a chronic worrier. On the other hand, a person upset only by specific situations to which he or she has been conditioned by past experience, or in which he or she anticipates threatening ego involvement, is said to be experiencing state anxiety.

Various scales such as the Cattell IPAT Anxiety Scale, the Taylor Manifest Anxiety Scale, or the Spielberger et al. State-Trait Anxiety Inventory have been devised to measure anxiety. The first two were devised to measure trait anxiety, although some research studies have attempted to use them as if they were measures of state anxiety. Saranson et al. express the opinion that, although there may be a general anxiety trait, science is not yet prepared to investigate it; and that the study of anxiety should begin with in-depth examination of particular stressful situations.[63]

There is some disagreement in the research as to whether anxiety affects learning or merely affects performance. Cofer and Appley, however, concluded that some relationship exists between drive strength and learning during the acquisition trials.[64] Various attempts have been made to measure the chronic-anxiety trait of certain individuals, and its relationship, if any, to learning and performance. The Taylor Manifest Anxiety Scale [65] and the Cattell IPAT Anxiety Scale [66] are supposed to be measures of trait anxiety; that is, measures of the degree of the individual's personality factor ordinarily labeled chronic anxiety or worry. Martens and Landers reported that their 1970 study [67] supported the chronic anxiety hypothesis. Martens comments that much of the research employing the MAS has actually used the scale as a *state* or situational anxiety measure under specific stressors.[68]

The review of anxiety and motor behavior by Martens in the June 1971 *Journal of Motor Behavior* presents a summary of the research on the scores, in the absence of a stressor, as related to motor learning and performance; and a summary of interaction effects when a stressor is also present. He finds no agreement among over thirty studies of the relationship of MAS and motor behavior when no situational stressor is present (thirteen consistent with drive theory, fifteen finding no difference, and seven uninterpretable). In the interaction effects of MAS on motor behavior with a stressor present, he summarizes the findings of some eighteen studies and finds equally conflicting results. He says:

> Insufficient evidence is available to discover any trends based on the learning versus performance dichotomy, the speed versus action distinction, or task difficulty.[69]

He thinks the time has come in progressive research to abandon the MAS. As to the IPAT as a trait anxiety measure, Martens says it is susceptible to immediate situations and is neither consistent nor stable. He does not recommend it as a state anxiety measure. He goes on to comment that the STAI (The State-Trait Anxiety Inventory) of Spielberger et al. is the best of such anxiety measures at present. It is constructed to attempt to assess both trait and state anxiety.[70]

Hammer completed two studies of athletes (high and low achievers), nonathletes, and their respective MAS scores. He found no significant difference among his various groups on MAS scores except for those of high-achiever wrestlers. He questions the Hullian theory as to drive and response relationship in sports.[71]

Effect of an Audience

Gates [72] reported a stimulating effect on performance of verbal and manual tasks when an audience was present for the group, but no improvement occurred for the better subjects in the group. Hartrick,[73] mentioned earlier, found improved performance over the control situation when an audience witnessed the performance on the bicycle ergometer. Travis [74] reported that over 80 percent of his subjects did better on an eye-hand coordination task with a small audience present, but that group differences did not reach significance.

Martens reports a study of arousal effect of an audience on the learning and performance of a coincident timing task. He used a palmar sweat print to measure arousal change. The highly anxious (trait scores) learned sooner in the presence of an audience, although the learning scores did not differ significantly when the audience was not present. Anxiety did seem to be aroused in both groups by audience presence.[75]

Empirical evidence indicates that background of the individual, general anxiety level, ego involvement, and previous experience of success or failure have much to do with the effects of an audience on performance. The beginner may stammer or forget his lines from stage fright but the experienced actor is inspired to superb performance by a large and interested audience. The first few times an athlete plays before a large crowd are likely to be moments of high emotional tension. With reasonable success, he or she finds less difficulty in appearing subsequently and in directing this energy from emotional stress into effective action. However, if he or she makes serious errors and is severely criticized on the first appearances, his or her level of anxiety may become too high to permit rapid and adequate adjustments in succeeding appearances. Let us examine a few studies of emotional stress in athletes.

DEGREE OF
AROUSAL IN ATHLETES

The aforementioned studies of Hammer reported little or no relationship between anxiety and skill level and performance in athletes. Warren Johnson completed a study of arousal states of athletes at the University of Denver [76] in which he used observation and interview plus measures of changes in heart rate, blood pressure, and blood sugar. The measures were taken (1) four to six days before the contest, (2) the day before the contest, (3) a few hours before the contest, (4) immediately before the contest, and (5) fifteen minutes after the contest. Johnson reported only mild precontest emotion in football players but a "very considerable" amount in wrestlers. In a later study,[77] Johnson used eighty-two winter sports athletes from New England colleges. His tools of measurement were a psychogalvanometer to measure changes in skin resistance under emotional disturbance and two word-association tests. He concluded in this second study that the precontest situation is characterized by "a tendency toward exaggerated psychogalvanic reactivity." He says:

> However, attention is called to the consideration that the "disturbed state" that so commonly characterizes the precontest situation is probably not detrimental to individuals who are comparatively free of profound personality disturbances.[78]

He also states that "In no case did men who were considered outstanding performers by their coaches react in an extreme manner." He agrees with Magda Arnold [79] that, within limits, varieties of emotional disturbance probably serve to improve neurological and endocrine integration for competitive action.

Harmon and Johnson [80] reported a study of like nature, using nineteen track men in a preliminary study and forty-two experienced football players later; the latter group had an average of seven years of playing experience. The subjects were all college men, and most of the football players were war veterans. The experimenters had the coaches rate the importance of the respective games early in the season. The subjects were given a base test that was separated far enough from any contest to permit a relaxed reaction. Then each subject was tested approximately twenty-five minutes before each contest. The measures used were a galvanic skin response, systolic blood pressure, and pulse rate.

All three measures revealed precontest "emotional disturbance." The experimenters reported a close relationship between the amount of "emotional disturbance" and the coaches' rating of the relative importance of each game. The investigators also concluded that the galvanic skin response was the best single indicator, and that the "regulars" were best for predicting degree of "upness."

Skubic [81] used a galvanic skin response measure to check excited state before participation of boys playing Little League and Middle League competitive baseball. She measured 206 boys ranging in age from nine through fifteen, and a group of eighty nonplayers of similar ages as a control group. All subjects were tested immediately before softball competition in physical education class, immediately after the class, and one and a half hours after the class. Then the Little League and Middle League team players were tested immediately before competition in baseball, immediately after the game was over, and again one and a half hours after the game. This procedure was repeated for three games. All subjects, both players and nonplayers, were also tested at other times when they were "in the most relaxed state possible."

Skubic reported that, in general, the players at all ages showed less change from the resting level than the nonplayers at all ages; that the players tended to show less emotionality than the nonplayers; and that league competition produced no more emotional reaction (as indicated by the galvanic skin response) than physical education class games in softball. Skubic cautions the reader not to take the galvanic skin response measure as a presentation of the whole picture of emotional response. Her findings agree with other studies in indicating that experience with stress tends to raise the threshold of stress.

SUMMARY

Motivation is a state of being aroused to action. This arousal may result from organic needs such as hunger or thirst, or from psychic needs such as the need for association with one's fellows, for affiliation and affection, or to explore and manipulate one's environment. Many needs are conditioned and directed through learning into secondary or derived motives, such as pride in one's work or in one's appearance, drive to complete a job once started, or drive to perfect one's skill in music, art, or sport.

Some degree of motivational arousal is essential for significant learning. Arousal states extend along a continuity from extreme lethargy or sound sleep to extremely high activation. The upper levels of the arousal continuity, or the accompanying awareness feeling tones rather than the physiological reactions, have traditionally been called emotion. Another way to describe this feeling-tone awareness is to call it psychological stress, although the word "stress" is more commonly applied to physiological imbalances and disequilibrium.

The higher arousal level, called emotion, is sometimes defined as deep psychic disturbance and generalized upset of homeostasis; but for our purposes in this chapter, we have defined emotion as *the conscious feeling tone* that accompanies degrees of motivation high enough to stimulate an excess of energy release, certain generalized reactions such as activity of the parasympathetic part of the autonomic nervous system, visceral and glandular reactions, and the chemical and physiological changes thereby initiated. We have limited the definition of emotional expression to include only certain learned patterns of stimulus situations and responses, psychic in nature and characterized by great depths of feeling. We use the word "certain" to exclude upsets caused by illnesses or physical injuries, except insofar as they also stimulate fear, anxiety, or anger.

Special types of arousal called chronic anxiety (trait anxiety) and situational anxiety (state anxiety) have been studied extensively for their effects on behavior. The research has been handicapped by the necessity to use indirect and often highly subjective measures, the great variation among individuals in specific physiological reactions to stress, and the difficulty of distinguishing between trait and state anxiety.

There seems to be some improvement in both learning and performance with additional arousal at the lower levels of the activation continuity, but a number of factors influence the effect of higher levels of arousal on learning and performance. Learning and previous experience, degree of conditioning and of appropriate automated response, simplicity or complexity of the task, needs and desires of the individual, and special aspects of personality all tend to affect both the learning and the performance curves. Many group studies tend to show the inverted U curve of *performance;* that is, improvement with increased arousal in the lower levels, then a tapering off and decline, and finally almost complete failure of adequate performance at the higher levels. The data, although not quite as complete on *learning* as related to arousal state, are somewhat similar. Nevertheless the above-mentioned factors cause great individual variation.

The term "stress," is usually used to represent efforts of the body to recover from a generalized upset or imbalance in its normal equilibrium or homeostasis. The upset of homeostasis may be caused by strong physical effort, strong psychic stimuli, toxic poisons, disease, or tissue injury. The term is generally used to describe the defense-reaction efforts of the body when it is seriously upset and imbalanced by stimuli strong enough to cause somewhat generalized visceral and glandular activity. Emotional arousal situations are only one type of the many stress-producing situations.

Praise and criticism, encouragement and discouragement, reward and punishment, and ego involvement (self-respect, status, prestige) are devices used to stimulate learning and/or performance. Previous denial of a need or desire, denial of recognition or praise, for example, strengthen the later effect of recognition or praise as an incentive. With much praise, however, its motivating effectiveness disappears. This principle of satiation applies to many incentives and drives. Reproof and punishment for maladapted action or error can be effective if they are not too strong or too frequent, and if they are followed by praise or reward for adjusted action. Competition and rivalry have strong arousal effects, but the results vary with the individual—with age, level of learning, previous experience of success or failure, and the presence of an interested audience. Thresholds of specific motivational stimuli seem to rise with experience; that is, one learns to perform effectively under stimuli whose strength would have been disruptive earlier in the learning stage.

Intrinsic motivation, a desire just to learn and be able to perform the task, is the most desirable type of motivation. This type occurs when the adolescent wants to learn to drive a car or to skate, for example. It can occur in many situations. To take an extreme example, it can occur in foreign language learning if the youngster wants to communicate with his associates when he is of necessity living in a foreign country as a result of his parents having moved there because of a job. However, intrinsic motivation is often not possible, especially when the student is first introduced to the new activity; hence the need for extra incentives. Incentives are external stimuli used to get people to do tasks irrespective of any satisfaction inherent in the doing of the task itself. Rewards, grades, bonuses, and special recognition are types of incentives. The type of motivational stimulus that will have the desired effect and the degree to which it should be used are problems of individual diagnosis and prescription by the teacher.

Automated acts of adjustment may occur so rapidly in an emergency situation that the heightened feeling tones only reach awareness after the act is completed. On the other hand, situations causing great awareness-level concern may be causal to and followed by extreme physiological stress. So-called psychological stress may cause physiological upset, or vice versa.

Athletes experience what is called emotional arousal before important contests, much as most students experience similar feelings with accompanying physiological changes before an important course examination. Unless it reaches an extreme degree, this additional stimulation tends to be beneficial rather than disruptive to the experienced person.

DISCUSSION QUESTIONS

1. Explain why play drives are considered at least partially innate.

2. What are the reasons for the theory that humans are not naturally lazy? Do these apply to all normal individuals?

3. Are the needs for affection and for affiliation with one's own kind learned motives? Explain your answer.

4. At what stage of learning of complex tasks is high arousal likely to be disruptive?

5. Explain the differences in the effects of strong arousal on learning and on performance.

6. Are the changes in physiological states under high arousal qualitative? quantitative? both?

7. What was William James's definition of emotion?

8. Does the field of psychosomatic medicine indicate that physiological changes may result from mental states? vice versa? Give examples of each.

9. Cite probable examples of Hellebrandt's theory that extreme stress is occasionally productive of much faster learning and better performance.

10. What need of persons seems to be assuaged by seeking and obtaining so-called highly emotional experiences?

11. Is competition an almost universal characteristic of human behavior?

12. Does the effect of praise on learning tend to diminish if it is continued over a considerable span of time?

13. Does the threshold of disruptive stress tend to rise with experience in situations that cause stress? Is this change in threshold specific to the particular stressful situation?

14. Girls seem to be less highly motivated than boys by the typical incentives used in physical fitness tests. Is this due to a difference in value concepts between the two sexes?

15. May the effectiveness of electric shock in accelerating certain types of learning merely be due to the stronger and more precise feedback of information as to results of action?

16. May learning often tend to cease completely when the arousal stimuli are excessively strong?

17. What factors affect the degree of arousal one can experience without decrease in learning? in performance?

18. Evidence indicates that there is often very high arousal accompanying athletic competition. Generally speaking, does this condition tend to be disruptive to highly skilled athletes?

NOTES

1. E. Duffy, "The Psychological Significance of the Concept of 'Arousal' or 'Activation,'" *Psychological Review*, 64 (September 1957), 265–75.

2. C. N. Cofer and M. H. Appley, *Motivation: Theory and Research* (New York: Wiley, 1964), p. 453.

3. Johan Huisinga, *Homo Ludens: A Study of the Play Element in Culture* (Boston: Beacon Press, 1950), pp. 2–4.

4. Walter B. Cannon, *Bodily Changes in Pain, Hunger, Fear, and Rage* (New York: Appleton-Century-Crofts, 1934).

5. Harry F. Harlow and Robert R. Zimmerman, "Affectional Responses in the Infant Monkey," *Science*, 130, 3373 (August 21, 1959), 421–32.

6. *Ibid.*, p. 423.

7. See Ranier Martens' excellent review, "Inverted-U Hypothesis," *Journal of Motor Behavior*, 3, 2 (1971), 167–69.

8. Wayland F. Vaughan, *The Lure of Superiority* (New York: Holt, Rinehart & Winston, 1928), p. 113.

9. E. L. Walker and R. D. Tarte, "Memory Storage as a Function of Arousal and Time with Homogeneous and Heterogeneous Lists," *Journal of Verbal Learning and Verbal Behavior*, 2 (1963), 113–19. See also R. G. Marteniuk and H. A. Wenger, "Facilitation of Pursuit Rotor Learning by Induced Stress," *Perceptual and Motor Skills*, 31 (1970), 471–77.

10. William James, *Psychology: The Briefer Course* (New York: Holt, Rinehart and Winston, 1893), p. 375.

11. Hans Selye, *The Story of the Adaptation Syndrome* (Montreal: Acta, 1952); *The Physiology and Pathology of Exposure to Stress* (Montreal: Acta, 1950); *The Stress of Life* (New York: McGraw-Hill, 1956).

12. Arne Lundervold, M.D., "The Measurement of Human Reaction During Training," in *Health and Fitness in the Modern World* (Chicago: The Athletic Institute, 1961), pp. 119–33.

13. Frances A. Hellebrandt, "The Physiology of Motor Learning," *Cerebral Palsy Review*, 19, 4 (July–August 1958), 12.

14. Norman Triplett, "The Dynamogenic Factors in Pace Making and Competition," *American Journal of Psychology*, 9, 4 (July 1897), 507–33.

15. P. T. Greenburg, "Competition in Children: An Experimental Study," *American Journal of Psychology*, 44, 2 (April 1932), 221–48.

16. Mehran K. Thomson, "Motivation in School Learning," in *Educational Psychology*, 4th ed., ed. Charles E. Skinner (Englewood Cliffs, N.J.: Prentice-Hall, 1959), chap. 16, pp. 465–66.

17. Jacob L. Gerwitz and Donald M. Baer, "Deprivation and Satiation of Social Reinforcers as Drive Conditions," *Journal of Abnormal and Social Psychology*, 57, 2 (September 1958), 165–72.

18. J. I. Lacey and B. C. Lacey, "Verification and Extension of the Principle of Autonomic Response Stereotype," *American Journal of Psychology*, 71, 50 (1958).

19. M. S. Krause, "The Measurement of Transitory Anxiety," *Psychological Review*, 68 (1961), 184.

20. Birger L. Johnson, "Influence of Puberal Development on Responses to Motivated Exercise," *Research Quarterly*, 27, 2 (May 1956), 182–93.

21. Carl N. Rexroad, "Administering Electric Shock for Inaccuracy on

Continuous Multiple-choice Reactions," *Journal of Experimental Psychology*, 9, 1 (February 1926), 1–18.

22. Ranier Martens, "Anxiety and Motor Behavior," *Journal of Motor Behavior*, 3, 2 (June 1971), 154–55. Albert V. Carron, "Motor Performance Under Stress," *Research Quarterly*, 39, 3 (October 1968), 463.

23. W. N. Runquist and L. E. Ross, "Relation Between Physiological Measures of Emotionality and Performance in Eye-lid Conditioning," *Journal of Experimental Psychology*, 57 (May, 1959), 329–32. W. N. Runquist and K. W. Spence, "Performance of Eye-lid Conditioning Related to Changes in Muscular Tension and Physiological Measures of Emotionality," *Journal of Experimental Psychology*, 58 (June 1959), 412–21.

24. In C. D. Spielberger, ed., "Drive and Drive Stimuli," *Anxiety and Behavior* (New York: Academic Press, 1966), pp. 291–326.

25. Albert V. Carron, "Motor Performance Under Stress," *Research Quarterly*, 39, 3 (October 1968), 463–69.

26. R. G. Stennett, "Relationship of Performance Level to Level of Arousal," *Journal of Experimental Psychology*, 54 (January 1957), 54–61.

27. E. Dean Ryan, "Effects of Stress on Motor Performance and Learning," *Research Quarterly*, 33 (March 1962), 111ff.

28. E. Dean Ryan, "Stress Effects as Related to Task Difficulty and Individual Proficiency," *Perceptual and Motor Skills*, 13 (1961), 103–06.

29. E. Dean Ryan, "Relationship Between Motor Performance and Arousal," *Research Quarterly*, 33, 2 (May 1962), 279–87.

30. Herbert G. Birch, "The Role of Motivational Factors in Insightful Problem-Solving," *Journal of Comparative Psychology*, 38 (1945), 295–317.

31. Edwin A. Fleishman, "A Relationship Between Incentive Motivation and Ability Level in Psychomotor Performance," *Journal of Experimental Psychology*, 56, 1 (July 1958), 78–81.

32. James Deese, *The Psychology of Learning* (New York: McGraw-Hill, 1952), pp. 322–23, citing Richard S. Lazarus and James Deese, "The Effects of Psychological Stress upon Performance," *Psychological Bulletin*, 49, 4, Part 1 (July 1952), 293–317.

33. Eugene A. Craig, "Perceptual-Motor Task Achievement Under Two Conditions of Stimulus Display," *Journal of General Psychology*, 53, Second Half (October 1955), 281–85.

34. Joseph D. Matarazzo, George A. Ulett, and George Saslow, "Human Maze Performance as a Function of Increased Levels of Anxiety," *Journal of General Psychology*, 53, First Half (July 1955), 79–93.

35. Celeste Ulrich, "Measurement of Stress Evidenced by College Women in Situations Involving Competition," *Research Quarterly*, 28, 2 (May 1957), 160–72.

36. John C. Mitchem and W. W. Tuttle, "Influence of Exercises, Emotional Stress, and Age on Static Neuromuscular Tremor Magnitude," *Research Quarterly*, 25, 1 (March, 1954), 65–74.

37. Lucille Chase, "Motivation of Young Children," *The University of Iowa Studies in Child Welfare*, 5, 3 (March 15, 1932), 9–119.

38. Clarence J. Leuba, "A Preliminary Experiment to Qualify an Incentive and Its Effects," *Journal of Abnormal and Social Psychology*, 25, 3 (October–December 1930), 275–88.

39. Lorraine B. Abel, "The Effects of Shifts in Motivation Upon the Learning of a Sensori-motor Task," *Archives of Psychology*, 29, 205 (June 1936), 1–57.

40. George Forlano, "An Experiment in Cooperation," *Journal of Educational Research*, 25, 2 (February 1932), 128–31.

41. Frederick John Hartrick, "The Effects of Various Incentives on Performance in an Endurance Exercise." Unpublished master of science thesis, Pennsylvania State University, 1960.

42. E. Dean Ryan, "Effect of Differential Motive-incentive Conditions on Physical Performance," *Research Quarterly*, 32, 1, Part 1 (March 1961), 83–87.

43. Clinton H. Strong, "Motivation Related to Performance of Physical Fitness Tests," *Research Quarterly*, 34, 4 (December 1963), 497–507.

44. Donald Laird, "Changes in Motor Control and Individual Variations Under the Influence of 'Razzing,' " *Journal of Experimental Psychology*, 6 (1923), 236–46.

45. William L. Lakie, "Relationship of Galvanic Skin Response to Task Difficulty, Personality Traits and Motivation," *Research Quarterly*, 38, 1 (March 1967), 56–63.

46. James A. Bayton and Harold W. Conley, "Duration of Success Background and the Effect of Failure upon Performance," *Journal of General Psychology*, 56, Second Half (April 1957), 179–85.

47. Celeste Ulrich and Roger K. Burke, "Effect of Motivational Stress upon Physical Performance," *Research Quarterly*, 28, 4 (December 1957), 403–12.

48. Jack L. Sparks, "Relative Effects of Various Verbal Incentives on Learning and Retention of a Gross Motor Skill." Unpublished master of science thesis, Pennsylvania State University, 1963.

49. Georgina Gates and Louise Rissland, "The Effect of Encouragement and of Discouragement upon Performance," *Journal of Educational Psychology*, 14, 1 (January 1923), 21–26.

50. Edward P. Gilchrist, "The Extent to Which Praise and Reproof Affect a Pupil's Work," *School and Society*, 4, 101 (December 2, 1916), 872–74.

51. Albert M. Johanson, "The Influence of Incentive and Punishment upon Reaction Time," *Archives of Psychology*, 8, 54 (May 1922), 1–53.

52. Marion E. Bunch, "The Effect of Electric Shock as Punishment for

Errors in Human Maze Learning," *Journal of Comparative Psychology,* 8, 4 (October 1928), 343–59.

53. Franklin M. Henry, "Increase in Speed of Movement by Motivation and by Transfer of Motivated Improvement," *Research Quarterly,* 22, 2 (May 1951), 219–28.

54. Maxwell L. Howell, "Influence of Emotional Tension on Speed of Reaction and Movement," *Research Quarterly,* 24, 1 (March 1953), 22–32.

55. Sanford J. Munro, "The Retention of the Increase in Speed of Movement Transferred from a Motivated Simpler Response," *Research Quarterly,* 22, 2 (May 1951), 229–33.

56. Joseph D. Matarazzo, George A. Ulett, and George Saslow, "Human Maze Performance as a Function of Increasing Levels of Anxiety."

57. Jack L. Sparks, "Relative Effects of Various Verbal Incentives on Learning and Retention of a Gross Motor Skill."

58. Wellman L. France, "A Study of Relationships Between Tests of Physical Performance and Varied Traits of Personality." Unpublished doctoral dissertation, Purdue University, 1953.

59. C. Etta Walters, "A Sociometric Study of Motivated and Non-motivated Bowling Groups," *Research Quarterly,* 26, 1 (March 1955), 107–12.

60. See Ranier Martens' "Anxiety and Motor Behavior: A Review," *Journal of Motor Behavior,* 3, 2 (June 1971), 151–79, and "Reactions" by Albert V. Carron, 181–88; Ronald G. Marteniuk, 189–92; and Janet Taylor Spence, 193–203.

61. Martens, "Anxiety and Motor Behavior: A Review," p. 151.

62. C. D. Spielberger, "Theory and Research on Anxiety," in *Anxiety and Behavior,* ed. C. D. Spielberger (New York: Academic Press, 1966), p. 17.

63. S. B. Saranson, K. S. Davidson, F. F. Lighthall, R. R. Waite, and B. K Roebush, *Anxiety and Elementary School Children* (New York: Wiley, 1960).

64. C. N. Cofer and M. H. Appley, *Motivation, Theory and Research* (New York: Wiley, 1964).

65. R. B. Cattell, *The IPAT Anxiety Scale* (Champaign, Ill.: Institute for Personality and Ability Testing, 1967).

66. J. A. Taylor, "A Personality Scale of Manifest Anxiety," *Journal of Abnormal and Social Psychology,* 48 (1953), 285–90.

67. R. Martens and D. M. Landers, "Motor Performance Under Stress: A Test of the Inverted-U Hypothesis," *Journal of Personal and Social Psychology,* 16 (1970), 29–37.

68. Martens, "Anxiety and Motor Behaivor: A Review."

69. *Ibid.,* pp. 163, 172.

70. *Ibid.,* p. 172.

71. W. H. Hammer, "A Comparison of Differences in Manifest Anxiety in University Athletes and Non-athletes," *Journal of Sport Medicine and Physical Fitness,* 7 (1967), 31–34; and W. H. Hammer, paper presented at 2nd International Congress of Sport Psychology, Washington, D.C., 1968.

72. Georgina Gates, "The Effect of an Audience upon Performance," *Journal of Abnormal and Social Psychology,* 18, 4 (January–March 1924), 334–44.

73. Hartrick, *op. cit.*

74. Lee E. Travis, "The Effect of a Small Audience upon Eye-Hand Coordinaion," *Journal of Abnormal and Social Psychology,* 20, 2 (July 1925), 142–46.

75. Raner Martens, "Effect of an Audience on Learning and Performance of a Complex Motor Skill," *Journal of Personality and Social Psychology,* 12 (1969), 252–60.

76. Warren R. Johnson, "A Study of Emotion Revealed in Two Types of Athletic Contests," *Research Quarterly,* 20, 1 (March 1949), 72–79.

77. Warren R. Johnson, "Psychogalvanic and Word Association Studies of Athletes," *Research Quarterly,* 22, 4 (December 1951), 427–33.

78. *Ibid.,* p. 432.

79. Magda Arnold, "Physiological Differentiation of Emotional States," *Psychological Review,* 52, 1 (January 1945), 35–48.

80. John M. Harmon and Warren R. Johnson, "The Emotional Reactions of College Athletes," *Research Quarterly,* 23, 4 (December 1952), 391–97.

81. Elvera Skubic, "Emotional Responses of Boys to Little League and Middle League Competitive Baseball," *Research Quarterly,* 26, 3 (October 1955), 342–52.

Eight

Measurement and Prediction of Learning and Performance

Children should be taught to play and sing themselves since it is difficult, if not impossible, for those who do not perform to be good judges of the performance of others.

ARISTOTLE, *Poetics* (VI)

It is necessary, first, to make clear to the reader just what we are trying to measure before we can discuss methods of measurement. The term "learning" will be used in this chapter to mean improvement—both rate of improvement and amount of improvement. Learning is an interpretation of improvements in performance as estimated from successive performance measures over a span of time. It is of necessity an inferred approximation, estimated from persisting, significant changes in performances as time goes on and additional practice is experienced. If we wish to compare individuals in their relative improvement on the same learning task, we must make sure that they have the same amounts of practice, equal motivation, and like procedures; and that the scores represent results from comparable amounts of practice which are interpretable in terms of the same units of difficulty in the learning process.

Numerical scores of rate and amount of improvement have no correlation or a negative correlation with initial skill measures. Scores of improvement at the lower (hence usually easier to learn) levels tend to be quantitatively larger and decrease in quantitative amount as one gets to the more complex, more difficult levels; that is, the higher the level of skill learning, the smaller the quantitative amount of improvement. Numerical scores of amount learned per session get smaller as one approaches the asymptote or peak level.

Initial skill represents the stage at which the individual has arrived as a result of aptitude for learning plus past practice and experience. Because of the wide variation in interest and experience among individuals, we cannot judge individual learning aptitude by observing initial level of skill; nor can we judge learning aptitude by *change* in gross score on skill tests. Improvement in performance is more difficult at higher levels, so that interpretation of improvement in terms of raw-score changes at various levels would make individuals starting at the higher level seem to be slower learners, for the amount of change in their performances would be numerically less. Moreover, individual performance at any one time may be affected by such factors as motivation, fatigue, or physiological fluctuations. Performance is different from learning. It is the way the skill is overtly expressed at any one time.

Performance is best measured in terms of degree of success in achieving the desired goal or objective. Goals may be those of the learner or may be those superimposed by the teacher or by society. Some skills such as required exercises in gymnastics or skating have a somewhat stereotyped pattern, partly imposed on the learner by established rules and regulations. For most skills, however, especially the open skills, movement patterns are adjusted by each individual to his specific situation—to the individual experiential background and capabilities, the desires of the moment, and the fluctuations of individual performances. Even the skill execution of the highly skilled individual varies in results from performance to performance. However, in most cases, *results* of the performance are evaluated to determine degree of success, *not* the method, style or form of the performer. As Locke says: "In the final analysis, skill from the learner's standpoint is concerned with results in the environment and not process in the performer." [1]

Skills build up into complex hierarchies of many subskills. The automatic nature of their performance, the speed involved, the variability in specific muscular patterns employed as they are adjusted to the specific conditions of the moment, both external and internal, all make evaluation of the quality and efficiency of a performance very difficult. When possible, skills are measured as objectively as possible by outcome in terms of time (track or swimming races), distance (throwing or putting), accuracy (archery or rifle), goals made (Lacrosse, hockey), runs scored (baseball), strokes taken (golf), and so on. Electric chronometers are gradually replacing human-operated stop-watch timing in races such as swimming. In track, chronometers can be started electrically by the starting gun and stopped by tape contact or cutting a light beam at the end of the race. Film replay has been advocated as a means to refine scoring by judges in championship gymnastic events.

When the skill result is a team effort (the results of a composite of various individuals' efforts), the relative contribution of the various team members is difficult to evaluate accurately. Successive tape replay of the action is a common aid used in such evaluation. The movie replay is being used more and more to determine individual performance effectiveness. It is also used to decide events such as close races in which a decision needs replay examination.

Measuring Skill, Not Value. One basic principle should be emphasized before delving into the details of the measurement of learning and performance. This principle is the statement that measurement does not determine value. Value is a feeling of worth. It is personal, subjective, and individual. Comparable value feelings, and hence judgments, may be held by groups or merely by a percentage of the group. If the majority are in agreement as to value and have influence and authority in society, they may be able to insist on acceptance of such value judgments and may advocate attempts of others to achieve measurable scores that, in their opinion, represent adequate degrees of such values. Measures indicating skill acquirement do not in themselves demonstrate the worth of that skill. How well one can juggle three balls, how accurately (high) one can score in bowling, how long one can climb and balance on a freestanding ladder, how well one can ride a unicycle, or walk on one's hands are measurable skills. How worthwhile it is to attain such skills is another question.

Performance Fluctuation. As mentioned above, individual fluctuation in performance makes it essential to compare several performances at spaced intervals to determine if the degree of change is more than chance fluctuation. For example, one's best time in a running event in track varies from day to day and from trial to trial. Heights or distances on jumps, distances on the shot put, the discus throw, the hammer or javelin throw usually vary considerably from performance to performance. Individual fluctuation occurs from performance to performance even at the expert levels. In skills in which the performer can be measured accurately in terms of time, distance, height, total strokes (golf), or percentage of success (basket shooting, marksmanship in rifle), an individual's scores on various performances are rarely identical and often vary significantly. If subsequent trials, days or weeks apart, show significant improvement on averages, we conclude that learning has caused the improvement.

Subjective Judgments. One difficulty in measurement occurs in performances in which quality must be judged and rated subjectively by experienced judges. In gymnastic performances, for example, the rating assigned to a single performance by an individual will vary considerably even among specially trained and so-classified expert judges. Marvin

Johnson made a study of the respective scores assigned individual gymnasts in the 1970 NCAA gymnastic meet at Temple University.[2] He intercorrelated the respective scores of the performers, as rated by the carefully selected judges, for both compulsory and optional events in the preliminaries. Of the seventy-two correlations of respective judges' ratings per individual, eleven of the judges' ratings varied so much as to produce a correlation below .80; thirteen correlated between .80 and .84. On the long horse compulsory performances, the various judges' ratings per individual had correlations ranging from .41 to .59, indicating very little agreement. Yet these judges were carefully selected and trained. Johnson questions the use of this event, the long horse, as a factor in individual or team titles. Note that this study was one of carefully selected judges scoring expert-level performers.

Back in 1962, Robert Johnson worked out a battery of skill tests for children in grades 1 through 6. The battery involved kicking, throwing and catching, a zigzag run, jump and reach, and batting as the respective skills. He tested both boys and girls from self-contained classrooms in which the teachers had close involvement with the students in all schoolwork including physical activity. The teachers tried to assess their students individually to determine to which fifth of the group they belonged insofar as skills were concerned. Johnson then correlated the actual scores of the individual students on the five skills tested with the teacher rankings. The correlations of the teachers' rankings with test scores ranged from .17 to .67. Only the teacher ranking with actual batting scores reached a correlation as high as the sixties. Even this highest correlation (.67) indicates a crude approximation, nonjustifiable for individual grading or diagnosis. In the other skills the correlations were so low as to invalidate skill classification of students by these teachers.[3]

THE MEASUREMENT OF LEARNING
AT VARIOUS LEVELS

Percentage Gain Over Initial Score

One of the ways used extensively in the past to measure improvement (learning) was to measure the initial performance, or perhaps the average of the first two or three trials, then compute the learning from following practices in terms of percentage of improvement over the initial score. McCraw gives a good example of the fallacy in this method of computing learning. He compares an improvement in the broad jump from 8 to 10 feet with an improvement from 20 to 22 feet. The first ratio of improvement to initial score (2:8) indicates 25 percent improvement, whereas the second ratio (2:20) indicates only 10 percent improvement. Yet, in relative difficulty, the second change would seem to be much harder to attain than the first.

Lack of Equivalency of Numerical Units

Failure to recognize the difference in difficulty at different levels in the measurement of learning occurs when teachers grade in terms of progress scores, regardless of the initial level of the learner. Those who start at the lower levels have much less difficulty in demonstrating progress. The basic principle proposed by McCraw,[4] which many other experimenters now stress, is that the numerical unit of gain after a high initial score represents more improvement per unit than a unit of the same numerical size at lower levels of learning. Counting the numerical change as equal at these different ability levels gives a distorted picture of learning. The change from 12 seconds to 11.8 seconds in the 100-yard dash surely does not represent the same amount of improvement as the change from 10 seconds to 9.8 seconds; or the change in a bowling score from 80 to 120 does not represent as much improvement as the change from 160 to 200.

When numerical progress is used as the measure of learning and of grading and rewarding, some individuals, knowing they must show "progress," learn not to score high on the initial tests. It is much easier to improve from a low initial score than from a high one. Actually, the relationship of the initial score both to the amount and the rate of improvement (in terms of raw-score changes) ranges from a very low to a negative correlation in most learning studies.

Methods of Computing Individual Improvement

Let us assume that valid measures of learning will take into account the increase in difficulty as one progresses toward one's maximum, that numerical increments are decreasing as one approaches one's limit, and that the method of measurement of improvement will in some way adjust the inequality due to different initial stages. A simple example of one method of computing percentage of improvement or learning rate follows:

$$\text{learning score per session} = \frac{\text{amount of change per session}}{\text{maximum score minus score at end of preceding session}}$$

If the task is to shoot 100 free throws, the maximum is 100. If, in the preceding session, the subject was successful in 60 out of 100 tries and is successful in 68 out of 100 tries in the current session, the learning in percentages is as follows:

$$\frac{68 - 60}{100 - 60} = \frac{8}{40}$$

or 20 percent. Later on, as he approaches his maximum, he has completed 85 out of 100 tries. In the next session, he is successful in 88 attempts out of 100 tries. The percentage of improvement then becomes:

$$\frac{88 - 85}{100 - 85} \text{ or } \frac{3}{15}$$

or 20 per cent. Note that 3 points in learning difficulty at this advanced stage is the equivalent of 8 points of learning at the lower levels.

Of course, the problem is not this simple. There are too many fluctuations due to uncontrollable factors to permit an increase with each practice that is a constant percentage of what is left to learn. Several successive practices would perhaps have to be averaged to see if the level would persist—perhaps scores for a week of practice in such a skill as the free throw of basketball, in order to smooth out the fluctuations. How many repetitions should occur in each practice unit, and whether to use highest score instead of average per practice unit, are other problems.

The individual's own limit or asymptote is very likely to be somewhere below perfection, the world's record, or whatever criterion we use for the limit of what is left to learn. In free-throw shooting, the perfect maximum may be far beyond the capabilities of all but a fraction of one percent of the subjects. It is doubtful if the average person would reach a limit beyond 85 out of the 100 in the above example. If we compute improvement on the basis of 100 instead of 85, we are introducing an error into McCraw's proposed formula; that is, we are computing his "per cent of learning of what is left to learn before he reaches his limit" with a denominator far beyond his capacity to learn. We are therefore underestimating the learning difficulty of each learning unit for this individual.

Another hypothesis is that those individuals who arrive at very high skill levels have practiced many more hours and studied procedures more intensely in order to accomplish each learning unit (so calculated by the above formula in terms of what is left to learn). If so, we are therefore underestimating the learning difficulty of the higher-level learning unit. In other words, the formula, although it represents a steadily diminishing numerical size as learning progresses, still may represent units that are more difficult at the higher levels than "equal percentage of improvement units" at the lower levels. The slope of the learning curve, calculated in terms of these so-called equal difficulty units (without holding constant time of practice, motivation, and work to achieve), may show a faster approach to the asymptote than true difficulty units would reveal.

We could compute the individual's improvement using the average plateau score of previous groups as our best approximation of his limit. If rate of improvement does not equal the group average in spite of like conditions of practice and motivation, we then assume he has less specific ability to learn this skill, a lower final maximum, or both. It is questionable whether a learning unit interpreted in terms of one individual's rate of learning, when other conditions are constant, is more or less meaningful than a group-average unit. The latter will afford the opportunity to compare the individual's score with a norm and determine his progress toward a desired level. Less than average progress may be due to lower learning ability, less motivation, or even an inefficient performance technique.

The truth is we cannot do a precise calculation and analysis of the individual difficulty of subjects' learning steps until they have reached their plateau and we have all the practice scores available. We do know that each individual will have a unique learning curve and that this curve will change if the learning task is changed; in other words, there is individual difference in learning aptitude and the amount of the difference is specific to the learning task.

In summary, if the units of measurement of an individual's learning are to be comparable to others of a group, they should represent the amount of improvement occurring under the same conditions and lengths of practice. At the higher and more complex levels where learning is more difficult, the amount of practice time necessary to make the change must be taken into account in the measurement of learning. The formula proposed for estimating learning units in terms of individual difficulty recommends that the computation of improvement be in proportion to what is yet to be learned by the particular individual before his or her individual learning limit is reached. Bachman, in reviewing the experimental studies in this area, says:

> It may reasonably be postulated that learning should taper off with increased practice, approaching a performance plateau, and that the amount of improvement caused by a stated amount of practice (for example, one trial at any point on the curve) should be a constant proportion of the amount still to be learned, this amount being defined as the difference between the skill or performance at that particular trial and the skill at the plateau. In other words, improvement should become relatively more difficult as the plateau is approached.[5]

STUDIES OF IMPROVEMENT COMPUTATION

McCraw,[6] in an extensive study of methods of scoring tests of motor learning, says that the method of percentage gain over initial score appears to be wholly invalid; that the methods of (1) adding the scores of all trials in the learning tests including the initial and final scores (the total learning score method), and (2) percentage gain of possible gain are the most valid methods to use when trying to compare individuals with different initial scores. He suggests that warm-up trials at the start not be counted as practice trials, nor should initial scores if they deviate greatly. However, one should be careful not to exclude so many of the first trials that the trials used as the measure of initial score will include improvement. He also calls attention to the fact that many individuals achieve maximum efficiency before final trials, and that this maximum performance should be considered in computations of percentage gain of possible gain.

Henry [7] reports a study of the problem of evaluating motor learning when the performance levels are heterogeneous—that is, when the initial scores of subjects vary widely. He evaluated the respective learning scores of his subjects in three motor skills: vertical jumping, a fast arm-movement task, and a balancing task. He found negative correlations (−.60, −.68, −.73) between initial performance raw scores and amount of raw-score improvement in all three learning tasks. Although the poorest showed the most improvement in the raw scores, they still scored poorly in final skill. Henry therefore says that it would be illogical to consider their motor educability as high. The raw learning scores were unrelated to final degree of skill. Henry proposed a formula for computing derived learning scores designed to hold constant the influence of initial skill. He says that, by the use of this formula, the corrected scores on the three learning tasks are found to be unrelated to initial skill but substantially correlated with raw learning scores and also with final skill attainment.[8]

MOTOR EDUCABILITY TESTS

There are in the literature various "motor educability tests" that purport to measure aptitude for motor learning, thereby enabling one to predict approximate degree of success in learning a new skill. The present stage of investigation indicates that these so-called educability tests do not measure motor learning aptitude or predict relative progress in learning. Gire and Espenschade [9] compared the scores on three of these educability tests with the achievement and learning of basketball, volleyball, and baseball skills, during a semester of instruction (eight weeks of basketball, three weeks of volleyball, and five weeks of baseball). The investigators correlated their skill-test scores in the three sports with three motor educability tests—the Brace Scale of Motor Ability, the Iowa Revision of the Brace test, and the Johnson Physical Skill Tests for Sectioning Classes into Homogeneous Groups. The investigators say:

> All correlations are very low and in most cases not significant. Negative relationships are the rule in the correlations of all "educability" tests with the criterion of "motor" learning. These negative relationships indicate that those individuals who are the best early in the season make the least progress; i.e., achieve less. . . . The degree of relationship in all cases is too low to obtain reliable prediction of any one criterion.[10]

The investigators conclude that

> . . . no test of "motor educability" studied measured accurately the ease with which the subjects in this study learned new skills or relearned old ones in basketball, volleyball, and baseball in regular physical education classes.[11]

Brace [12] reported a series of studies at the University of Texas in which scores on the Brace Motor Ability and the Iowa-Brace Motor Ability tests were compared with scores of 275 high school girls learning five motor activities. The number of trials needed to perform perfectly was taken as the score for each activity. The activities where (1) a dance step to be performed correctly to count; (2) scoring twelve points with three balls in driving a hockey ball at a target; (3) bouncing a tennis ball on a racket ten consecutive times while standing in a three-foot circle; (4) executing a headstand and handstand for ten seconds, in any form; and (5) bouncing a volleyball against a wall with both hands six times in succession. Brace states:

> Conclusions from the data would seem to indicate that either the so-called learning tests do not measure ability to learn or that the other measures obtained have little relationship to ability to learn motor skills.[13]

In the same article, Brace reports a learning study in swimming, using eighty-nine girls from grades six, seven, and eight, all beginning swimmers. The number of trials needed by each girl to pass ten swimming tests was correlated with scores on the Brace and Iowa-Brace tests. Brace say: ". . . . the data indicate that neither of these tests has predictive value, and no proof has been produced that these tests are tests of motor educability."

Gross, Griesel, and Stull [14] conducted a study of various measures of learning in a wrestling class of fifty-six college students, none of whom had ever had any wrestling experience before. The subjects were given the Iowa Revision of the Brace test and the Metheny Revision of the Johnson test during the first week of the course. The investigators reported a correlation of only .40 between the scores on these two tests. Ratings of progress and achievement were made by the instructors, who had watched the students during the course in class competition bouts, and by outside experts in wrestling who evaluated them at the last part of the course. The correlation between the Iowa-Brace test scores and the combined rating on wrestling was .46; and between the Metheny Revision of the Johnson test and the wrestling rating, it was .33.

Various tests purport to measure "general motor ability" or to predict future performance of individuals in various fine and gross motor activities. Authorities are not in agreement as to what constitutes the abilities that are described as *general traits of the individual,* as contrasted with specific abilities. Fleishman [15] has emphasized motor abilities ("more general traits of the individual which have been inferred from certain response consistencies") as well as specific skills. Henry, on the other hand, tends to emphasize the specific nature of motor learning. He says:

> The theory of specific motor abilities implies that some individuals are gifted with many specific abilities and others with only a few; it follows that there will inevitably be significant correlations between total test battery scores when tests involving many abilities are lumped together. The general motor factor which thus makes its appearance is a sample, fundamentally, of how many specifics the individual has, and general motor ability does exist in this sense.[16]

Most of the so-called general motor ability batteries seem to have about the same predictive value as the motor educability batteries discussed above. For historical reasons, one such battery, developed outside the physical education field, will be discussed briefly below.

The Stanford Motor Skills Unit

The Stanford Motor Skills Unit [17] is a battery of motor tasks designed to predict an individual's performance on various types of manual motor skills. The battery is made up of the six tasks listed below:

Spool packing—speed of bimanual coordination

Koerth pursuit rotor—accuracy in following a moving target

Motor rhythmic—precision in repeating an auditory rhythm on a tapping key

Serial discrimination—quickness in making discriminatory finger responses to number signals

Tapping speed—measured on a telegraph key

Speed rotor—speed on arm, wrist, and finger movements in turning a hand drill

Three studies will be cited relative to its effectiveness in prediction.

Walker and Adams [18] used the Stanford Motor Skills Unit in an experiment in which they tried to predict typing progress and achievement. They used seventy male students ranging in age from fifteen to seventeen years. The subjects were first tested on the Stanford Motor Skills Unit, then trained in typing for seven months. They were then tested with two typing tests. The investigators reported finding no significant relationship between the Stanford Motor Skills Unit scores and the typing scores.

Sigfrid Seashore [19] conducted an extensive study of prediction with the Stanford Motor Skills Unit in the Jantzen Knitting Mills in Portland, Oregon. He administered the Skills Unit to fifty employees in an attempt to predict their proficiency in operating a knitting machine. The scores on the machines were in terms of amount of work done and amount of yarn used. The men's work was scored for the first two weeks and for the last two weeks of their training period. The correlation between the scores on the Stanford Unit and on the machines was .14. Seashore then tested ten men who had been dropped from the industry because of their failure to maintain satisfactory standards of production. A comparison of the scores of these unsuccessful men with the scores of the ten most successful machine operators revealed that each group excelled in three of the tests. Seashore concluded that skills are highly individual and specific, and that many factors influence an individual's performance on motor-skill tests.

Many investigators have reported similar results with so-called motor educability and motor ability tests. For example, in a study involving methods in teaching swimming, Dillon [20] reported a correlation of −.02 between the Iowa Revision of the Brace test and improvement in swimming speed. Stull,[21] in a study of effects of distribution of practice on the learning of swimming, found no correlation between the JCR test (Sargent jump, chin-ups, and shuttle run) and the various measures of swimming. However, the problem of measuring needs much more analysis than merely the correlating of performance scores on such tests with learning rates and achievement.

STUDIES OF TASK SPECIFICITY

There is much evidence that individuals do not have a general motor-learning ability. Not only do individuals vary greatly in learning rates under comparable conditions, but each individual varies in learning rate from activity to activity. In a study of specificity of learning and performance in two similar speed tasks, Marteniuk [22] reported that there was no general speed factor—that ability to learn is task-specific and depends on innate ability, previous experience, motivation, and specific strategies developed. Henry, who has been investigating this area for a number of years, says:

> . . . it is no longer possible to justify the concept of unitary abilities such as coordination and agility, since the evidence shows that these abilities are specific to the test or activity.[23]

> . . . [T]he evidence from controlled research gives no indication that there is any quantitatively important unitary function that can be called general coordination. On the contrary, it must be conceded that coordinations are highly specific—it it largely a matter of chance whether an individual who is highly coordinated in one type of performance will be well or poorly coordinated in another. This does not of course exclude the possibility of a few "natural athletes" who are so fortunate as to be gifted with a large number of specifics, or the "motor moron," that unfortunate individual who has few or none.[24]

Studies of various types of motor behavior and the intercorrelation between their measures follow. It is hoped that the sampling of such studies is extensive enough to permit the reader some tentative generalizations as to specificity of motor learning and performance.

Almost half a century ago, R. H. Seashore published his much-quoted study, "Individual Differences in Motor Skills."[25] He tested fifty subjects on eight fine motor skills and found that the intercorrelations averaged only .25. He stated that his findings argued against any theory of general motor ability and in favor of specific skills, and that the theory of determining motor skills by measuring a relatively small number of motor capacities was very questionable. In 1934 Ragsdale and Breckenfield [26] tested junior high school boys in various skills from four different athletic sports. Although they intimated that certain group factors, such as strength, speed, and accuracy, might exist, they concluded from the low intercorrelations of the different tests that it was erroneous to speak of general motor ability.

In his doctoral thesis at Columbia University in 1935, Jones [27] reported intercorrelations of test scores of over 2,000 college men in five athletic tasks. The tasks were: running high jump, standing bar vault, rope climb, sprint run, and baseball throw for accuracy. His correlations were all so low as to indicate great specificity of motor ability. Rarick [28] attempted to analyze the speed factor in simple athletic activities through factor analysis of scores of college men in strength, vertical jumping, sprint, and shot put. He reported low correlations except for that between the sprint and the vertical jump (.63). This higher correlation between jumping and sprinting has been reported since in other studies and may indicate common elements between the jump and the strong explosive push on each stride in the sprints, for the length and rapidity of the dash man's strides indicate extensive springing action.

Harold Seashore [29] reported two studies at Springfield College, Adrian's on balance and steadiness and Wollenberger's comparison of physical education majors and nonmajors. He says that Adrian's study permits the conclusion that "groups of college men of known differences in gross motor ability . . . do not differ significantly in the two types of finer coordinations measured." He concludes, in part, that Wollenberger's results furnish added evidence of a lack of relationship between fine and gross motor abilities. Seashore then did an elaborate intercorrelational analysis of scores of a sample of 103 men who had taken a large battery of motor ability tests, including both fine and gross motor tasks. He again finds "essential independence" of fine and gross motor abilities. However, the intercorrelations among the gross motor tasks reveal the same lack of significant relationship. The average correlation between these gross tasks was .26; and only nine out of fifty-five correlations computed between the various gross motor tasks exceeded .40. The great similarity in the nature of the task seemed to explain some of these nine, such as the r of .69 between chinning and dips and the r of .53 between the vertical jump and the standing broadjump.

Scott,[30] in an attempt to establish tests for the measurement of kinesthesis, administered twenty-eight measures of kinesthesis and two of motor ability to a hundred college women. In a second sample, she tested seventy college women with fifteen of the previous tests and a new test which supposedly measured kinesthetic influences in space orientation. Scott reported little interrelationship among the tests, and no evidence of a general kinesthetic capacity.

Fleishman [31] investigated differences between terminal accuracy (moving limbs to specific points) and steadiness (holding a limb steady while in a fixed position) such as are required in piloting aircraft. He reported over 200 correlations. Most of these correlations were quite low. Fleishman says, however, in a 1966 publication:

From the patterns of correlations obtained, we have been able to account for performance on this wide range of tasks in terms of a relatively small number of abilities. In subsequent studies our definitions of these abilities and their distinctions from one another are becoming more clearly delineated.[32]

In a study called "Age Differences and Interrelationships Between Skill and Learning in Gross Motor Performance of Ten- and Fifteen-year-old Boys," [33] Henry and Nelson tested seventy-two boys on the learning of three sensory-motor skills. They make the following statements with respect to task specificity:

> None of the intertask correlations of amount of learning is significantly different from zero at the 1-per-cent level of confidence. . . .
>
> Evidently the learning of motor tasks, at least those of the type used in this experiment, is not a matter of motor learning ability—rather, it is a matter of specific aptitudes for learning specific tasks. . . .
>
> Even among gross tasks that are similar, task-specificity is great; it tends, however, to be less in the younger boy.[34]

Henry and Whitley [35] reported finding no significant correlation between static strength and strength in action (arm mass times speed of movement) in two experiments with college men as subjects. They state:

> . . . individual differences in static strength can not predict "strength in action," in particular as it is exhibited by maximal speed of movement in a 90 degree horizontal arm swing from the shoulder pivot. Neuromuscular control patterns are apparently specific and different when the muscle is moving a limb as compared with causing simple static tension.[36]
>
> The results agree with the concept that strength as ordinarily measured is determined by a neuromuscular coordination pattern rather than the ultimate physiological capacity of the muscle.[37]

Lotter [38] completed a study relative to the specificity or generality of speed in systematically related movements. His subjects, eighty college men, were tested for speed of single and repetitive movements of each arm and each leg and in speed of pedaling, first with the two hands, then with the two feet. He found very little generality—six of his r_2 computations ranged from 2 percent to .4 percent. He did find 15 percent and 17 percent, respectively, of generality between the single-arm and single-leg pedaling task, and between the two-arm and two-leg pedaling task.

Smith [39] explored the problem of the specificity of the details of a particular motor act; that is, whether or not individual differences are specific not only to the particular limb but also to the direction of the movement and to the particular element measured (strength, speed, reaction latency). Smith reports from his findings:

> Individual differences in limb action abilities (considering reaction latency, strength, and speed as the components of such action) tend to be highly specific to the component, to the limb involved in the action (arm or leg), the direction it is moved (forward or backward), the dynamic or static nature of the action (speed vs. measured strength), and the phase of the action (reaction latency vs. speed of movement). For some of the findings, cross-

validation using other published data is available and lends additional support to the hypothesis.[40]

In a study of specificity and generality in learning and performing two large-muscle tasks, Bachman [41] reported "little more than zero correlation" between the individual scores of 320 subjects on the learning of two motor tasks. The tasks were balancing on a stabilometer and climbing a free-standing ladder. The correlations between the two tasks were not significant either for learning scores or for performance scores. He reported 3 percent or less in generality in the skills.

Tyler,[42] in a study of the interrelationships of scores on various balance tests and abilities in three sports (basketball, gymnastics, and swimming), found significant though low correlations between swimming and some of his balance measures, somewhat less correlation with gymnastics, and no correlation between basketball abilities and any of his balance measures. His average r between the various balance tests was .26 with a range from .10 to .45.

Valentine [43] completed a study of various measures of balance and their relationship to improvement and skill in dancing and skating. She found very little correlation between her various measures of balance. These measures were a balance board, a balance stick (administered with eyes open and with eyes closed), and a balance beam. The average of her intercorrelations between the various balance measures was .29, including th r of .53 between the eyes-open and eyes-closed measures on the balance stick. She found significant correlations between certain of the balance measures and both skill and improvement in skating and *advanced* dance.

Reeves [44] administered seven different types of balance tests to a group of eighty-three college men in a study of balance as related to swimming. As part of his study, he computed the intercorrelations between the various balance-test scores. Out of the twenty-one correlations, only three were significant. The range was −.17 to .53 and the average was .12. He found that certain of the balances measured improved during the course in swimming, but the correlation between improvement in swimming and improvement in balance was not significant.

Evaluation

That the low intercorrelations between balance tests indicate a high degree of specificity is clear. It is also clear that only certain types of balance tests have any significant correlation with even those skills in which balance seems to be an important factor. If we define balance as adjustment in body control with respect to the pull of gravity, we are faced with the fact that some type of balance is a part of every activity. We can hardly say that this adjustment is an "insignificant" part of sport skill. The findings of low or no relationship between certain sport skills and selected balance measures seem to mean that we did not measure the balances involved; that is, balance is highly specific to each position, static or dynamic. Of course, the many other variables in a complex skill may obscure any variation due to differences in the levels of the balances involved. Granting basic amounts of balance abilities to all subjects who can walk, run, and change direction, perhaps *additional amounts* are of minor importance, having little to do with the relative rank of these individuals as they progress to higher levels in certain activities. This hypothesis is applicable to other correlational studies reporting no significant rs, and to certain hypotheses about transfer. If the basic amounts are already present in all subjects previous to the training, additional amounts are of so little importance as to be indiscernible.

The early balancing, crawling, standing, walking, running, and changing direction, not to mention the rolling, skipping, climbing, and so on that average individuals do as children in their motor-developing processes produced many of the subskills utilized in later skill learning. The error in many studies that report lack of transfer from one physical activity to another is that the control groups used in the research already have these long-established bases to build on. The relatively short training of the experimental groups in a specific activity may add little or nothing to another specific skill, but these postural and dynamic body controls are already far advanced in both the experimental and the control groups. Beyond these bases, highly precise pattern transfer must depend on considerable similarity in movement patterns—for example, transfer from baseball to softball or from tennis to squash.

The view of McGeoch, Hebb, and others that new learning is built on past learning, and that adult learning is almost always affected by transfer, was presented in earlier chapters. Hebb expressed the opinion that the reason we do not find transfer in learning experiments is because the transfer effects have already taken place before the experiment starts.[45] This concept is closely related to the "basic abilities" hypothesis —that is, one learns ways to learn and one acquires abilities applicable in many similar situations. There seem to be many abilities that affect the earliest stages of learning in the beginner, and many of these are nonmotor. Those of the readers who have attempted to teach skills to groups with very low IQs will be aware of the lack in many of these subjects of the ability to "get the general idea" of what to do.

It seems to me that we cannot entirely divorce previously developed bases, motor and nonmotor, from the learning of a new skill; and that many of these bases do not seem to be "identical elements." However, the amount of specificity in the learning of the particular motor task is extremely high, as hundreds of low to zero correlations have shown. Failure to recognize this fact has lead to much wasted time and many false predictions through use of "general motor ability" and "motor educability" tests. Henry's interpretation [46] of the differences in aptitudes (and the positive correlation of some of these motor-ability batteries with achievement) as being due to variation in the number of specific abilities individuals possess seems to describe most learning beyond infancy and the earliest stages of the novice. It will certainly not lead us into as many *cul-de-sacs* as has the general-ability hypothesis.

One other point seems to be suggested by the review of the previous studies on specificity: the fallacy of trying to draw a line of demarcation between fine and gross motor skills. On the one hand, the so-called fine motor skills must be built over a postural base involving many larger muscles. The degree of involvement of the gross musculature seems to vary along a continuum, but never approaches zero. Fine precisions involve precise postural controls. On the other hand, higher levels of so-called gross motor skills involve small muscle action and many controls of a delicate nature.

LEARNING CURVES AND PREDICTION

In his study evaluating motor learning with heterogeneous groups, Henry says:

> Using the method of residuals to hold statistically constant the influence of initial skill, it is possible to compute derived learning scores which are unrelated to initial skill and at the same time substantially correlated with learning and also with post-learning performance.[47]

In Henry and Nelson's study cited earlier, in which they examine the learning rates at different age levels, they say:

> Attempts to fit a mathematical curve system to these graphs in order to quantify the learning rates with greater accuracy have not been fully satisfactory due to the irregularity of the points.[48]

They conclude as follows:

> Evidently, the 10-year-old differs from the 15-year-old in being slower in motor performance of the type measured. On the average, he learns more than the older boy before the plateau is reached, but probably approaches the plateau at the same rate. His final skill is more determined by his ability to learn than is characteristic of the 15-year-old.[49]

Bachman [50] compared the learning curves of ten groups of male subjects and ten groups of female subjects during learning sessions on a stabilometer and on a free-standing ladder. He reported that rate of learning was not influenced by age or sex over the range of six to twenty-six years. Performance level (skill) varied considerably with age and was relatively poor in postadolescent females. The average learning rate was considerably slower for the free-standing ladder climb than it was for the balance-board stabilometer. He noted a slowing of learning rate on the stabilometer during adolescence but a speeding up of the rate for the ladder climb during the same period. Welch [51] extended Bachman's study, having her subjects practice the free-standing ladder climb for six days (sixty trials), where Bachman had used ten trials. She reported a multiple r of .75 by the thirtieth practice, using initial score and improvement as her factors for predicting final level. In other words, the prediction was relatively poor halfway through the training period.

Trussell [52] had forty college women learn a three-ball juggling skill during twenty-seven practice periods spaced over nine weeks. She found no appreciable correlation between any of the cumulated learning scores and the initial score (range from − .19 to .09). Cumulated learning scores correlated progressively higher with final success score as the practice continued. She combined periods 1 and 2 for her initial score, then combined periods 3 and 4, 5 and 6, 8 through 11, 12 through 15, and 16 through 19. The complete learning score was the improvement from periods 1 and 2 to periods 24 through 27. The correlations of cumulated learning with final score were .09, .32, .38, .52, .54, and .59 (cumulative starting with 3 and 4 and continuing up to and including 16 through 19, correlated with 24 through 27). Trussell concludes in part as follows:

> . . . [T]he learning curve of 3-ball juggling shows that this skill is acquired relatively slowly compared with other laboratory-type motor-learning tasks. While 50 per cent of the learning is achieved after 4 days of practice, 11 days of practice are needed to secure 75 per cent of the learning and approximately 21 days of practice are required to reach 90 per cent.
>
> The effectiveness of prediction of individual differences in final success, made on the basis of multiple correlations using initial skill and some specified amount of practice, rises almost linearly during the first 60 per cent of practice. Relatively little increase in predictability is achieved by including the last 40 per cent of practice even though nearly 20 per cent of the learning occurs during this interval. [53]

These findings of slight improvement in predictability during the last 40 percent of the learning might very well be accounted for by the variations in levels at which individuals reach their limit. If individuals were reaching plateaus at differing levels during this last 40 percent of the learning, the wide individual variation in improvement rates would account for the low increase in predictability from the later practice scores.

Hengst [54] completed a study using thirty-two female subjects in the learning of a dynamic balance skill. Her apparatus was a continuous seventy-two-foot balance beam that decreased in width one-quarter inch every twelve feet. The beam was one and one-half inches wide for the first twelve feet, and one-quarter inch wide for the last twelve feet. Each subject practiced ten days, four trials each day, for a total of forty trials. She calculated a first-order correlation between cumulative learning score at each session and the final score. Her Pearson product-moment r was .867 using cumulative scores at the sixth day, but only .876 between the ninth day and the final score of the tenth day. Morehouse [55] used the raw data from Hengst's problem to determine if prediction of final success in this balancing skill could be improved by multiple correlation techniques. A multiple correlation of .764 with final performance (tenth day) was found by using a combination of initial performance and cumulative learning over the first three days of practice. These results seem to be consistent with the correlations obtained by Trussell in the three-ball juggling skill.

IQ and Motor Learning

The literature on the relationship of academic intelligence test scores to motor learning scores is so extensive and so uniform in its findings that mere mention will be made of it. In general, correlations range from zero to .50, with the average being .20 or less. When motor learning is correlated with intelligence in groups of lower intelligence levels, a somewhat higher relationship tends to appear. From the moron level down in the scale, the correlation tends to become higher; that is, the moron tends to be superior to the imbecile in learning motor skills. In selected samples of those well above IQ 100, such as senior high school or college students, the correlations tend to approach zero.

PREDICTION OF ATHLETIC SUCCESS [56]

The same conclusions as those reported by industrial psychologists in their field have been reached from studies of prediction of athletic success at the high levels; namely, the best predictive test of ability is a sampling of performance in the activity in which prediction is desired. However, as pointed out above with regard to studies of learning, initial score on skill-test batteries has little or no relationship to amount or rate of improvement. One can use such batteries of tests to sort out the opposite tails of the curve if doing so is necessary and desirable. However, observation at one practice would probably be at least as effective unless the number of subjects was quite large. The discriminations between individuals near the mean are much more difficult to make, and the test prediction is always a certain score plus or minus the standard error. For example, a correlation of .80 between the criterion and the test used for prediction means that the distribution can be limited to 60 percent of its original size; that is, instead of picking by pure chance from the entire distribution, we can now pick the individuals from a distribution only 60 percent as large ($k = \sqrt{1 - r^2}$). However, individual selection of the most skillful presents additional problems. Morehouse summarizes these as follows:[57]

1. Ability to predict at extremes is dependent on the spread of the scores in the skill test. The more widely spread the scores are, the better are the chances of prediction.
2. Individuals vary in performance from day to day and even from hour to hour.
3. The criterion with which the test is correlated is not a true criterion in itself because of errors in judgment of even the most expert raters.
4. The basic assumption of prediction is that the distributions of both skill-test scores and criteria are normal. This assumption could scarcely be made of the subjects in the typical athletic squad that reports for practice.

Computed probabilities of selecting from one to five of the best players from a squad of twenty-five by use of scores in a test correlating .80 with a completely valid and reliable criterion follow. These estimates are based on a normal distribution in which the estimate of the variance is an adjustment of individual predictions, using rank scores.[58]

Estimate of the probability of getting all five correct or one chance out of 100	.0102
Estimate of the probability of being wrong on all five	.0776
Estimate of the probability of being correct on four and wrong on one	.0767
Estimate of the probability of being correct on one and wrong on four	.2592
Estimate of the probability of being correct on three and wrong on two	.2334
Estimate of the probability of being correct on two and wrong on three	.3461

Prediction of future national or world records in various individual sports events has been attempted many times, along an exponential decline. Henry's [59] short article and graph of the records in the mile run over a century is quite interesting in the light of such attempts. He presents the graph and says:

> Recent events can best be appreciated by examining the lower right corner of the graph in relation to earlier data. The lesson is clear. Neither consistency of performance nor trend of the empirical improvement curve gives us any dependable information about the physiological limits of human performance.[60]

There are numerous examples of misinterpretation of athletic prediction tests in the literature. A study by Boyd et al.,[61] abstracted in the October 1955 issue of *Research Quarterly*, has been quoted in a recent tests and measurement text as evidence that the Knox Test of Basketball Ability is an excellent instrument for prediction of basketball success. The one figure which is quoted is the biserial r of .96 between the best scores and membership or nonmembership on the basketball squad (after the coach cut his squad to less than half its original size). The investigators deserve a more thorough report because they present much more valuable evidence in their study than the biserial correlation involving forty-two men and what may not have been a normal distribution.

The additional data, besides the statistics on retention (eighteen men) and dropping (twenty-four men) from the squad, included:

1. Knox test scores
2. Coach ranking of all squad members after three weeks of practice
3. Coach ranking of retained players at end of season
4. $\dfrac{\text{Total minutes played}}{\text{Number of games played}}$, or average playing time per game.
5. $\dfrac{\text{Points scored}}{\text{Total minutes of game participation}}$, or average points per minutes of play.

The respective correlations were (rho was used for those involving rank):

$$r_{12} = .17 \qquad r_{24} = .23$$
$$r_{13} = .10 \qquad r_{25} = .52$$
$$r_{14} = .00 \qquad r_{34} = .85$$
$$r_{15} = .11 \qquad r_{35} = .79$$
$$r_{23} = .27 \qquad r_{45} = .11$$

An examination of the correlation of the Knox test scores with all the other criteria (r_{12}, r_{13}, r_{14}, r_{15}) indicates no value. As to the coach's original gross selection and its high biserial correlation with the Knox test, the coach would probably prefer to make the judgment because he has additional data as to player personal characteristics, academic aptitude, and attitudes toward improvement, training, work, and winning. The inexperienced coach or teacher might wish to use a test to make the release from the squad seem to the student to be more impersonal and objective.

The Predictive Index (times 100) gives in percentage terms the probability of predicting a dependent variable from an independent variable. PI (predictive index) is calculated from the formula $PI = 1 - \sqrt{1 - r^2}$, and, when multiplied by 100, gives the percentage better than pure chance of predicting the dependent variable (say playing performance) from the independent variable (say test-battery score). If the $r = .80$, PI $\times$ 100 would by this formula equal 40 percent, which means that prediction from the r of .80 is 40 percent better than pure chance ($PI = 1 - \sqrt{1 - .64} = .40$). If the r is as high as .866, the PI is then by this formula merely 50 percent better than pure chance.

The coefficient of determination, r^2, is used to find the percentage of the total variation of the dependent variable that can be accounted for by the relationship between the independent variable and the dependent variable. In other words, the above correlation of .80 means that only 64 percent of the total variation of the dependent variable can be accounted for by the relationship between the independent variable and the dependent variable. In other words, 36 percent of the variation of the dependent variable has no relationship to the independent variable. What this 36 percent can do to your individual predictions, you can now consider.

I recall some extensive work a graduate school committee of experienced basketball coaches did some years ago in trying to construct and select a battery of basketball skills to pick the best players from a group of twenty-five varsity squad players from various universities. After much experimental work of skill testing and correlating with subjective judgments, the committee was finally able to put together a battery that correlated .82 with the mean ranking of the individual subjective judgments of the five coaches. The coaches' judgments were completed only after they had observed, rated, and rerated the players over two weeks of scrimmage. The coaches were dissatisfied with their own battery selection of the best five. They picked out two different teams from the players not selected as the best five by the battery, both of which defeated the battery-selected team. It was apparent to the coaches that they were unable to construct a test battery of skills that included all the factors important in team-play superiority.

Perhaps one additional factor should be mentioned in connection with these correlations: They refer to linear relationships. As you noted in the earlier discussions of emotion and arousal, the relationships of arousal to learning and performance does not seem to be linear. Moreover, as mentioned earlier, the selection and integration of skills into patterns in response to the various cues arising in a game situation involves much more than a numerical sum of scores on individual skills.

Attempts to Select Superior Athletes

Scouts for professional athletic teams and recruiters for university athletic teams have the responsibility for predicting future success of those they select and subsidize or put under contract. They rely on background history of the individual's athletic performances, recommendations of those who are quite experienced in athletics and know the prospective athlete well, and personal observation of several competitive performances. The custom is to try to secure quite a number of prospective athletes because it is well known that predictions will be far from 100 percent correct. By 1975, NCAA regulations for university recruiting for football limited the number to be recruited per year to thirty. The year before this rule went into effect, one famous university coach was reported to have recruited eighty-two new prospective football players for the ensuing fall.

When extensive tryouts are legal before signing, they are also used and include many specific skill tests. These tryouts are more common among professional teams. When they are not legal before signing, in the universities for example, the long weeks of spring and fall practice serve as a sorting as well as a training procedure for a squad that contains a much larger number of individuals than the number later used in sports contests. Olympic teams are usually selected from winners in a number of grueling pre-Olympic contests. Additional tests of various kinds are also employed. One interesting one in rowing follows.

Hagerman and Howie [62] constructed and administered a test of a combination of physiological and performance measures of rowing. They were attempting to predict which individuals should be selected as crew members for the New Zealand national rowing team. They used an ergometer that practically duplicated the situation in rowing. The body position approximated the actual rowing position and twelve pounds of resistance opposed each pull. The subjects worked six minutes at maximum effort. The total number of strokes and the total force of the pulls were recorded. Heart rate was also recorded for each subject at the end of each minute of exercise, and at the end of every minute of the ten-minute recovery period after exercise. Resting heart rate had also been recorded. The physiological tests substantiated the selection committee's choices for the most part, but did discover two new rowers whose follow-up rowing performances justified their selection as a part of the team. These two subjects "rowed creditably" in the 1967 New Zealand eight, which later won the United States National Championship, the North American Rowing Championship, and the Mexican Invitation Regatta. A year later these two rowers made up half of the crew of the four-with-coxswain that won the gold medal at the Olympic Games in Mexico City. Two other subjects with excellent ratings in this test were also selected for the 1967 training squad.

Skill and Performance

It should be remembered that most competitive athletic sports are made up of a relatively large variety of skills. Success in such sports involves not only use of specific skills but also the decision about when to use the particular skills, how to integrate them and adjust their timing to meet the exigencies of the situation. In dual and team sports, most of the selections and integrations involve rapid cue recognitions and rapid responses without time for thinking through the problem or weighing various possible responses. The individual who must think through suitable responses before acting on the quick-appearing cues in a contest is usually too late in responding to be successful. This weighing of possible response before acting is characteristic of the beginner in fast-action contests and must be reduced to automatic response to cue before the individual can progress to high-level competition.

A seemingly contradictory situation arises at times in sports in which an individual who seems to perform at a lower level than opponents in the individual skills nevertheless puts them together in such a way as to win. An old saying describing such an individual is that "He doesn't know how to do anything very well except win." In the so-called open skills particularly, cue recognition, prompt decision as to most effective response, and automatic response that secures a desired result do not necessarily imply grace, ease, and beauty of performance. An infielder blocking the baseball grounder with his body, picking up the ball, and throwing the runner out at first base is just as effective as a player who catches the ball on the bounce and then throws the runner out at first. Sometimes the former will stop more hard-hit grounders than the latter, and thus prevent runners from advancing as far. It should be remembered that success in most physical events is judged in terms of results, and not particularly in manner of performing. Most skill performers, except perhaps a few in such activities as diving, figure skating, or gymnastics, are judged entirely by results rather than method of performing. However individual and unique the forms used in the performances may be, those which seem to produce the best results for that individual are usually chosen.

SPORT SKILL TESTS

Studies have been published describing construction and validation of numerous sport-skill tests for badminton, basketball, baseball, softball, field hockey, touch football, golf, gymnastics and tumbling, handball, soccer, diving and swimming, tennis, volleyball, and other sports. One common procedure in constructing such tests is to correlate individual scores on various skills selected from the sport with experts' rating of those same individuals in that sport. The assumption is that a high correlation of skill scores with judges' ratings establishes the validity of the test. Items that do not correlate significantly with expert ratings are deleted from the battery.

Other procedures are to correlate the skill scores and total battery score with the subjects' ranks in a round-robin tournament; to correlate skill test battery scores of teams with team success in games (wins) within the group tested; and to correlate scores on a newly constructed test with other tests already available. Reliability is computed by the test-retest method. One problem in the determination of reliability by the test-retest method in sports is the fact that players fluctuate considerably from performance to performance; hence a reliability coefficient close to 1.00 would not only be very difficult to obtain but would not actually be a true measure; it would have to be so crude in discrimination as to gloss over the individual fluctuations.

A check of reported validities of twenty-five different sport-skill tests reported in the literature revealed five that reported a validity coefficient of .85 or higher, seven in the .80 to .84 range, two in the .75 to .79 range, one in the .70 to .74 range, four in the .65 to .69 range, four in the .60 to .64 range, and one reporting a validity coefficient of only .44. Most of these validities are too low to be of much value for individual prediction. These tests can perhaps be used with advantage for teaching purposes, motivating purposes, or gross classification with large numbers, although even in gross classification only the extremes of the curve are valuable. The discrimination is not fine enough to classify the middle 68 percent.

It is unfortunate that we are not able to measure objectively and then predict accurately in the sports field, but so far we have not found objective tests in team and dual sports to replace the subjective judgment of the expert. Fortunately, individual sports—track, archery, marksmanship, bowling—can be objectively measured by chronometers and measures of distance or of accuracy. Three major problems seem to account for the difficulty in constructing skill tests with high enough validity to serve for individual selection or for prediction of later success. The problem of predicting rate and amount of improvement has already been discussed in the first part of this chapter. Initial scores, even if they are well above average, have too low a relationship with improvement scores and final scores for use in prediction. A second problem is the impossibility of measuring many of the factors that contribute to success in highly complex sports; for example, personality factors, attitudes, adjustment to stress. A third problem is that the specific items used, even if they are parts taken from the activity itself, are not the same when isolated as when integrated into the larger patterns of whole-activity performance.

This last problem, mentioned by Morehouse in prediction of athletic success, is also applicable to those sport-skill tests in which "expert judgment" is used as a criterion. I am reminded of a conclusion that appeared at the end of a study in the *Research Quarterly* many years ago (March 1952):

> There is no relation between improvement in swimming form and improvement in swimming speed for either the crawl stroke or the breast stroke. The coefficients of correlation between improvement in form and improvement in speed ranged from −0.11 to 0.11.[63]

This statement startled me because form (implying efficient form) is a way of doing, a work method; and what better criterion do we have for efficient form in this type of skill than actual achievement in performance! Here we can clearly see how variations in viewpoint enter into one common criterion for skill-test validity, the "judgment of experts." In precisely measurable individual events involving distance, speed, or accuracy (marksmanship, track and field, bowling), and perhaps round-robin or ladder tournaments in individual sports, we do not have to rely so much on expert judgment. But in spite of its subjectivity and the varying ratings assigned by individual judges, we have not yet been able to find any means of evaluation of an individual's team sport ability that even approaches the validity of expert judgment. In some skills subjective judgment is the necessary method of scoring—for example, diving or gymnastics. In these cases the aspects of the skills to be scored are carefully itemized and described, and the judges are given much practice in rating; nevertheless, individual rankings by respective judges tend to vary significantly. There are, however, certain basic conditions:

1. The one so judging must be really expert, not just some dubious "authority."
2. The expert must have first made careful observations of the individuals

to be judged over an adequate span of time, and he must have been able to make comparisons of the respective individuals during performance.

3. The expert must have made (at least mentally) a rough outline of a case history of each individual to be judged in the various behavior situations and performances, competitive and otherwise.

SUMMARY

Learning is measured in terms of rate, amount, and difficulty of improvement. Rates and amounts of learning by individuals cannot be compared unless the levels at which they are working are the same; hence the measurement must be adjusted to take into account the difficulty of improving as one advances to the higher levels. If we wish to compare rates of learning of individuals who are at different levels of skill, we must interpret the scores so that they represent results of equivalent lengths and conditions of practice.

Perhaps an average rate per skill, established by large groups at each level, would be the best standard for comparison and analysis of the individual learner. Insofar as learning is specific to the skill, we would have to establish such learning curves for each skill; that is, we could not predict from one skill the learning rate in another.

Individual performance at any one time varies with background of experience and training, fatigue, interest and motivation, and physiological variations. Initial scores are of little or no predictive value as to rate of learning and final achievement level.

Neither percentage gain of initial scores nor amount of change in raw scores is a valid measure of improvement. With practice time held constant, cumulative learning scores and percentage gain of "amount left before limit is reached" seem to produce reasonably valid and comparable measures of improvement.

So-called motor educability and general motor-ability tests do not measure individual aptitude for learning or predict an individual's approximate degree of final attainment. General motor-ability tests are invalid because motor abilities are specific to the learning task. An individual has specific aptitudes, not general motor ability. These aptitudes are specific to the skill being learned; that is, individual rate of learning varies from task to task. Those individuals who seem to be "very good" in physical activities merely have a lot of special aptitudes; those who seem "poor" have very few.

Great breadth and quantity of background experience in motor learning does seem to build bases that accelerate the learning of similar types of motor skills, at least in the earlier stages. The further one progresses in the complex physical skills, the more specific they seem to become; that is, training in one skill does not seem to improve performance in another skill unless there is great similarity in the motor acts.

As mentioned previously, the final level of attainment in a motor skill cannot be predicted from an initial score. Combinations of initial scores with cumulative learning scores (in a multiple r) begin to have some predictive value about halfway through the learning in simpler skills. Academic intelligence does not seem to be a factor related to the learning of motor skills except at the lower end of the IQ range.

So far, no tests of much value in predicting individual success in athletics have been devised. Subjective as it is, the expert teacher's or coach's judgment is generally superior to test batteries for individual selection. The numerous sport-skill tests in the field of physical education may be of value as teaching devices, for motivation purposes, or for a crude classification of the extremes (not the group $\pm$ 1 sigma) when very large numbers make individual observation impractical. Such tests are not an adequate measure to use for evidence of either learning or final achievement in the instructional program (course grade). As to predictive value for future learning, the principle is the same as that reported under prediction of learning; initial score has no correlation or a negative correlation with improvement.

DISCUSSION QUESTIONS

1. Why is initial performance in a motor skill not a good indication of the final skill level the individual will attain?

2. Explain why the rate of improvement in skill learning tends to be negatively correlated with initial score.

3. What is the fallacy in measuring learning of a skill in terms of the initial score represented by each practice gain?

4. Why should the same quantity in a raw improvement score have different values at higher and lower levels of learning?

5. Do motor educability tests measure aptness for learning? Explain your answer.

6. Is there such a thing as "general motor ability?"

7. Does aptness for motor learning vary with the skill being practiced?

8. Is the Stanford Motor Skills Unit an excellent predictor of level of success in industrial manual-motor skills?

9. Does specificity of learning rule out the possibility of transferable basic abilities? Give an example to illustrate your answer.

10. Do group learning curves vary from skill to skill?

11. How well can final attainment in skill learning be predicted halfway through the training period?

12. Should athletic- or sport-skill tests be used by the coach or teacher as the criterion for squad and team selection? On what should selection be based?

13. Should the teacher use objective sport-skill tests as measures of skill-course outcomes and as a basis for student grades in the course?

14. Is academic intelligence of a high order essential for high achievement in motor-skill learning? Give examples to illustrate your answer.

15. Is balance a general factor? an innate ability? an ability depending only on kinesthetic stimuli to guide appropriate action?

16. Explain transfer in terms of primary motor learning and the development of skill hierarchies. What is your hypothetical explanation of the apparent decrease of the general factors with advance in age and skill level?

17. Is skill retained only in the muscles that acquire it? Explain your answer.

18. Does the level of skill performance indicate the value of such a performance to the individual so performing? How is value determined?

NOTES

1. Lawrence F. Locke, "Movement Education—A Description and Critique," in *New Perspectives of Man in Action,* ed. R. C. Brown and Bryant J. Cratty (Englewood Cliffs, N.J.: Prentice-Hall, 1969), p. 222.
2. Marvin Johnson, "Objectivity of Judging at the National Collegiate Athletic Association Gymnastic Meet: A Twenty-year Follow-up Study," *Research Quarterly,* 42, 4 (December 1971), 454–55.
3. Robert Johnson, "Teachers Ranking of Five Tests on a 5-Point Scale Correlated with Test Results," *Research Quarterly,* 33, 1 (March 1962), pp. 94–103.

4. L. W. McCraw, "Comparative Analysis of Methods of Scoring Tests of Motor Learning," *Research Quarterly*, 26, 4 (December 1955), 440–53.

5. John C. Bachman. "Motor Learning and Performance as Related to Age and Sex in Two Measures of Balance Coordination," *Research Quarterly*, 32, 2 (May 1961), 124.

6. McCraw, *op. cit.*

7. Franklin M. Henry, "Evaluation of Motor Learning When Performance Levels Are Heterogeneous," *Research Quarterly*, 27, 2 (May 1956), 176–81.

8. Henry uses the method of residuals to hold statistically constant the influence of initial skill. His formula is $W = Y - bX + C$ where W is the attainment score, Y is the individual's learning score, C is bM_x and b is $r_{xy} (\sigma y / \sigma x)$. Note that r_{xy} is usually negative. In addition to the article by Franklin M. Henry already cited, see two other articles by him: "Condition Ratings and Endurance Measures," *Research Quarterly*, 20, 2 (May 1949), 126–33; and "Errors in Measurement," in *Research Methods Applied to Health, Physical Education and Recreation* (Washington, D.C.: The American Association for Health, Physical Education, and Recreation, 1949), p. 463.

9. Eugenia Gire and Anna Espenschade, "The Relationship Between Measures of Motor Educability and the Learning of Specific Motor Skills," *Research Quarterly*, 13, 1 (March 1942), 43–56.

10. *Ibid.,* p. 53.

11. *Ibid.*

12. D. K. Brace, "Studies in the Rate of Learning Gross Bodily Motor Skills," *Research Quarterly*, 12, 2 (May 1941), 181–85.

13. *Ibid.,* p. 182.

14. E. A. Gross, Donald C. Griesel, and Alan Stull, "Relationship Between Two Motor Educability Tests, a Strength Test, and Wrestling Ability After Eight Weeks' Instruction," *Research Quarterly*, 27, 4 (December 1956), 395–402.

15. E. A. Fleishman, *The Structure and Measurement of Physical Fitness* (Englewood Cliffs, N.J.: Prentice-Hall, 1964), chap. 2; "An Analysis of Positioning Movements and Static Reactions," *Journal of Experimental Psychology*, 55, 1 (January 1958), 13.

16. Franklin M. Henry, "Specificity vs. Generality in Learning Motor Skills," *Proceedings of College Physical Education Association*, 61 (1958), 127.

17. R. H. Seashore, "Stanford Motor Skills Unit," *Psychological Monographs*, 39 (1929), 51–56.

18. Robert Walker and Raymond Adams, "Motor Skill: The Validity of Serial Motor Tests for Predicting Typewriting Proficiency," *Journal of General Psychology*, 11 (July 1934), 173–86.

19. Sigfrid Seashore, "Aptitude Hypothesis in Motor Skills," *Journal of Experimental Psychology*, 14 (1931), 555–61.

20. Evelyn K. Dillon, "A Study of the Use of Music as an Aid in Teaching Swimming," *Research Quarterly*, 23, 1 (March 1952), 1–8.

21. G. Alan Stull, "Relationship of Quantity and Distribution of Practice to Endurance, Speed, and Skill Development by Beginners." Unpublished doctoral dissertation, Pennsylvania State University, 1961.

22. Ronald G. Marteniuk, "Generality and Specificity of Learning and Performance of Two Similar Speed Tasks," *Research Quarterly*, 40, 3 (October 1969), 522.

23. Henry, "Specificity vs. Generality in Learning Motor Skills," p. 126.

24. Franklin M. Henry, "Coordination and Motor Learning," *Proceedings of College Physical Education Association*, 59 (1956), 68–69.

25. R. H. Seashore, "Individual Differences in Motor Skills," *Journal of General Psychology*, 3 (1930), 38–65.

26. C. E. Ragsdale and I. J. Breckenfield, "The Organization of Physical and Motor Traits in Junior High School Boys," *Research Quarterly*, 5, 3 (October 1934), 47–55.

27. L. M. Jones. *Factorial Ability in Fundamental Motor Skills*, Contributions to Education No. 665 (New York: Columbia University Bureau of Publications, 1935).

28. Lawrence Rarick, "An Analysis of the Speed Factor in Simple Athletic Activities," *Research Quarterly*, 8, 4 (December 1937), 89–92.

29. H. G. Seashore, "Some Relationships of Fine and Gross Motor Abilities," *Research Quarterly*, 13, 3 (October 1942), 259–74.

30. M. Gladys Scott, "Measurement of Kinesthesis," *Research Quarterly*, 26, 3 (October 1955), 324–41.

31. E. A. Fleishman, "An Analysis of Positioning Movements and Static Reactions," *Journal of Experimental Psychology*, 55 (1958), 13–246.

32. E. A. Fleishman, "Human Abilities and the Acquisition of Skill," comments on the paper "Individual Differences," presented by Marshall B. Jones at a conference on acquisition of skill, New Orleans, March 8–12, 1966. See Edward A. Bilodeau, ed., *Acquisition of Skill* (New York: Academic Press, 1966), p .152.

33. Franklin M. Henry and Gaylord H. Nelson, "Age Differences and Interrelationships Between Skill and Learning in Gross Motor Performance of Ten- and Fifteen-year-old Boys," *Research Quarterly*, 27. 2 (May 1956), 162–75.

34. *Ibid.*, pp. 167, 168–69, 175.

35. Franklin M. Henry and J. D. Whitley, "Relationship Between Individual Differences in Strength, Speed, and Mass in an Arm Movement," *Research Quarterly*, 31, 1 (March 1960), 24–33.

36. *Ibid.*, pp. 32–33.

37. *Ibid.*, p. 24 (in abstract).

38. William S. Lotter, "Specificity or Generality of Speed of Systematically Related Movements," *Research Quarterly*, 32, 1 (March 1961), 55–62.

39. Leon E. Smith, "Individual Differences in Strength, Reaction Latency, Mass and Length of Limbs, and Their Relation to Maximal Speed of Movement," *Research Quarterly*, 32, 2 (May 1961), 208–20.
40. *Ibid.*, p. 219.
41. John C. Bachman, "Specificity vs. Generality in Learning and Performing Two Large Muscle Motor Tasks, *Research Quarterly*, 32, 1, Part 1 (March 1961), 3–11.
42. Robert William Tyler, "Interrelationships Among Dynamic and Static Balance Measures, and Their Correlation with Certain Sport Skills." Unpublished master's thesis, Pennsylvania State University, 1960.
43. Ann Valentine, "The Effect of Selected Physical Education Activities on the Balancing Ability of College Women." Unpublished master's thesis, Pennsylvania State University, 1961.
44. John A. Reeves, "A Study of Various Types of Balance and Their Relationship to Swimming Endurance and Speed." Unpublished master's thesis, Pennsylvania State University, 1962.
45. D. O. Hebb, *The Organization of Behavior* (New York: Science Editions, 1961), p. 110.
46. Henry, "Specificity vs. Generality in Learning Motor Skills," p. 127.
47. Henry, "Evaluation of Motor Learning When Performance Levels are Heterogeneous," p. 176.
48. Henry and Nelson, *op. cit.*, p. 172.
49. *Ibid.*, p. 175.
50. Bachman, "Motor Learning and Performance as Related to Age and Sex in Two Measures of Balance Coordination."
51. Marya Welch, "Prediction of Motor Skill Attainment from Early Learning," *Perceptual and Motor Skills*, 17 (1963), 263–66.
52. Ella Trussell, "Prediction of Success in a Motor Skill on the Basis of Early Learning Achievement," *Research Quarterly*, 36, 3 (October 1965), 342–47.
53. *Ibid.*, pp. 346–47.
54. Virginia G. Hengst, "Predictive Ability of the Modified Springfield Beam Walking Test and a Seventy-Two-Foot Balance Beam Walking Test." Unpublished master of education problem, Pennsylvania State University, 1965.
55. C. A. Morehouse, "Addendum" to Hengst, *op. cit.*
56. John D. Lawther, *Psychology of Coaching* (Englewood Cliffs, N.J.: Prentice-Hall, 1951), pp. 67–70.
57. If $r = .00$, $\sigma = 7.36$; if $r = .80$, $\sigma = 4.416$. The computations and statements were prepared and summarized by C. H. Morehouse.
58. See Robert G. Steel and James H. Torrie, *Principles and Procedures of Statistics* (New York: McGraw-Hill, 1960), esp. p. 175 under "A Prediction and Its Variance."

59. Franklin M. Henry, "A Note on Physiological Limits and the History of the Mile Run," *Research Quarterly*, 25, 4 (December 1954), 483–84.

60. *Ibid.,* p. 484.

61. C. A. Boyd, J. R. McCachren, and I. F. Waglow, "Predictive Ability of a Selected Basketball Test," *Research Quarterly*, 23, 3 (October 1955), 364–65.

62. Frederick C. Hagerman and G. Angus Howie, "Use of Certain Physiological Variables in the Selection of the 1967 New Zealand Crew," *Research Quarterly*, 42, 3 (October 1971), 264–73.

63. Dillon, *op. cit.,* p. 8.

Author Index

Subject Index

Feedback, 5-7, 59, 184
  augmented, 59
  automatic, 3, 6, 96-97, 138
  loop control (exteroceptive, propriocep-
    tive, preprogrammed release), 64-66
  precision in, 155
Feel of the act, 6-7
Form, 94
  variability among individuals, 120
  variability in individual performances,
    121-24

Generalizations, 82-83, 120, 138
General idea of the skill, 97
General readiness training, 108-9
Generality vs specificity in learning, 207-8,
    208-12, 214

Hierarchies in development, 3, 108, 120,
    199
  linking of subskills, 40
  progression in complexity, 108
High skill level, 37-38, 138

Imitation, 89
Inadequate neurological organization, 25-
    28
Incentives, 171-72, 187
Indefinable knowledge, 40-41
Individual differences, 11-12, 120
Individuation, 12, 13-14
Institute for Achievement of Human Po-
    tential, 25-26
Interval between responses (latency pe-
    riod), 4

Hemispheric dominance, 26, 28

Juggling, 97-99, 143, 152, 215

Kinesthesis, 97
Knowledge of mechanical principles, 155-
    57
Knowledge of results, 155

Learning
  adaptation and progression, 7-8
  adult, differences from child, 8, 119-20
  limiting factors, 44-45

Learning (*cont.*)
  amount of, method of computation, 205,
    214
  analogy to computer, 2-3
  animal versus human, 21
  automatic action, 11, 37, 39, 120
  beginner characteristics, 112
  change with age, 7-8
  child development hypotheses, 25-30
    early training and potential, 41-42
    quantity of experience a major factor,
      32-33
  conditioning, 56-58
  connectionism (bond formation), 58-59
  continuum, a, 54
  definition, 2, 54, 198
  drive (*see* Motivation)
  gross-framework idea, 11, 90-91
  gestalt, 59-62
  hemispheric dominance, 25-26, 27-29
  hierarchies, 3, 7, 40, 108, 120, 199
  individuation, 12, 13-14
  kinds of, 55-62
  latent, 56
  laterality, 28
  levels of learning and stress effects, 179-
    81
  maturation, 10
  meaningfulness, 80-82, 154-55
    gestalt, 62
  meaningfulness in motor learning, 80-
    81, 154
  measurement of, 198ff
  retarded children, 25-30
  unskilled adults, 43-44, 119-20

Man, ancient versus modern, 1-2
  experience handed down, 1-2
  growth, causes of, 1
  maturation as distinct from learning, 10
  progressive adaptation, 2
  size of, 1
  skill records and causes, 1-2
Measurement, 199-200
  computation of individual improve-
    ment, 201-5
  percentage gain over initial score, 201-2
  skill measures versus rates of improve-
    ment, 198
  skill versus value, 200
  subjective judgment, 200-1
Mental imagery, 126-27
Methods
  beginner, 91-92
  comparison of, 101-4
  demonstration, 102-3